The Bouvier Affair

A TRUE STORY

BY ALEXANDRA BREGMAN

The Bouvier Affair

Text copyright © 2019 by Alexandra Bregman

Amazon E-book: 978-1-7338345-0-6
Amazon Softcover: 978-1-7338345-7-5
Ingram Spark Softcover: 978-1-7338345-2-0

Cover Artwork:
Gustav Klimt (1862-1918) - *Wasserschlangen II (Water Serpents II)*,
painted in 1904 and 1906-07, oil on canvas, 80 x 145 cm

First Edition

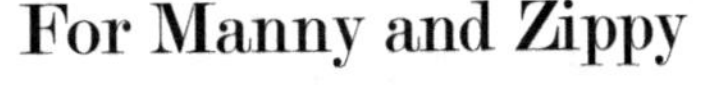

For Manny and Zippy

TABLE OF CONTENTS

I. Savior of the World

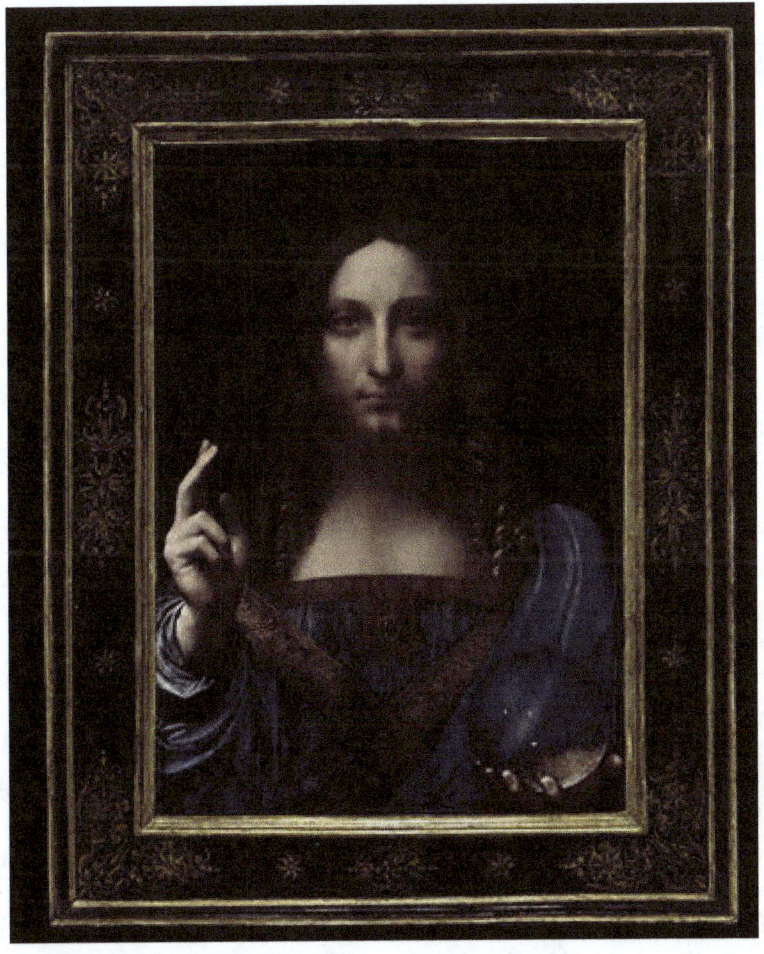

Leonardo da Vinci (1452-1519)
Christ as Salvator Mundi (c. 1499-onwards), oil on walnut, 65.5 x 45.1 cm

1

A GRIPPING MASTERPIECE

'Masterpiece': a word as timeless as the works it has come to represent. The power of even the idea of a masterpiece echoes through the art historical lexicon. Of course, it is occasionally overused; when an artwork sells at auction for an obscene amount of money, so-called experts are quick to decree its exceptionality. At worst, this is backpedaling—an excuse to hammer through stores of value and ship off canvases and sculptures to secret tax havens in the name of security rather than beauty. But in the case of the *Salvator Mundi* by Leonardo da Vinci (1452-1519), masterpiece was the perfectly appropriate loaded term, covering all manner of controversies.

Translated as 'Savior of the World,' fascination with this painting—just one of 15 still known to exist by Leonardo da Vinci—eclipsed at Christie's in Rockefeller Center on November 15th, 2017. In just 20 minutes that evening, the course of art history was forever altered.

Jussi Pylkkänen, the Finnish-born auctioneer, stood at the podium with a carefully balanced demeanor, striking a practiced but energized intersection of poise and excitement. He had stood before the crowd many times before, cultivating a career of hammering down some of the most expensive works ever sold. President of Christie's Europe and the Middle East, he got his start buying at auction and selling to his friends' parents at King's College School in Wimbledon. His subtle strategies of art business had little to do with the merits of a painting, because in the heat of a deal, it was all about profits.

Yet to sell a da Vinci was the kind of lifetime achievement for an auctioneer that could never be replicated…and the crowds were well-aware.

The formula was predictable at the many auctions that took place at the illustrious houses of Christie's and Sotheby's every year. To those in the know, the familiar rhythm was ritual. Often a wry, bespectacled Brit leads a room of suited dealers and specialists to lift paddles over and over, prodding millions to be passed over in the name of so-called masterpieces. Tobias Meyer heralded in the era of blue-chip art sales in the early 2000s, and Pylkkänen followed in his footsteps.

For this sale, press representatives were prominently placed to report the hammer price, the value before the totals of buyer's premium of various taxes, external expenses, etc., all added after the final sale. Various methods of possible buyers defined the layout from there: Alongside the auctioneer taking center stage, top specialists spoke in hushed tones to remote collectors on the phones. They were called phone bidders. A few seasoned but discreet dealers, collectors and their respective representatives clutched big, simple numbered bidding paddles. They had been vetted to pre-authenticate whether they could actually pay if they won such a valuable painting. On the digital sidelines, online bids were placed with increased anonymity, but the dramatic, theatric effect of the energy in the room made the sale much more interesting.

The evening's audience was unusually bubbly, and rightfully so. A steady buildup of marketing, controversy, and deep emotional connections to the artwork had drawn huge numbers. The ad agency Droga5 created marketing materials in which they focused exclusively on the viewer reaction, not even showing the painting itself. To imprint in the mind of aesthetes and neophytes alike, content featured viewer after viewer standing in front of it—awestruck; teary; even amused—all without ever actually showing the work of art.

The provocation practically spoke for itself.

One elite following the sale was a beautiful blonde, texting her father with updates. She did not stand out among well-to-do Manhattanites and art lovers, but her position was exceptional. Ekaterina Rybolovleva, then 28, was the daughter of Dmitry Rybolovlev. Her father had purchased the da Vinci in 2013 for a cool $127.5 million through his Swiss art dealer, Yves Bouvier by way of one of the family trusts. It hung in her father's Monaco home with a cabinet they had specially designed, purchased in part with funds protected by a family trust in her own name. She remained relatively anonymous, however, primarily in the interest of security.

Since the dawn of the auction house structure in the 18th century (Sotheby's was founded in 1744, Christie's in 1766) one could expect to see a few classic roles and devices, modified over the centuries with the advent of various technologies.

So while the old adage of 'death, debt and divorce' tended to put art on the market, with an estimated net worth of $9.8 billion at his peak, it was safe to assume that the Rybolovlev was not in the red, and was very much alive. Divorce, on the other hand, soon revealed an entirely different matter.

In terms of debt, the bidders would have been present even if a work did not sell, termed 'bought in' at auction. While the fanfare was a testament to the enduring legacy of auction house traditions, auctions of high-value artworks often had an agreed-upon monetary amount pre-paid by Christie's or Sotheby's.

For all the excitement around the sale or otherwise, the opportunities for profit were not confined to these two categories. In the case of the sale of another watershed work in Rybolovlev's collection, *Nu au coussin bleu* (1917) by Amedeo Modigliani, for example, the Christie's lot description had noted, "a direct financial interest in the outcome of the sale," in which a minimal sale price would be granted to the seller, regardless of the auction's results.

Guaranteed sales were just one source of financial innovation in the art world. Increasingly, many art collectors were lending money against their art's value, spurred on by banks like JP Morgan and US Trust assisting high-net worth individuals to capitalize.

Evan Beard, in charge of Art Finance at the latter, was something of an art market evolution expert. Citing *The Economics of Taste* by Gerald Reitlinger, he noted that artworks had functioned as cultural trophies since the 19th century to elevate both the art collection itself and the status of the collector. Art was purchased not just for aesthetic pleasure, but social and cultural capital. In this same vein, the 21st century's new breed of collector, coming from hedge funds, private equity, and oligarchy, viewed art just as much for its asset behavior as an expressive good.

Beard explained, "If you're a good collector, many—I would say most—put credit facilities against their art collection. While maintaining art collections, they unlock the capital and plough it into other aspects of their financial life. That pays them a dividend which their art does not."

During the current period of art investment, this practice was widespread. "If you went to the *ArtNews* list of top 200 collectors and took those in the US," Beard continued, "You'd probably see 10 billion dollars in art lending facilities for the group on that list."

"And so, ladies and gentlemen," Pylkkänen began from the podium, "We move to the Leonardo da Vinci, the *Salvator Mundi,* masterpiece by Leonardo of Christ the Savior, previously in the collection of three kings of England. At 90 million..." He trailed off, enticing the captive audience to challenge. An opening bid of 90 million in itself was rare. Footage from the evening pans smug Christie's staffers, all but snickering with anticipation.

The painting appeared. In a way, the aesthetics mirrored its journey: dark, shrouded in mystery, and challenging the everyday world in a way that was supernatural.

From a black background, the face of an ethereal Christ figure emerged from the darkness. He glowed, all-knowing in a dimensionality shaped by a lightly smoky pallor rather than heavy shadow. The fingers of his right hand caught the light from a golden source unseen, undulating down the ripples of his blue sleeve. The pose was commanding, but the expression and chiaroscuro gentle, with the ripples emanating an implacably delicate spirituality.

On the left side, bright golden ringlets dangled almost feminine against the finery of a robe fit for the son of God. Male yet feminized, captivating yet elusive, it had all the notations synonymous with the coveted *Mona Lisa* by Leonardo da Vinci hanging at the Louvre in Paris.

"Discovering a new painting by da Vinci is like finding a new planet," exclaimed art critic Alistair Sooke for Christie's marketing materials in the buildup to the sale. More succinctly, Christie's called it, "Without question the greatest artistic rediscovery of the 21st century…the male Mona Lisa."

The most profound element was the light, as it carried the eye to a clear orb. Round and beautifully lit, inside there was nothing but a spattering of stars, revealing only a fraction of the left palm behind it, and merely alluding to a cosmos within.

One unusual feature to the crystal ball was that it was entirely transparent. It did not distort the image in a swirl as was commonly seen in other works. While this puzzled some art viewers, the da Vinci specialists marveled at its precision. The reason behind the use of the clarity was twofold: firstly, that the swirl would be a distraction, and secondly, because they felt it would be inaccurate.

"It's actually false. If you hold out a crystal ball at arm's length, it will upend in the image, reverse the image. But if you hold it next to your body, it won't…," Simon said. "I have a crystal ball in my office."

The fact this needed justification spoke to the constant scrutiny surrounding the work. Because while the *Salvator Mundi* quite literally had its 'come to Jesus' moment at this auction in 2017, it had a few naysayers in its wake, who felt its demarcations were almost too literal. Jerry Saltz, celebrated contemporary art critic, was the most vocal. As he wrote in Vulture, "The painting is absolutely dead. Its surface is inert, varnished, lurid, scrubbed over, and repainted so many times that it looks simultaneously new and old." [1]

"When one is standing in front of the painting, regardless of the artist," echoed art advisor Todd Levin in the Associated Foreign Press that December, "It's not a gripping masterpiece."

To this eye, the sense of magic was outpaced by an alarming flatness. Christ's light eyes on the wooden panel could be deemed as hollow as they were boundless. The stark contrast of the thick background and the whispered features of the face could feel cartoonish in its most modern sense.

In response, Simon said, "There's a lot of hyperbole…I find it pretty offensive."

The extensive conservation process did much to revive the work, but it may not have been enough. When the painting first came to prominence after centuries when it had been considered lost, it was in a deep state of disrepair. The wood panel it was painted on had a significant crack, and years of overpainting had obscured the original intent of the artist. To the untrained eye, many felt it was not a da Vinci at all.

2

A CHANGE OF HEART

CONSERVATION for this work was done primarily by Dianne Dwyer Modestini. Over six years beginning in 2007, punctuated most heart-wrenchingly by the death of her husband and fellow art historian Mario Modestini the year prior, she brought the painting from a state of uncertainty to one of electrifying da Vinci-worthy splendor. With her own shaking hands,[2] painstaking cleaning to strip overpainting revealed the artist's indecision. She used in-painting with the perfect replacement colors, and soon a supple lip to rival the Mona Lisa was uncovered as well.

For many specialists in the field of Renaissance art history and conservation, there was no doubt that this was da Vinci. Certainly, it fit nicely into his canon. *Leonardo* biographer Walter Isaacson did extensive research and spoke to the man widely accepted as the foremost da Vinci expert, Martin Kemp, at length. His book pointed out a number of works made by Leonardo, which incorporated many motifs present in the *Salvator Mundi*. Among them, a fascination with male beauty, perhaps stemming from his homosexuality, a preoccupation with ringlet hairstyles, and positioning around light that prioritized composition over reality. *St John the Baptist* (1513-1516), like the *Salvator Mundi*, was oil on wood, with a feminized man painting his hand to the sky. A less alluring work from a much earlier period, 1490, is *Portrait of a Musician*, most likely of lyre player Atalante Migliorotti, Leonardo's companion when he moved from Florence to Milan. As with the *Salvator Mundi*, a pale man's face gazed into the light.

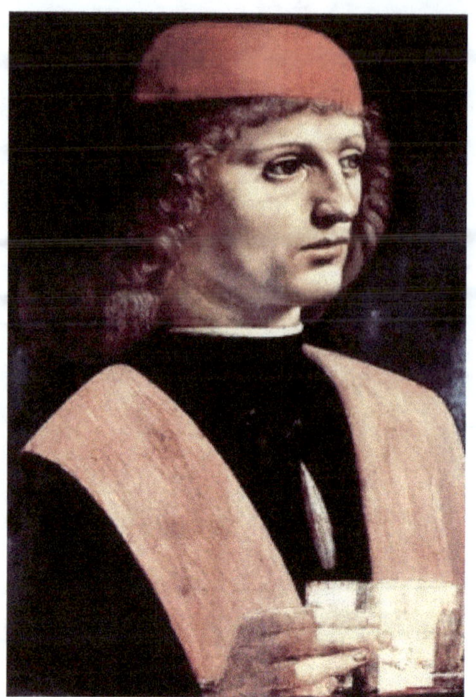

Leonardo da Vinci (1452-1519)
Portrait of a Musician (c. 1485), oil on panel, 43 x 31 cm

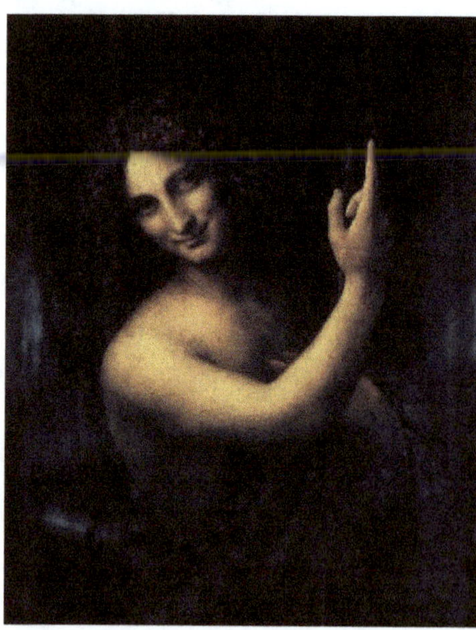

Leonardo da Vinci (1452-1519)
St John the Baptist (c. 1513-1516)

But because the depiction of Christ was charged with questions of symmetry and idealism,   Christ faced the viewer straight-on. His fanciful robe was carefully constructed with lapis, and the clear orb in the deity's hand did not obscure his perfection.

The experts never doubted it was real. Above all, a recurrent theme in Leonardo da Vinci's work endured as a dichotomy: the impossibly beautiful or the impossibly aged, male features with female allure, velvety darkness and the holy light of daybreak…these stemmed from a fascination with the ideology behind each work of art. In the modern moment, the questions of authenticity versus sensationalism arose in similar fashion.

That questions surrounded the cleaning process was surprising, especially within Modestini's home base, the Metropolitan Museum of Art. Former museum director Thomas Campbell sparked an Instagram war with the likes of auction royalty Loic Gouzer and Robert Simon, (the latter of whom held the image rights to the work, and was responsible for elevating it out of obscurity). He commented beside an image of the painting before it was restored.

"450 million dollars?!" Campbell blasted on Instagram, "Hope the buyer understands conservation issues… @christiesinc #leonardodavinci#salvatormundi #readthesmallprint"

Ex-Christie's art world power player Brett Gorvy wrote back, "Would love to see the condition report on the Mona Lisa or the Last Supper …" in a charmingly defensive rebuttal.

Robert Simon was far less sympathetic. He had a personal investment in the sale, and wrote angrily:

"@thomaspcampbell @brettgorvy Dr. Campbell, this is an incredibly ill-informed and mean-spirited comment about one of the most respected painting conservators in the world, one who incidentally spent many years diligently working at your former institution. I personally observed the conseravation process on the Salvator Mundi and can attest to the absolute honesty, modesty, and respect that Dianne Modestini brought to her work on the painting — carried out at the highest ethical standards of the profession. Given the prevalence of so many foolish remarks in both serious and social media, I have refrained from responding, but feel compelled to do so now."

Meanwhile, skeptical art critic Jerry Saltz simply wrote across two comments, "You are right to the core! #BogosityRules @christiesinc."

Simon spoke succinctly about his frustration more than a year later, still appalled.

"She is the most scrupulous, ethical restorer on the planet." He said evenly. "She has spoken very clearly and published all the information, but that's not what people want to hear."

Simon insisted the skeptics were ill-informed on the processes surrounding cleaning Old Master paintings. These were, he said, "people who have no concept of what old master paintings look like when they're cleaned. Go to the National Gallery, go to the Metropolitan Museum, see how many paintings are left unrestored."

Three books concerning the provenance and legitimacy of the *Salvator Mundi* were due to release as of spring 2019, and the film rights to Isaacson's biography were optioned to great fanfare to Leonardo DiCaprio, who was set to star in the film about his namesake. DiCaprio was also a prominent art collector in his own right, known to have owned a Picasso[3] and attended Warhol exhibitions; he considered Loic Gouzer a friend.[4] Gouzer and DiCaprio were equally passionate about environmental conservation and preserving the oceans, so much so that DiCaprio was honored by Prince Albert of Monaco for his activism two months before the da Vinci was sold.[5]

One particular aspect of the work that encouraged the idea it was an authentic da Vinci was the usage of *pentimento*. Contemporary Italian linguistics claimed it was a derivative of repentance,[6] and in art history, *pentimento* most closely aligned to 'a change of heart'. Indecision and correction were detected with X-ray and infrared technology before the paint layers were peeled back, revealing the mind's eye of an artist in real time. The Christ painting had *pentimento* around the position of the hand.

While Martin Kemp's forthcoming book with Robert Simon suggested he was eager to share this story, he was reluctant to speak to individuals, not least due in part to the barrage of misinformation and sensationalism detracting from their life's work. Kemp referred to some of his inquirers as "Leonardo Loonies," a term for laymen and conspiracists alike who bombarded him with odd, incessant requests.

In the meantime, the debate that began around aesthetics had since become one of both ethics and financials. Julian Baumgartner, the head of his eponymous family restoration business of more than 35 years, had worked on paintings by Botticelli, Michelangelo, and countless other masters of the period. He weighed in on Modestini's process as a bystander.

"It was really just the ghost of a painting, and in that state, it was much more difficult to attribute the painting and to appreciate it…The smoke left after the fire," he said, "So the conservator has to make a decision – how far do we go in bringing the painting back?"

With this in mind, Baumgartner defended a fellow conservator. "[Modestini] is an expert for a reason. When she decides to make a decision, it should be understood that it's done with all of her experience, her technical prowess and her education. It's not done in a vacuum."

When thinking critically about the conservation components, he maintained that an even-keeled and practical approach is imperative to making the right choices as objectively as possible.

He compared it to a patient's experience at a hospital emergency room. A celebrity should not be given special treatment at the expense of a lesser-known person. In that case, generalized standards of medical practice would not be forcibly upheld.

"Frankly, no artwork has any real value," he offered, "It's worth $100 in materials. You could burn it and make some BTUs and it would be worth, $2 or $3 bucks?…We decide the value. We decide the stakes. I'm sure [Modestini] would have loved to work on the painting even if it weren't worth half a billion dollars. I'm sure it wouldn't have changed her perspective."

Ben Lewis, author of *The Last Leonardo*, pointed to another version of the Christ that may have been the one traced through the 19th century provenance: Giampietrino's Salvator Mundi, painted circa 1500, and in the Pushkin Museum of Arts in Moscow. This panel had a "CR," for Charles Rex, proving it was in the court of the King. The story broke in November 2018, but no updates came through on the Rybolovlev da Vinci.[7]

Perspective, undoubtedly, was essential to the viewing process of a painting, but also to its embodiment of cultural significance.

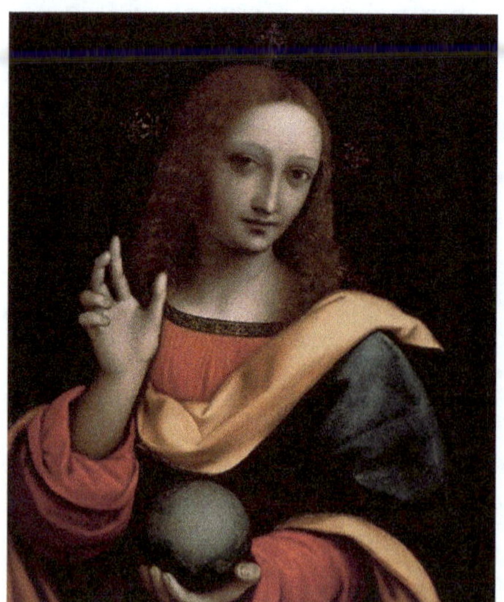

Giampietrino (ca. 1495-1553)
Christ as Salvator Mundi (c. 1499-onwards), tempera on wood, 50 x 30 cm

Would the *Mona Lisa* be such an enduring part of the western world's cultural canon if it were not prominently located at one of the most heavily trafficked museums, the Louvre in Paris, with Mona's enigmatic face judiciously imprinted on t-shirts and mugs in small towns and cliched in popular culture, solidifying her role in popular culture from communities large to small? Would she have mattered to the masses if this had not been the case? In other words, how did you determine the legacy of a masterpiece?

To Rybolovlev when he first saw the da Vinci painting, he was struck by its eminence of light. On March 22nd, 2013, he viewed the piece at his 15 Central Park West apartment. The property was purchased for $88 million in 2011,[8] still far less than the painting's sale price to him two years later. As he regarded the gaze of da Vinci's Christ, sunshine from the window spilled onto it. Upon reflection, Rybolovlev decided it was his favorite painting he had ever purchased.

Without the projection of real life's possibility, the painting could have been—and was—overlooked. The provenance was almost as fantastical as the subject matter itself.

3

THE DARK ONE

LEONARDO DA VINCI was born in 1452 in Vinci, outside of Florence to a well-to-do father and a humble mother. Out of wedlock and openly homosexual, he relied on his exceptionally inventive and curious mind to find patrons and steady work. 7,200 notes and sketches survived from his curious musings and intensive study, but this fascination with nature and humanity only produced 15 paintings known to exist today. Beyond the perfectionism and genteel approach of the painter, this limitation unto itself lent a quantifiable value to the artworks. In other words, they became precious.

Isaacson's book explained how at 24, Leonardo was arrested in Florence on sodomy charges, but a member of the group he was traveling with had married into the Medici family and the charges were dropped. In a later interview with Neil deGrasse Tyson, he said with a smile, "Things were slightly corrupt then."

Tyson replied, "If you get arrested, get arrested with someone rich." [9]

To which Isaacson responded, "I think people already know that in this audience. You're preaching to the choir."

Though salacious, the timelessness of powerplay and corruption was as relevant as the stunning mastery of paint. Leonardo da Vinci was a breathtaking painter, but he was also forced to be shrewdly political and maneuver in a city dominated by wealth and strategy. In the contemporary narrative around this artwork, its history of patronage and diplomacy grew equally important.

At 30 years old, largely untrained, da Vinci decided to move to the up-and-coming Milan from the oversaturated art community of Florence in the hopes of leveraging political connections. This was a way to differentiate himself from the Florentine bastion of expertise, and to make a name for himself with the politicians thriving in the new city. His first patron was Lorenzo de Medici, and soon he began working as a military engineer for Duke Ludovico Sforza, also 30.[10]

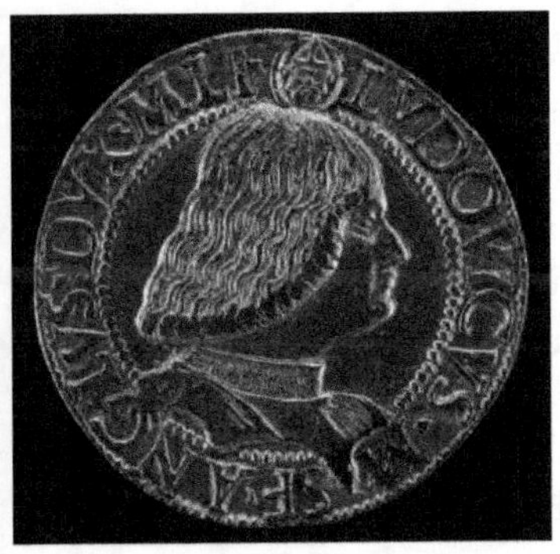

A coin featuring Duke Ludovico Sforza

Da Vinci's relationship with the duke, known by his childhood nickname of 'Il Moro' (typically translated as the 'dark one'…often used interchangeably to mean Arab or African, given for the duke's dark features) was complicated. Da Vinci was widely respected as diplomatic if impulsive, loyal if eccentric, and passionate if easily distracted. He fostered strong friendships with his patrons and fellow artists alike, with few exceptions.

Il Moro, on the other hand, was a more fearsome and divisive figure. It was the era of Machiavellian logic, in which Niccolò Machiavelli studied the behaviors of those around him, most notably the powerful Cesar Borgia, whose practices inspired Machiavelli's *The Prince* in the early 16th century. These characters informed the life and times of da Vinci, and potentially, his own behavior.

Like the Borgias, Ludovico used tactical prowess to maintain and elevate his own power. While their partnership began innocently enough with da Vinci's mastery of theatrical sets (using precious materials to great fanfare, as was later the case in the *Salvator Mundi*) its evolution into war materials spoke as much to the duke's interests as it did to the need for defense in trying times.

His grandfather, Filippo Maria (1412-1447) was described in *The Civilization of the Renaissance in Italy* by Jacob Burckhardt, first published in 1860 accordingly:

"What a man of uncommon gifts and high position can be made by the passion of fear, is here shown with what may be called a mathematical completeness. All the resources of the State were devoted to the one end of securing his personal safety, though happily his cruel egotism did not degenerate into a purposeless thirst for blood…

Whoever entered the citadel was watched by a hundred eyes; it was forbidden even to stand at the window, lest signs should be given to those without. All who were admitted among the personal followers of the Prince were subjected to a series of the strictest examinations; then, once accepted, were charged with the highest diplomatic commissions, as well as with the humblest personal services both in this Court being alike honorable. And this was the man who conducted long and difficult wars, who dealt habitually with political affairs of the first importance, and every day sent his plenipotentiaries to all parts of Italy.

His safety lay in the fact that none of his servants trusted the others, that his *Condottieri* [mercenaries] were watched and misled by spies, and that the ambassadors and higher officials were baffled and kept apart by artificially nourished jealousies, and in particular by the device of coupling an honest man with a knave."

The viciousness of rampant political subterfuge was a way to maintain power. Filippo's son-in-law was Ludovico's father, Condottiere Francesco Sforza (1450-1466), whose wife, presumably Ludovico's mother, had Francesco's mistress murdered. Francesco's sons, Ludovico and Galeazzo, were described by Burckhardt with a similar veil of tragedy. "Those children, beautiful as angels, carefully and thoroughly educated as they were, fell victims, when they grew up, to the corruption of a measureless egotism."

Burckhardt explained that Galeazzo was prone to "fits of senseless debauchery and of revolting cruelty to his nearest friends," who ultimately conspired to have him murdered during Christmas.[11-12]

Ludovico's seven-year-old nephew,[13] Gian Galeazzo, was thus made Duke of Milan. When Leonardo da Vinci first met Ludovico Sforza, the aristocrat had not yet assumed the title from his young relative. However, as a father figure, Ludovico malignantly encouraged his nephew's indulgences as he grew up, gaining more power as he built relationships around him. Eventually, Gian died at the age of just 25 in 1494, and the dark one was able to step in.

Da Vinci played a critical role to legitimize the Duke's rule by providing narrative artwork, lavish theatrical sets, and even military equipment, with humility and loyalty. His career as a designer, as much as a painter, continued to advance. So how did a gentle soul become entrenched with such a treacherous network?

Walter Isaacson speculated in his book that, "Much of Leonardo's career was consumed by his quest for patrons who would be unconditionally paternalistic, supportive, and indulgent in ways that his own father had only occasionally been."

In art, an enduring conception was that provenance was merely a set of locations, simply qualifying a history of changing hands. But provenance was also context. In this case, it was the understanding of the interplay between loyalty and deceit in patronage, and how it paved the way for centuries of conflict, all anchored in the beautiful art of a master.

Christie's noted that the *Salvator Mundi* painting was likely commissioned by King Louis XII of France and Anne of Brittany around 1500. Louis' father, King Charles VIII, had been a connection of the Duke's.

Hundreds of years of the painting changing hands grew daringly complex: It traveled with Queen Henrietta Maria from France to England when she married King Charles I in 1625, but he prompted the sale of the painting in 1651, and records were then lost until 1763, where it was left in storage and largely forgotten. It came to America in the late 19th century, then sold at a Christie's London auction in 1958 for £45 to a Houston-based American named, Warren E. Kuntz. At the time, it was attributed to Giovanni Antonio Boltraffio (1467-1516) in "the da Vinci school."

Martin Kemp's research suggested that this was not unusual. The *Mona Lisa* had gaps in its history, between 1519 and 1550, and the *Lady With the Ermine* of Cecilia Gallerani only reappeared in the 19th century.

The Kuntz lineage was carefully traced by a *Wall Street Journal* team of Denise Blostein, Kelly Crow, and Robert Libetti in 2018. Before that, even Simon and Parrish were unable to fully confirm its origins.

By 2004, Warren Kuntz's wife's nephew's daughter, Ms. Hendry Tureau, had put the work up for auction. The *Salvator Mundi* was purchased for the still-hardly noteworthy $10,000 at an estate sale by Alexander Parrish in 2005. He then worked with art dealers Robert Simon and Warren Adelson on the authentication, restoration, and exhibition of the work to prepare it for resale.

Initially, Parish and Simon had acquired the *Salvator Mundi* together, and Warren Adelson was considering buying a partial-share in the work at a $10 million investment. He reached out to George Wachter, Chairman of Sotheby's North and South America, and Co-Chairman of Old Masters, to ask his opinion on whether the work was real. Hearing back in the affirmative, Adelson went in on the deal.

It was still very uncommon for multiple collectors or dealers to take public partial shares of an artwork, and as such, what was later better known as fractional ownership was still a minuscule, up-and-coming part of the art market.

They also created the painting as a company, Salvator Mundi LLC for tax purposes, in Delaware.

"We were advised that that was the intelligent way to do it," said Robert Simon, "But I really don't know why these things are done."

Especially when compared to New York state laws, Delaware property law was considerably more protective and lenient. In both Chapter 7 and Chapter 13 bankruptcy cases, property is generally protected from any kind of asset-related seizure.[14] McClatchy noted that of the 515 companies either owned or connected to President Donald Trump in his disclosure statements, 378 were located in Delaware. In short, it was a way to avoid taxes.[15]

Swiss legal experts were quick to point out that the United States had a much-appreciated value as an international tax haven, even if it was under-reported.

"LLCs currently are the most potent tool if you want to have secrecy…," said Swiss lawyer David Wallace Wilson, who represented Ekaterina Rybolovleva during the high-profile divorce of her parents, the da Vinci buyers. "Everybody knows this."

With the ability to have secrets, he explained, there was also the ability to conduct illegal business. There was simply no way of knowing.

Speaking rapid-fire and liberally peppering his phrasing with the word "obviously," he went so far as to say, "Everyone is exchanging now. We're giving information to other countries. You cannot hide…but the U.S. is the current biggest black hole in the world if you want to hide money illegally. It's quite well-known…Delaware, Wyoming, Alaska, Nevada, all those places…There's been a big move of assets there to avoid automatic exchange tax for clients."

As he grew more heated and even more animated, Wilson said, "It's filthy out there, and they do nothing…Everyone in the world hates the U.S. for that."

It was a smart (and legal) move to place the painting in an LLC either way for the sake of discretion. As general practice, Rybolovlev himself had each painting registered as its own company.

What truly made this work exceptional was the sale in 2012. After the restorative process and the hype around the 'real' da Vinci, it was exhibited at the Dallas Museum of Art. There was talk that it could be sold for $200 million, surpassing the existing record-breaker of a $170 million Picasso.

But while expectations mounted, the three New York investors were unable to sell the da Vinci. They offered it to the Kimbell Art Museum in Fort Worth, Texas for $125 million, and to an undisclosed buyer in Boston, Massachusetts, for $200 million, who both declined. From a market perspective, the failed attempts to sell the work may have devalued it, posing a potentially massive bargain opportunity for someone serious about purchasing a masterpiece.

Sotheby's went to the trio in 2013, who hoped to sell the painting for $150 million. They alluded to a Russian buyer who had been close to purchasing the work for $125 million. In response, Sotheby's initially purchased insurance at the previous asking price—$150 million—just in case anything terrible happened.

The insurance valuation was revised down to $113.4 million (€100 million), after Parish, Adelson and Simon were able to sell through Sotheby's, in May 2013, for $80 million. The private sale was brokered by Sotheby's New York by Senior Director/Vice Chairman Samuel Valette, in the Impressionist and Modern Art departments, and it was shrouded in layers of mystery, later only uncovered in litigation.

A year after the sale, Scott Reyburn ferreted out the existence of the transaction, breaking the story in *The New York Times* in May 2013. He noted that it had occurred, but not the buyer, who still remained unknown.

This undisclosed buyer was later confirmed as freeport magnate Yves Bouvier, who had procured the work for his most important art client, Russian oligarch Dmitry Rybolovlev.

The oligarch saw the article, and gradually realized he had actually paid much more than Bouvier brokered. It appeared that, through what was deemed mischievous upselling, Bouvier had obtained a $47.5 million profit on the da Vinci painting alone.

In March of 2013, Yves Bouvier coordinated with Sotheby's and arranged for Rybolovlev to see the Salvator Mundi at his home. Bouvier's contact at the auction house, Samuel Valette, arrived at 15 Central Park West, and was escorted into the apartment. There, he saw someone he described as a vaguely familiar-looking man from Bouvier's art dealings in Europe, along with a small group of his associates. There was no introduction, and apparently, no conversation at all.

The third man, of course, was the eventual buyer: Russian oligarch Dmitry Rybolovlev.

The legal filings expressed doubts about Valette's willful ignorance:

> "It is inconceivable that Sotheby's would arrange a viewing of one of the world's most valuable masterworks in one of the world's most expensive apartments, in the presence of the person widely reported by the press to be the apartment's owner and entirely for his benefit, without knowing who he was."

They added:

> "Sotheby's was trying to arrange a private sale of *Salvator Mundi*. In that capacity, according to its website, its job was to 'discreetly offer [*Salvator Mundi*] to individual potential purchasers.' It would have been professional malpractice for Sotheby's not to know who Rybolovlev was…Sotheby's claim to have no knowledge of Rybolovlev is not credible."

Bouvier and Rybolovlev then went into a separate room and viewed the painting without the others.

Valette's lack of knowledge continued. He claimed he had no idea what Bouvier's plans for the da Vinci were after it was purchased, with no connection to the final transaction. He only knew the exchange occurred for sure once he saw it in the media.

While he may not have been a part of the relationship with the Russian, Valette's relationship with Bouvier was instrumental in facilitating not just this watershed sale, but ongoing client opportunities. As the so-called "Freeport King," Bouvier had access to a multitude of high-end art collectors, who stored their items in his specially bonded warehouses. Moreover, Valette personally reached out to Bouvier and suggested works for Rybolovlev's collection, sourcing works on behalf of Sotheby's—not just for the da Vinci sale, but for many other works he later bought.

"Independently of Rybolovlev, I was a regular client of Sotheby's, especially in 2005/2006," He explained later, "They provided a lot of the administrative work and controller documents."

After the viewing, Bouvier coordinated with the owners of the da Vinci, Adelson, Parrish, and Simon through Sotheby's to facilitate the sale at the bargain price of $80 million.

During negotiations through Alexander Bell, another Sotheby's representative, offered to give the sellers a paltry $68 million, along with Pablo Picasso's *Le Fumeur* (the Smoker, at a value of $12 million). From there, the sellers could place the additional work up for auction at Sotheby's.

But Bouvier told his client a very different story. Speaking to Rybolovlev's team, he wrote, that their original offer of $100 million was "rejected without a moment's hesitation." In emails, he said, the seller was "[o]ne tough nut, but I'll fight and take as long as necessary."

The legal documents explained, "Bouvier later said that a deal was 'clinched' at $127.5 million—"[t]erribly difficult, but it's a very good deal with regard to this unique masterpiece by Leonardo./ All of these representations were false. The negotiations were fabricated."

For the $127.5 sale, Bouvier received $1.275 million in accordance with his agreement with Rybolovlev for due diligence and administrative expenses, which dated back to their dealings as early as 2003. This was only one percent.

Bouvier also paid Tania Rappo, a close family friend, $4.92 million kickback on this transaction. Rybolovlev, who had made Rappo his younger daughter's godmother, had no idea.

PURCHASE YEAR	TITLE	ARTIST	CREATION YEAR	SALE PRICE
2004	*Les Noces de Pierrette*	Pablo Picasso	1905	$43.8 million
2006	*Nu couché aux bras levés*	Amedeo Modigliani	1916	$26.75 million
2006	*Mousquetaire à la pipe*	Pablo Picasso	1968	$12.5 million
2007	*Jeune fille blonde en buste*	Amedeo Modigliani	1919	€17.5 million
2008	*La danseuse rose*	Edward Degas	1877-80	€25 million
2008	*Te fare hymenée (La maison des chants)*	Paul Gaugin	1892	€54 million
2008	*Madame Hébuterne aux épaules nues*	Amedeo Modigliani	1919	€17 million
2008	*Nu dolent*	Amedeo Modigliani	1908	€18 million
2008	*Nu debout (Nu Medici, Vénus)*	Amedeo Modigliani	1917	$39 million
2008	*Nymphéas*	Claude Monet	1897-98	€46.5 million
2008	*Nymphéas*	Claude Monet	1914 –17	€42 million
2008	*La soeur de l'artiste*	Pablo Picasso	1899	€37.5 million
2009	*N° 1 - Royal Red and Blue*	Mark Rothko	1949	$24 million
2009	*Le Baiser*	Henri de Toulouse Lautrec	1892	€18 million
2009	*Paysage avec olivier montagnes en arrière plan*	Vincent Van Gogh	1889	€18 million
2011	*Saint Sebastian*	El Greco	1600	undisclosed
2011	*Femme de Venise IX*	Alberto Giacometti	1956	45 million CHF
2011	*La Méditerranée (Bronze)*	Aristide Maillol	1902-03	
2011	*Nu au châle vert*	Henri Matisse	1921-22	undisclosed
2011	*L'Homme assis au verre*	Pablo Picasso	1914	undisclosed
2011	*Jouer de flûte et femme nue*	Pablo Picasso	1970	€25 million
2011	*Jeunes filles au bord de I'eau*	Pierre Auguste Renoir	1885	$2.5 million
2011	*Eternel printemps (marble)*	Auguste Rodin	1901-02	£ 30 million
2011	*Le Baiser (Bronze)*	Auguste Rodin	1886	€7.5 million
2012	*Jesus et Madonna (Christ taking leave of his mother)*	El Greco	1579-80	€48 million
2011	*Le domaine d'Arnheim*	René Magritte	1938	$43.5 million
2012	*Nu couché au coussin bleu*	Amedeo Modigliani	1916	$118 million
2012	*Eve*	Auguste Rodin	1881	$26.25 million
2013	*Christ as Salvator Mundi*	Leonarda da Vinci	1499	$127.5 million
2013	*Otahi/Seule*	Paul Gaugin	1893	€120 million
2013	*Wasserschlangen II (Water Serpents)*	Gustav Klimt	1904-07	$183.8 million
2013	*Espagnole à l'éventail,*	Pablo Picasso	1957-58	€27 million
2013	*Femme se coiffant (Tête de femme)*	Pablo Picasso	1957	included
2013	*Au lit - le baiser*	Henri de Toulouse Lautrec	1892	€13.75 million
2013	*N° 6 (Violet, vert et rouge)*	Mark Rothko	1951	€140 million
2014	*Tête*	Amedeo Modigliani	1911-12	undisclosed

He later alleged that the team at Sotheby's had access to Bouvier's exchanges, knowing how much he purchased the work for, and for how much he sold it to Rybolovlev. When Bouvier was found to have inflated the prices, they did not provide the Russian team with related correspondence.

This behavior was later decried as fraud.

Both Rybolovlev and the sellers had been kept in the dark, and filed their own lawsuits: *Salvator Mundi. Sotheby's, Inc. v. R.W. Chandler, LLC et al*, in which the sellers demanded a larger percentage of the painting given Bouvier's $127.5 million, and *Accent Delight International LTD and Xitrans Finance LTD. v. Sotheby's and Sotheby's, Inc.* The former case, by the sellers, was the result of dismay at the defrauding, and a demand for their own compensation.

"While the Defendants' legal theories have been difficult to discern, they have asserted that Sotheby's should pay them, at a minimum, the difference in price between the $80 million they were paid and the $127.5 million that Rybolovlev paid Bouvier," the legal reporter explained, "They also have asserted that they intend to bring a civil action asserting, among other causes of action, claims alleging breach of fiduciary duty, fraud, and a violation of the civil RICO statute."

Ultimately, this was settled out of court with the legalese version of 'you should have known better'.

"The Defendants' claims are entirely without merit," the reporter read in closing, "These Defendants are experienced art professionals, experts in their fields, who voluntarily sold the Leonardo for a huge profit at a price they agreed to after direct, arms-length negotiations. Once Bouvier purchased the Leonardo, it was Bouvier's to hold or sell as Bouvier saw fit."

Bouvier himself echoed these sentiments. "I did nothing wrong," he said. "100% fair."

"If a hotel concierge gets a commission when he orders a taxi for me, he doesn't have to tell me," he clarified later. "It's the same thing at auction. If I buy a work of art from Sotheby's, I don't have to inform my client. Many art dealers buy in these houses. It's common practice."

But the latter lawsuit, spearheaded by the Russian oligarch, kept going. It was part of a wider assault against Bouvier in New York, Paris, Monaco and Singapore. In New York, documents implicated Sotheby's for facilitating the sale of 12 of the 37 artworks in question to Bouvier, for a total of 38 pieces (including furniture). They consigned for auction two of the works on Bouvier's behalf, one of which it previously sold him), and conducted valuations for four of the works, all of which the auction house had previously sold him themselves.

Per many records of exchanges between Rybolovlev's trustee liaison, Mikhail Sazonov in Geneva, Bouvier, and Valette at Sotheby's. Price inflation by Bouvier undoubtedly occurred. Whether the auction house "materially assisted the largest art fraud in history," remained to be confirmed in ongoing litigation as of 2018, because the precedents were as gray as the culpability.

In subsequent statements from Bouvier's lawyer, Daniel Levy, the emails in Rybolovlev's legal filings have been disputed.

"This is incorrect," Levy wrote. "Bouvier bought at one price and sold to Rybolovlev at a higher price. This is not price 'inflation.' Bouvier was a dealer entitled to buy and sale at prices that he saw fit."

During the sale process, Bouvier did not share his plans to resell da Vinci to Rybolovlev with Sotheby's. He reached out to them on his own as late as January 2015 to provide an updated insurance report on the da Vinci, which, according to the legal filings, insinuated not just that he may have still been the current owner, but as a potential way to validate the inflated price Rybolovlev had paid.

Bouvier's end defended this practice, saying that Rybolovlev had asked him for the insurance reports himself, as a way to earn credit on the paintings—the way that Evan Beard assured collectors had been doing industry-wide.

The logic on both sides worked out.

But one thing was for certain: Yves Bouvier had taken a total of $1 billion from Dmitry Rybolovlev.

In subsequent conversations with Bouvier's lawyer, Daniel Levy, this statement has been heatedly disputed as factually incorrect. "Bouvier had not 'taken' anything," Mr. Levy wrote by email. "He earned various amounts."

It was important to note that Bouvier and Rybolovlev did not create written sales contracts after the first two sales in 2003 and 2006. Instead, they generated two invoices, one for the sale of the work and the other for due diligence and administrative expenses performed by Bouvier's company, amounting to two percent.

Less than one year after the publication of the da Vinci price in the New York Times, Bouvier was arrested in Monaco. In 2017, Rybolovlev decided to sell the prized masterpiece at a prestigious auction house.

Christie's.

4

AUCTION

THE MINIMUM for the sale was $100 million, and the sale bids quickly shot up to $140 within seconds. Most likely, some of those bids had been placed in advance of the auction, but it was also common that many people bid early on at the lower end of a value proposition.

Pyklannen held the crowd's attention.

"95 and I go 110 over. 110. I have it. At 110. 100 million. Who will give me 120? 140. 130 million. 140 million is bid. At 140 million, with Alex."

Alex was Alex Rotter, Chairman of Post-War & Contemporary Art at Christie's. The decision to include an Old Master in a contemporary art sale was unusual, but it was intended to attract the trophy hunters who often seek out well-known works.

"140 million. 150 might take it. At 140 million holding at the moment."

The auctioneer's eyes darted around the room expectantly, then lit up with a bid.

"Where is that? 150. Welcome. At 150 million on the left. 160 might take it. At 150 million. Many takers still."

Again he darted. The words took on a singsong, lackadaisical quality as anticipation built.

"160 is bid back to…Alex, at 160 million. At 190 million give me 200. 190 is bid."

"200!" shouted Alex Rotter.

"200 million is bid." Repeated Pylkkänen, "At 200 million. At 200 million."

The auctioneer paused ever so slightly, not giving the crowd a moment to share in his shock. At 200 million, this painting had effectively surpassed any auction record in history, far beyond Picasso's *les femmes d'Algers* at $170 million in 2015. This transaction officially occurred in less than 60 seconds.

But hoots erupted from a normally clipped art crowd. It was very unusual behavior, but then again, this was a very unusual price.

"Shh!" Exclaimed Pylkkänen. Not only were the hoots indecorous in an auction tradition where so much as a fidget was deemed distracting to an auctioneer looking for raised paddles, but much more bidding was still to come.

"200 million. Please! 200 million is bid."

The crowd obliged and quieted down, more stupefied than obedient.

"Give me 10. At 200 million is bid. 200 million is *here*. Currently hanging with Alex on my right."

Pylkkänen practically chided the audience, like a disappointed schoolteacher. Were the antics really ending so soon?

"At 200 million…" he trailed, "For the Leonardo. At 200 million looking for 210."

And then an uptick, "Sir, are you back coming in? At 240 million. Currently.

"245 million…," he trailed, "…is bid. At 245 million."

He leaned over the podium and paused eagerly, looking at Loic Gouzer and Alex Rotter gesticulating and muttering on the phones.

Loic Gouzer was the Hollywood handsome 37-year-old contemporary art co-Chairman at Christie's, also on the phone bidders' block. Spearfisher, shark swimmer, passionate environmental fundraiser and close friend to Leonardo DiCaprio, it was he who was credited[16] with the strong relationships and the inclusion of the old master on the contemporary list. He corresponded directly with Dmitry Rybolovlev's replacement art dealer, Sandy Heller.

"250 million is bid." Pylkkänen shuffled a paper. "And back to Francois de Poortere."

Francois de Poortere was the Head of Old Masters. With this single sale, the increased revenues for Old Masters overall had already skyrocketed, breaking records across departments.

"At 266 million dollars." Pylkkänen said slowly, drawing out the impressive number.

"268 million; you heard it, ladies and gentlemen." He mused. Then he straightened up, using his commanding voice to keep the conversation going. "Back to Alex, at 268 million. Are we all out here?"

He gestured to the bidders.

"270 million. The hand goes up. 270 against you. Alex, would you like two-seven-five?" He asked, almost casually, as if they were ordering drinks. Then he quipped, ever-so-British, "Might do the trick."

Was he using humor to relax the audience, or a dose of sarcasm in his own bemusement? Perhaps it was both.

"270 million. Back to Francois de Poortere. Loic, are you out?"

Loic Gouzer shifted his head back and forth playfully, undecided.

"You all done? Pop back in with a five?" He prodded.

And then, emboldened Pylkkänen said firmly, "280. 280 million. An increment of 10 million, ladies and gentlemen, 280 million. With Alex. At 280 million dollars." He raised his arms triumphantly. "Are we all done?"

And the arms moved stage left. "…Maybe not. Don't take the photograph quite yet."

There was laughter from the audience, as the crowd stood poised with smartphones.

"286 million. 286 million. Would you give me 290, Alex?"

Pylkkänen gestured to Alex Rotter, who had his hand cupped over his mouth on the phone. Rotter nodded.

"I thought so," confirmed Pylkkänen. The crowd oohed. "300 million."

They erupted in applause.

"Let's see if that's done it. 300 million. At 300 million is still with Alex."

While the room waited, Pylkkänen prepared the hammer. "At 300 million dollars, *Salvator Mundi*, by Leonardo da Vinci, at 350 million dollars. Not yours at the moment. Give me a bid…"

And then a hand shot up.

"318 is bid," Pylkkänen said sharply. "The hand went up at 318 million now." He leaned back up against the podium, tempting the audience.

"At 318 million dollars. With François. 320 million we're still not done. At 320 million." He looked to his left. "At 320 million now. Give me 5 François. 320 I have 320 million. I'll have to hire you. At 320. 328 million.

"328 million back to François de Poortere. 330 million. At 330 million now. 330 million. Would you like five? 330 million is bid, ladies and gentlemen, and selling. At 330 million…with Alex's clients, ahead of you here at three…" he breathed, "Hundred and thirty-two million, back to Francois." He puckered for a moment, and then refocused, "At 332 million."

The auctioneer nearly giggled as he said, "Three-three-two is the number. Three-three-five?"

After a long pause, those in the room cooed again in surprise.

"For those of you following online you may not have heard it. The bid was 350, it was called, on the telephone. At 350 million, the Leonardo Salvator Mundi. At 350 million. Here at Christie's. At 350 million and looking for…another bid please, François."

The room laughed at the ridiculousness of such an ask, but Pylkkänen did not falter.

"At 350."

There was another long pause as the phone bidders debated.

"The conversation continues," he said in disbelief, "So we pause. At 350 million. 352 million." He sipped a glass of water, not breaking eye contact with the bidding area. He set the glass down to a quiet clink – evocative of the hammer soon to come. "352 million," he said again, eyes cast down, prepared to close out the most exciting sale of his life, "is bid. At 352 million dollars."

And with yet another pause, he announced gravely, "355 million dollars is bid." Then he turned to the phone bidders and asked, "Would you like 340?"

He meant 360 and was too flustered by the shattering record, "360, I beg your pardon. 360 million. 355 is bid. 355 is bid. 360 will be next. 370 is bid. 370 million. 370 million back to François' client."

And then Rotter shouted, "400 million."

The crowd gasped in unison, audibly shocked.

"400 million!" Pylkkänen all but exclaimed. He stared sassily at the crowd, then checked his paper. "400 million it's a bid. Here in the sale room at 400 million. With Alex Rotter. The bid is here at 400 million dollars," he breathed, face flushed, "The *Salvator Mundi* at 400 million."

But he still didn't miss a beat. "François is out. Are you sure, François? At 400 million then. Thank you all for your bidding here," he gestured to the room. "And on the telephone as well. And of course with François. It is with Alex Rotter, at 400 million.

"Selling here, at Christie's, 400 million is the bid and the piece…is…"

He hammered.

"Sold."

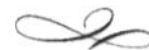

Everyone clapped. After the buyer's premium was added, the total for the da Vinci painting was $450.3 million.

Though the buyer at that time was still largely unknown, Dmitry Rybolovlev had just turned a profit of $322.5 million. For reference, as of August 2018, that was 2.5 million more than the net worth of Taylor Swift. The previously most expensive painting, the Picasso, had sold for less than half of the da Vinci.

That said, the comparisons to the Mona Lisa meant that, if true, this painting was rather accurately valued. The Mona Lisa was insured for $100 million, approximately $800 million in today's time.[17] Meanwhile, the ripple effect of this financial investment was undeniable. The Louvre in Paris, where the Mona Lisa was housed, noted it expected to receive 12 million visitors per year by 2025.[18]

So opening this painting to the public was a lifetime goldmine for both the buyer and its seller. But the seller, Rybolovlev, was still not satisfied.

LOUVRE ANNUAL VISITS (In Millions)	
2010	8.4
2011	8.9
2012	9.7
2013	9.3
2014	9.3
2015	8.6
2016	7.1
2017	8.1 (+14%)
2025	12 (projected)

He was still incensed at Yves Bouvier, and on principle, no painting's sum could quell his rage. Rybolovlev sought his justice relentlessly.

Rybolovlev had decided to sell the painting not for the money, but because it was a symbol of distrust. As one source close to the Russian attempted to explain, "What's the word? It was contaminated. It spoiled the enjoyment of the art."

Before the fallout, Bouvier had enlisted a team to compile a catalogue of all the works he sold to Rybolovlev. The book was meant to be impressive: it was large, heavy, and more than 500 pages, complete with vivid plates and reflective essays by art historian Joachim Pissarro. Paris-based Pissarro was the grandson of celebrated artist Camille Pissarro, and he liberally quoted legendary art historian John Richardson, who lived among the artists mentioned from the 20th century. Pissarro's essays were translated from the French by a group that included Vera Voitenkova, whose father, Geneva-based Alexandre Voitenkov, headed translation at the United Nations in Switzerland. She also did extensive Russian work for the Rybolovlevs.

Like the relationship between Bouvier and Rybolovlev, however, the catalogue was fractured. Each essay had its own story, and the entirety of the catalogue, while pedigreed, was rife with typos, duplicities and inconsistencies, alluding to the later holes and gaps in communication between the oligarch and his dealer.

Because ultimately, as the book quoted Albert Camus, "To collect is to be able to live one's past." The collection and the lives of the men who acquired it were blurred together, in a historic collaboration as much about art as it was about finance, politics, and the qualifications of loyalty.

It began when Rybolovlev was born in Russia.

II. The Potash Tsar

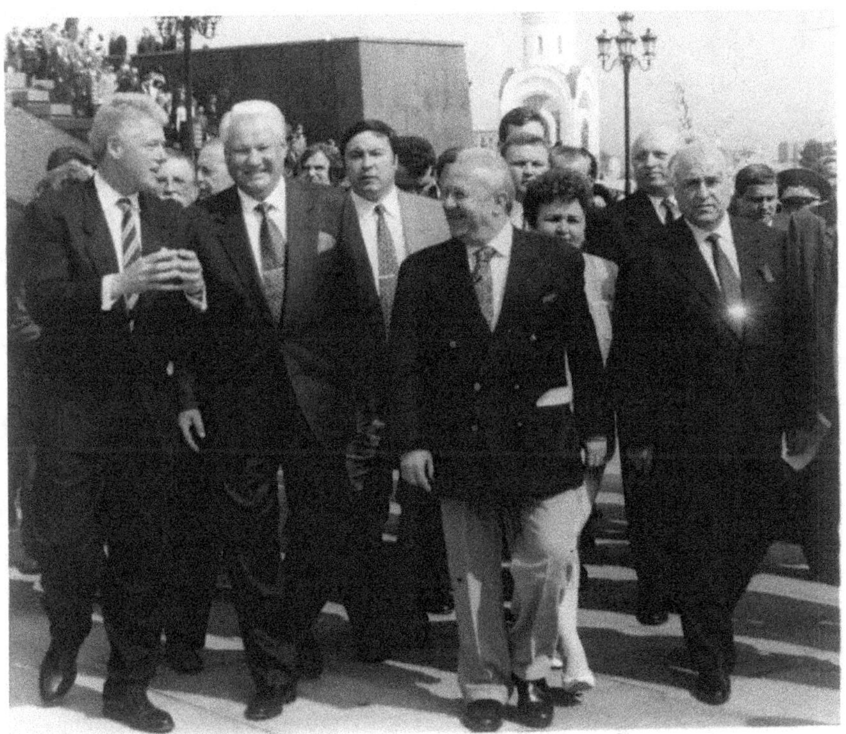

Then-President of the United States Bill Clinton walked with Boris Yeltsin on a tour of Russian art sites with Zurab Tsereteli, c. mid-1990s.

5

HEART PROBLEMS

Oligarchs eventually became near-mythical creatures in modern lore: omnipotent supervillains conquesting corporations and territories, tantalizing American audiences with their imperviousness. The recipe to acquire such a title in Post-Soviet Russia required state support, a large sum of money, and a sense of ruthlessness. The title came to embody seizure of opportunity; only through a series of choices and acts of fate was an oligarch molded by destiny.

Dmitry Yvegenyveich Rybolovlev was born on November 22nd, 1966 in a small town within Perm, Russia. He was the only child of Eugene and Zinaida, both doctors and professors at the Medical Academy of the State of Perm. Even-keeled, calculating, and academic, his father was a cardiologist—the kind of doctor who specialized in heart defects—and taught radiology. At the age of 11, young Rybolovlev was coincidentally diagnosed with myocarditis.

The disorder was marked by shortness of breath and fatigue, which was tied to lung issues and a general weakness for the young boy. Speaking to Rybolovlev in adulthood, biographer Arnaud Ramsay noted that he struggled with loneliness during this period, but nevertheless, had access to great education and relative physical freedom.

He followed in his parents' footsteps when it came time to pursue graduate education; he decided to attend the Medical Academy and pursue heart-related study, beginning his first semester in 1986. In the enrollment line, he met a beautiful blonde named Elena. Like him, he soon learned, she planned to study cardiology—heart medicine.

Rybolovlev and Elena quickly discovered that they had much more in common. They were the same age, both only children, and shared a love for arts and culture. Perm was known as much for its opera and ballet as its medical school, and the couple spent weeks together admiring the museums, theater, and myriad performances Perm had to offer. They were inseparable, and by July 1987, when Rybolovlev was still just 20 years old, they were married.

The first of two daughters, Elena, was born in 1989, and the couple graduated medical school together in 1990. Both parents were quoted as saying that the early years of their marriage were idyllic.

One tabloid did dispute that all was well. An article titled, "From Russia With Major Daddy Issues," in the *New York Post* claimed that Elena tried to leave her husband as early as 1989 with the newborn baby, staying with her mother. Enraged, Rybolovlev broke into the grandmother's apartment and tried to abduct the child, involved in a literal wrestling match.

Whether or not the marriage was stable, Rybolovlev forged ahead in his career after medical school. He worked briefly with his father on magnetics in medicine, but soon saw opportunity in the climate of a falling regime and transitioned to finance. After quickly finishing off a short course at the Ministry of Finance in Moscow in 1992, he founded his first company.[19-20]

Whereas many referred to as oligarchs were gifted state-owned enterprises, Rybolovlev was not—instead, he was both admired and feared for his cunning. Those close to him alleged he made his first million by reselling beer, never paying the original cost of the purchased goods.

Then he went into business with a man well-connected to the KGB, who let him know about the voucher system. Flanked by intimidating bodyguards, he went to the auction…for privatization.

As the Soviet Union fell, there was a scramble to capitalize on national resources. Corporations previously owned by the state were being offered to private entities—and individuals—with vouchers. Low-priced agreements were poorly publicized, and only those with ambition and shrewd strategic foresight were able to enter the discourse. In so doing, a select few in Russia became exorbitantly wealthy. These were the future oligarchs.

Privatization was not looked upon well by everyone. Mikhail Gorbachev, the last USSR President, was appalled at the rush on wealth. When the oligarchs soon became synonymous with a capitalist Russia, to him, they also became synonymous with greed.

"Bureaucrats," he told the BBC, "Stole the nation's riches and began to create corporations."[21]

However, Gorbachev was believed to have actively contributed to the downfall of his governing structure by facilitating positive relations with the West. He was not only perceived as a pawn of American interests, but also as a failure.

Gorbachev had worked closely with then-American President, George H. W. Bush, and thought they had reached an understanding, wherein the Soviet Union would remain intact as the Iron Curtain fell. Instead, when Bill Clinton became president in 1993, the initial agreements fell apart, along with the Russian economy.

It was Gorbachev's administration which allowed the Russian government to borrow mass amounts of U.S. Government funds, ultimately responsible for severely undervaluing Russian industry: 150,000 companies were valued at a grand total of 9.8 billion dollars by the foreign powers of the World Bank and the IMF. At one time, this was Rybolovlev's estimated net worth on his own.

Understandably, this devaluation caused massive financial upheaval. As American economist James Shelbourne Henry explained, "There was no way to protect those savings against the hyperinflation they decided to unleash…It was a Wild West."

The country was falling apart.

"With Gorbachev, people were sleeping in the streets!" Cried another businessman, with a proud portrait of current president Vladimir Putin and diamonds on display behind him. He declined to be named for safety reasons.

The fiscal and political ramifications of the strategy were undoubtedly catastrophic for the Russian economy. Gorbachev's successor, Boris Yeltsin, was also considered to be a pawn of Western interests. He was a comical figure ridiculed for his repeatedly debilitating drunk and disorderly conduct[22], whose economic ineptitude left the country in even more uncertainty by the end of his tenure, resulting in the Russian ruble crash of 1998.[23] One Russian spokesman compared his attitude, misbehavior, and collusion to a modern day Donald Trump.

Former *Forbes Russia* editor and author of *Godfather of the Kremlin* Paul Klebnikov (1963-2004, unsolved assassination), took a similarly sensationalistic view of the scramble for power in Yeltsin's Russia, writing, "For the Russian people, the Yeltsin era was the biggest disaster since the Nazi invasion of 1941."[24] Industry was at an all-time low, hyperinflation of Russian currency was at an all-time high, and the savings and access of the individual were depleted beyond control. Unemployment was at 30%, there was no pension program, and no healthcare. As companies privatized, fear, uncertainty and doubt abounded.

Most smaller companies and shops were cashed out locally, while companies widely responsible for natural and industrial resources, largely fell into the voucher program. Rybolovlev's later potash (a potassium fertilizer) venture fell into this category, while health and education sectors remained state subsidized. There were also corporatized businesses that became stockholder companies.[25]

"On the face of it, [privatization is] a very noble idea," Klebnikov said in a 2002 interview.[26] "Theoretically, it could create a kind of Jeffersonian broad-based middle class of small property owners, who, in turn, would be the foundation for a democratic Russia. It all went terribly wrong."

Sounder economic alternatives less attuned to Western interests may have prevented the financial uncertainty, such as a Marshall Plan. Instances of corruption by Americans in Russia during the period were arguably just as prevalent as those by well-connected citizens. Based on the policy decisions of the period, there was a case to be made that Americans in the region were even more suspect.

Russian or American, anyone with the advantageous knowledge of the low-priced industrial vouchers was able to purchase them for far below market value, capitalizing by any means necessary. Ill-informed citizens outside the realms of business and crime were either willfully or accidentally left out of the discourse, and by proxy, the discourse of Russian corporate history.

Later, this fiscal reality became important in terms of art investment. Tangible goods could be safer than volatile currency, especially when they maintained status as cultural heritage.

The select few who were able to obtain vouchers usually did so in bulk, paving their way to careers as oligarchs without any consequences for the way business was handled during this frenetic and uncertain period. Some oligarchs were deliberately presented with state vouchers during privatization as a gesture of goodwill.

But Rybolovlev did not fall into the favored category right away. He was only 28 in 1994, making the transition from medicine to investment banking in troubled times. His family still lived in their modest home in Perm, and his daughter was five.

Rybolovlev's intentions were the source of mild debate in his circles. To some, he was a resilient underdog, triumphing over his humble origins as a medical scholar in the Machiavellian world of Russian mob tactics through calculated moves. To others, navigating the complexities of privatizing Russia rendered him hopelessly corrupt.

Fending off criminal organizations of corporate mercenaries and gangs was a prerequisite to defending these shares. To do business meant to protect one's life simultaneously. The threat of murder, as one Russian associate shared matter-of-factly, "Was the method of settling the problem."

Bill Browder, a rare American to come to prominence during this period, succinctly summed up his perspective on the dangers of Russian business in his tell-all book about his experiences.[27]

First, he detailed the bidding process. It was an auction: the buyer announced he wanted to purchase a company voucher, then quite literally, another man waved a card. The buyer went to the table with the appropriate amount of cash per share, and the vouchers were presented. Though decidedly less glamorous, the process was much like the blue-chip auctions where Rybolovlev's art was later sold.

The differences were the level of safety and the possibility for grave consequence.

"In Russia there is no respect for the individual and his or her rights." Browder wrote, "People can be sacrificed for the needs of the state, used as shields, trading chips, or even simple fodder. If necessary, anyone can disappear. A famous expression of Stalin's drives right to the point: 'If there is no man, there is no problem.'"

Whether Rybolovlev was exceptionally criminal was thus a question of perspective.

"Rybolovlev's profile is absolutely no different from others who built their fortunes on the fall of the USSR," said one source to Ramsay, "If, as criteria for determining who is an oligarch, you refer to the false bankruptcies and other methods of theft for taking control of production capital that the original shareholders divided among themselves, or to government corruption, he is clearly among them."

Nevertheless, Rybolovlev persisted as a determined money manager. He bought up 20 companies through the bank utilizing the voucher program, singlehandedly joining the ranks of Russia's increasingly powerful men.

He was not alone in this astute venture. Other increasingly wealthy investors were using any means necessary to obtain their shares.

To be the owner of privatized companies through these frenzied yet strategic means was step one in earning the title of oligarch, but it was not everything. Work ethic was undoubtedly a factor as well, as became apparent when Rybolovlev took the helm at the Perm-based fertilizer company, Uralkali.

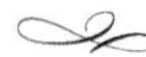

Uralkali was a potash company based in Berezniki, 200 kilometers from Perm, Russia. Thanks to the new management and a reputedly terrifying corporate culture of output and accountability, the potash, a locally sourced potassium carbonate fertilizer, was being exported across BRIC markets, particularly to new markets in China. It was distributed through the International Potash Company, or IPC.

The Ural region was relatively rural and picturesque, but has its place in Russia's complex history. Named for the Ural mountains that divided Europe and Asia, the nearby Kama River was one of the largest in the` country. Trees dotted the landscape through the spring and summer in a vivid green, and come winter, snowfalls render the region worthy of Olympic skiers.[28]

The president of Russia when Rybolovlev took over Uralkali, Boris Yeltsin, was born in the Ural region in 1931,[29] just three years before potash mining began there. Yeltsin's father moved the family to Berezniki after he was released from a Gulag work camp, which were common in the Perm region, seeking work as a laborer in 1937. Young Boris lost two fingers during the period while throwing a hand grenade into a church—even more ironic as the town of Berezniki was briefly called 'Molotov,' though the namesake of the Molotov cocktail arose tangentially during the Spanish Civil War.[30]

The namesake of Molotov was apt in that it suggested a characterization of violence, and Post-Cold War Perm abounded in danger and subsequent paranoia. During this period, Rybolovlev first earned his reputation as cold, icy, and protected, with a general distrust that remained part of perceptions of him for decades to come.

When asked about this characterization during an evening in Monaco decades later, a source close to the oligarch laughed and answered, "I was touching him today and he's quite warm. He's absolutely normal, like everybody."

Then the laughter stopped abruptly.

"OK, first impression: he's a bit suspicious, as it is around any person with money and power," he added, before quickly returning to a strong defense.

He had never been charismatic or friendly, but he had earned respect as a man of few words, anticipating others' next moves and staying on top in his business dealings.

Rybolovlev was already using bodyguards as early as 1993.[31] He was also wearing a bulletproof vest, which he slept in.

To be sure, it was not without reason. Snipers lurked in dark corners, waiting specifically for him. As a majority stakeholder in a number of powerful companies, his life was in the way of many powerful entities.
The problem was endemic. Mafia hitmen were regularly killing translators as well, to send the ultimate "shoot the messenger" warning.

Two years later, in 1995, Rybolovlev held a 66% company stake at Uralkali and was Chairman of the Board, overseeing decisions for the entire potash company. His family was sent to live in Switzerland for their protection, and Rybolovlev joined them a few months later.

Not only was the move imperative to protect both family and financial security, but the Swiss banking system was widely known for its discretion. Rybolovlev was protecting his assets as much as his family. Throughout all conflict, he continued to fly to Russia from his mainstay in Geneva, maintaining business there into present day.

And in a world where law was suspect, loyalty was the true currency. Looking intensely into someone's eyes, the Russian team claimed, became far more important than any contract.

At the time, IPC held 40% of the shares of Neftekhimik, a subsidiary, and 44-year-old Yevgeny Panteleimonov was at the helm. He had only become the General Director at Neftekhimik earlier that year, following the resignation of his predecessor in anticipation of the shareholder meeting.[32]

That summer, Panteleimonov urged Rybolovlev to quell mafia involvement at Neftekhimik, which the budding oligarch approved. However, unlike the oligarch with his seemingly drastic security measures, Panteleimonov decided not to enlist a bodyguard.

On September 3rd, 1995, company shareholders voted to divest from IPC.

On September 4th, 1995, Panteleimonov woke early for his breakfast at home. He lived on the 10th floor, and went to his landing at the top of his stairwell around 8am. There, a hitman shot him four times, and he died instantly. No one claimed they saw the killer as he left.

An elderly neighbor living on the 16th floor heard the shots. She found the body at the foot of the stairs.

After a large-scale investigation, a man named Oleg Lomakin was traced. During his plea deal offering, he claimed Rybolovlev had purchased two unlicensed pistols[33] for the contract killers and ordered the hit. Lomakin recounted his version of events in great detail, citing that the killers had not been paid the money they had been promised.

Confidants told a version of the story that said Rybolovlev was framed by the board, who blackmailed him to gain control of his shares. Since he refused to give them up, he had to pay the price with prison time.

It was a negotiation tactic, to terrorize him.

He insisted that murdering Panteleimonov himself did not make sense. After all, as he told *Forbes Russia*, why would you kill a director you'd just appointed?

Regardless of his culpability, the initial wealth of evidence was unforgiving. Rybolovlev was arrested for Evgeny Panteleimonov's murder. He was sent to prison in 1995.

6

WHITE SWAN

THE PRISON where Rybolovlev landed was for not-yet-convicted felons in Perm. He never made it to White Swan, where the long-term criminals languished, and the prison's eerily innocent nickname was gleaned from its blindingly white walls. Regardless, life was lived in darkness.

In prison, the wealthy businessman was stripped of his identity. Hair shorn and dressed in the uniform, nothing about him stood out, and he was treated like any other convicted felon. Prison guards patrolled the halls at all hours, selecting inmates to abuse one at a time.

When the summer arrived, the ventilation was exceptionally terrible, and Rybolovlev was not the only inmate who struggled to breathe. What was worse, his myocarditis, the heart problems from childhood, returned to exacerbate his symptoms as they spread to his lungs.

Conditions quickly became unbearable. One weekend, biographer Arnaud Ramsay reported, Rybolovlev was crammed into a single cell with 12 other inmates, and one died from the ventilation blockages in the room. Another night, 60 people were crammed into a room, with not enough room for everyone to sit.

He approached the guards and informed them his health was too poor to endure these cramped quarters. It was positioned as a threat rather than a complaint. "If I die," he told them, "You will have so many problems."

Horrific though it was, Rybolovlev used his medical training to help those close to him with untreated ailments. He cautiously began his time at the prison saying he was a doctor, not a wealthy executive, to avoid any consequential business dealings or animosities. To say imprisonment was isolating would be an understatement: he withdrew from his parents, wife and daughter, in a hole of poor health and depression.

Soon he developed kidney stones from the dehydration. These went untreated because the guards thought he was lying, but without help, the kidney damage could have proved fatal.

In November 1996, Rybolovlev celebrated his 30th birthday behind bars. By this point, friends and connections on the outside were concerned, and managed to get his favorite song on television with a subtitled message. He watched wistfully as Hotel California played on the screen, and the message below the English words said, "We wish you a happy birthday. And we hope you'll soon be out."

Eventually, legal dealings outside the jail did start to turn his life around. Interventions by noted regional politicos were persistent enough that the case was reopened. Lomakin recanted his statement, claiming that he had slandered Rybolovlev, and received a sentence of 15 years in 1997. He served 12 years of the terms, released on parole in 2009. Like Ryobolovlev, Lomakin maintained his financial holdings from before his detainment.[34]

Thanks to Lomakin's reversal, Rybolovlev was released on a bail of 1 billion rubles after 11 months, then fully acquitted by the High Court. He had survived, along with his continued majority stake in Uralkali. As the primary stakeholder, he earned the nickname in the media—the Potash Tsar.

But the emotional toll was severe. Long baths, silverware, and even the light of day felt surreal. In the end, the release from prison was a turning point in his life. Financial security could not trump personal safety again; he ruthlessly strove for both.

Returning to his home in Geneva, Rybolovlev sent three identical cars to the same pickup and drop-off locations—same model, same color, even identical license plates. This tactic was designed to protect him from assassins. No one could be sure which car was his.

He had escaped.

III. Fine Art Protectors

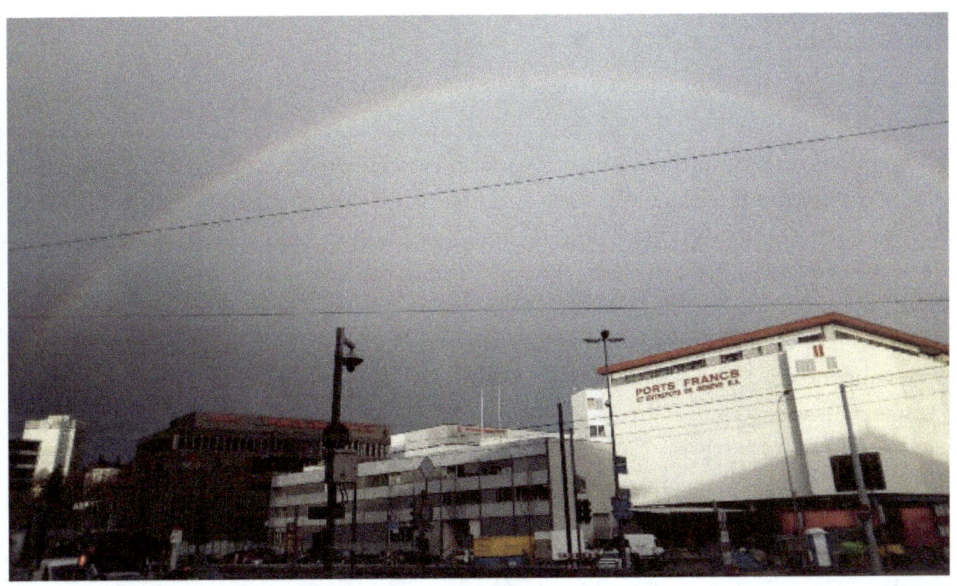

The Geneva Freeport, taken by Alexandra Bregman

7

FIXTURES

Recovering from the harrowing prison experience, Geneva in 1996 was a refuge. Its famous clear lakes and history of peace must have provided a sense of instant relief to the Rybolovlev family, constantly threatened whenever they were back in Perm. Perhaps the landscape bore reference to their hometown, with the winding streams of water and snow-covered mountains a distant drive away. There was a Russian Orthodox church a 10-minute drive from the new home, and a museum in neighboring Lausanne called The Hermitage Foundation, not so unlike the Hermitage in St. Petersburg. The only white swans were the beautiful birds on Lake Geneva.

But based on the accounts of those in her orbit, it seemed Elena Rybolovleva felt entirely lost in her new home city. She had spent the first few months there by herself with her young daughter while her husband languished in jail, and spoke no French or English. Encumbered by these emotional burdens, she was having some difficulties navigating her new home.

Then she went to the dentist, a Swiss man named Jacques-Olivier Rappo. He took pity on his client, who was miserable and alone while her husband was imprisoned in Russia. Olivier, as he was known, suggested Elena meet his wife, who spoke Russian, in addition to her native Bulgarian, French and English. Olivier himself spoke at least English, French and German fluently. Together, they were easygoing, open, and very communicative. It wasn't long before the whole family went to his dentistry office, and they spent many hours getting to know each other as the years began to pass.

To Elena, Tania Rappo was a warm and important friend.

No doubt, they were different: Where Elena struggled with language, Tania was a talented translator. Where Elena was tense, even stilted, her new friend Tania was indisputably gregarious and excitable. Where Elena was blonde and uneasy, Tania Rappo had jet black hair and sparked conversation and connection wherever she went. Where Elena felt young and insecure, Tania was more than a decade older and wiser, born November 20th, 1950—just two days before her husband, though 15 years his senior.

The Rappos were also deeply passionate about culture. Olivier was a well-to-do dentist, but he had been very artistic as a child, painting and drawing. He even had an uncle connected to the prestigious Beaux-Arts institute in Geneva in the early 1960s. When he had expressed interest in pursuing an artistic career path as a young boy, he was dissuaded at his Catholic school. The teacher leaned in and whispered, "You know, you'll have to paint naked women. Are you sure you want to do that?"

Later, in his thirties, he returned to art and took figure drawing classes at night—with the very nude models his teachers had warned him about. The Rappo family's two children later pursued careers in musical composition and architecture, educated and working around the globe.

Tania Rappo herself was an avid reader. She had worked in publishing in Bulgaria at the dawn of a new literary age, translating French to English. Later, she worked for a Russian cultural foundation, once again leveraging her language skills.

But she was also a true aesthete. She had a love of Asiatic art, with Japanese folding screens and Buddhist hanging scrolls. She juxtaposed French crown molding with Eastern European gold, with English books about Roman saints beside Chinese porcelains on her bookshelf. She was the kind of person who would go to an Egon Schiele exhibition more than once.

Rappo was literary, aesthetic, and passionately curious, laughing, smiling and charming. She later found a love of Instagram, capturing the most beautiful moments from her travels around London, Paris and Monaco as a way to find joy in the every day, coping with hardships that had arisen.

In the beginning, Elena was in awe.

"That's what Elena always said, you know?" said Sixtine Crutchfield, a source close to Bouvier's affairs, who heard about her needs secondhand. "'You're so comfortable. Show me how to behave. Show me how to dress. Show me what to say. Show me how to be.'"

Crutchfield was the quintessential Geneva woman. She was well-educated, well-connected, and as down-to-earth as she was knowledgeable. With German and French parentage, a British boarding school and American university education, 15 years in Australia and decades in Geneva, she was effortlessly international and open to helping out. She was also very important to the underpinnings of the Swiss art market.

But like a good Swiss citizen, Crutchfield was so discreet as to be anonymous. To the overt Russian culture of status that Elena had been living in, she went largely unnoticed, much to her annoyance. Meanwhile, Rappo instantly became a fixture in the family's life, and they felt indebted to their new friend.

Loyalty was paramount to the Rybolovlevs. In the cutthroat world of imprisonment and assassinations they had just left behind, trust was a priceless asset, and its power was boundless. As Dmitry later told *Tatler,* "It's a Russian trait. When you have a friend, you trust them absolutely. It's probably not the right way."

Although closeness with Elena came with Dmitry, Rappo remained very wary of her friend's important husband. "He's a fascinating man," Rappo recalled in *Monaco Matin,* "But will immediately turn your blood to ice. He's someone hard and cold, who does not speak much."

It was a question of boundaries. In cases of people like Tania, the Russian oligarch expected more than complete trust; he expected subservience. Rappo worked closely to procure whatever they desired, but she was secretly frustrated. She was chafing against the feeling that she was a slave to their demands. Elena was difficult, and Rappo was practically their concierge.

Because the Rybolovlev family had essentially come to Geneva completely green. Their new Swiss compatriots considered them unsophisticated even by Russian standards, coming from a low-brow mining region rather than the sleeker city of Moscow. Their overt requests (and not just from Rappo) for favors grew larger, even as the family grew more dissatisfied with Switzerland and each other.

To be sure, Elena threw herself into her assimilation and self-improvement, and quietly earned respect for her diligence and determination. She hired English and French tutors, and was eager to find herself in the right circles. With Crutchfield's connections helping her navigate the locality through a connection to Tania Rappo, many of the doors she sought were opened.

It started with writing a letter here or there, and with each of these odds and ends, Elena came to rely on her more and more, and Rappo reportedly took advantage of her friendship. Rumor had it that when Elena went into one of Geneva's designer shops like Chanel and Celine, Rappo would walk behind her and quietly take a commission. On her end, the friend denied the kickbacks.

The requests gradually grew more outlandish. Elena asked for an introduction to join the Fondation pour Genève, a society for the wives of expats to enjoy the finer points of flower arrangement and strolling by the lake where admission was normally by invitation only. Then it was assistance gaining entry to the Golf Club of Geneva, hailed on their website as "a haven of peace." [35] Elena and her husband even asked for their daughter, Ekaterina, to have tea at a royal equestrian club, where she might have a chance to meet and marry one of the British princes. Sixtine Crutchfield's boarding school friend, the school's founder, did her the favor and obliged…though the prince was not there that day.

In one particularly surprising story, Elena requested a butler, and had managed to procure an English butler from the Queen of Sweden. He did not last, but somehow found work in Trinidad with the British Ambassador there. That kind of pedigree had not been good enough for Elena.

Despite all of her requests, Elena was rarely seen. She was a ghost at the Fondation pour Geneve.

"I was the one who knew her," Crutchfield said, "Whether she actually knows that, I don't know. But I've never seen her."

She continued, "The president once told me, 'Oh your friend Elena? She never participates.'"

More than awkward, she was an absentee.

"Geneva's small. You do meet people," Crutchfield explained. "At the art things, I'm there all the time…I'm often out there. She's never there. I've never seen her once."

The couple was also not philanthropic, which bothered Crutchfield, active in many charitable organizations.

"It wasn't that they gave too little," Crutchfield said, "It was that they gave nothing."

Nevertheless, Rappo deeply understood the importance of connections, and provided support when Elena needed it most. In 2000, Elena became pregnant with her second child, and her husband went on what she thought was a business trip. Shortly afterwards, she received an anonymous FedEx containing explicit photos of him in a compromising position. She was sent into a shock so strong, it looked like she was going to miscarry. Elena spent the next five months bedridden to prevent further harm.

Anna was born in 2001, and Tania Rappo was named godmother.

By then the Rybolovlevs were living in the posh, exclusive neighborhood of just 5000 in Cologny, where they immediately began building the ultimate dream home. They bought the neighboring properties with the intention to create their own "Petit Trianon," inspired by the Palais de Versailles in Paris. The vision for the Rybolovlev version was estimated at a cost of €70 million, with a swimming pool overlooking Lake Geneva.

Like the Rybolovlevs, Marie Antoinette was rich and powerful, but technically foreign and vulnerable. The young queen arrived to France from Austria as a bride in her teens, unfamiliar with her new home, and during her reign as queen, she was eager to make an impression. She wore the latest and most provocative fashions, and was willfully imaginative and theatrical. Trying to make the marriage work, King Louis XVI bequeathed her the Petit Trianon as a place where she could be herself, spend time with her friends, and surround herself with her favorite things. She was eager to decorate…even as the property later became a symbol of her untimely demise.

While it was a place to impress, Elena's Trianon was also a place to protect herself, insulated away from critics and prying eyes. Once again, the value on security was paramount to the Rybolovlev family.

Noting that the walls in Cologny were fitted with light sconces designed to show off installed paintings, it was natural for the homeowners to take advantage of these existing accoutrements and start buying top-quality paintings. But this innocent comment about the light fixtures was seen as gauche by the art lovers of Geneva's upper-crust. Despite their best efforts, the Rybolovlevs were still not fitting in. The construction was viewed as over-the-top and an eyesore, and the newfound love of art was seen as rudimentary and fumbling. Either way, it was a pivotal moment in Rybolovlev's wealth acquisition. It was time for him to start buying art.

True to form, Dmitry allegedly told Elena, Rappo, and later Yves Bouvier that it could not be just any art collection.

"He only wanted exceptional paintings," said Bouvier. In French, *que des tableaux d'exceptions.*

In the catalogue Bouvier eventually compiled on Rybolovlev's behalf, essayists compared Rybolovlev's collection to the two most important individual collectors in Russian history: Sergei Ivanovitch Shchukin (1854-1939) and Ivan Abramovitch Morozov (1871-1921) who together were instrumental in creating the Pushkin Museum in Moscow and the Hermitage Museum in Saint Petersburg. Like Rybolovlev, both these individuals collected rapid-fire: in Morozov's case, under a decade, and in Shchukin's, less than two.

Both the Russian collectors were equally passionate about Impressionists, working with Cézanne, Matisse, and Picasso. Through his comparable fervor, Rybolovlev was poised to become an equally meaningful part of this same art collector cannon, as his purchases and warehouses went on to span the globe.

"This stunning collection…immediately reveals Rybolovlev's extraordinary eye, which is never satisfied by anything less than iconic works," the catalogue explained, "And whose fine-tuned sensibility can be seen in the masterpieces that make up this collection. They clearly indicate the standard to which Dmitry Rybolovlev has sworn allegiance: pure and simple excellence, or nothing."

Rappo rose to the occasion and came to the rescue again, though with hesitation.

As Rappo later recalled, his request was simple and explicit.

"He said, 'I want somebody to sell me paintings.'"

"I said, 'Listen, I am not very good,'" she shared with Sam Knight at the *New Yorker*. "I knew it was quite a tricky world."

In the subsequent conversation, she explained, "I didn't have a lot of friends in the art world. I didn't understand anything commercial. I'm a great art lover, but I didn't know anything about the commerce of art."

Without being intimately familiar with the innerworkings of the art market or even private sales etiquette whatsoever, Rappo had leveraged existing contacts.

She called friends who had a gallery in Baden-Baden, and told them, "I have a Russian friend who wants to buy something."

She procured the Rybolovlev family's first major acquisition: *Le Grand Cirque* by Marc Chagall, an oil on canvas.[36]

8

GRAND CIRCUS

MARC CHAGALL was born Moyshe Segal in Vitebsk, a small town in modern-day Belarus in 1887. He came from modest origins even by the standards of the day, longing for a grander life rife with imagination. Like Rybolovlev, he came of age at a pivotal time in Russia's revolutionary tide, in which a man of modest circumstances had a chance to become something bigger. Turning 30 in 1918, he bore witness to the fall of the Russian monarchy, and the rise of the proletariat.

There were many factors involved in the end of Russia's ruling family in favor of communist sentiments, but arguably the richest narrative of the period concerned the reigning Romanovs. Tsar Nicholas the II was the handsome heir to the Russian Empire, descended through the hereditary kingdom for centuries. He was not an exceptionally prudent political leader, instead making a name for himself by falling deeply in love with his distant German cousin, who after a charmed courtship went onto become Tsarina Alexandra.[37] Nicholas and Alexandra were considered alarmingly casual by their aristocratic peers, parading their passion for one another and family excursions in play clothes following the births of their four ebullient daughters (Maria, Olga, Tatiana and Anastasia). Tensions and misunderstandings only escalated with their youngest child, and only son's, diagnosis of hemophilia.

This was also the apex of Alexandra's anxiety. Her precious sense of security in family, an oasis away from courtly politics, faltered, and her reliance on a single friend weighed intensely—a self-proclaimed healer and mystic named Grigori Rasputin.

Rasputin's mystic man tendencies seemed to quell both her son's seemingly unstoppable bursts of bleeding, the young boy's most terrifying symptom, and

Alexandra's own mounting anxiety. She ignored rumors of Rasputin's sexual and interpersonal propriety, craving the peace of mind he gave her in the short-term.

But the quick fix only made matters worse: by insulating herself from other important connections and advisors, Alexandra left the family vulnerable to political adversaries from all directions. They were assassination targets as the nation teetered on the brink of a massive coup. The threat was not empty: shortly after the alliance with Rasputin tightened, the monarchy was overthrown, and the family was assassinated one by one. The moral was acute: trusted friends may have provided much-needed love and support in times of vulnerability, but ambition negated calculation and a wide network to maintain strength. Lacking foresight, consequences were fatal.

In contrast, the revolution was anything but tragic for Chagall. It was cataclysmically positive. Changing legislation allowed Jews like himself to leave their designated ghettos, newly immunized against discrimination.[38] It was a time for all manner of possibilities.

As a tastemaker in his own lifetime, Chagall was not initially a definitive figure among the avant-gardists and the conceptual abstractionists. This held true in Russia, where geometrics were more aligned with the parred-down communist ideology radically renouncing the old regime. What Chagall had to offer was an infectious sense of joy. Happiness superseded trend, and later became highly collectible as a symbol of resilience in revolt.

Galvanized by the shifting tectonics of change, Chagall painted his euphoria. Scenes of everything from landscapes and marital bliss to circus performers swinging swollen in vibrant helter-skelter motions, the figures tilted around in compositions as revolutionary as the political climate that surrounded him with ecstasy. *Le Grand Cirque* was a recurrent motif in Chagall's work, stemming from a formative childhood memory of a circus performance he saw with his family. The elements of whimsy and unpredictability coupled with deep, strong tones of red, green and blue, with tinges of golden yellow underscoring the dually melancholic and joyful shapes that have come to define his canon.

The schema first appeared as a series of drawings encouraged by Chagall's Paris print dealer, Ambroise Vollard.[39] While in France, Chagall reinvented himself with his Francophone spelling and life as a successful artist removed from the social trappings of Russian society, but he never lost his love for the fanfare of a grand circus performance. He attended the more ornate circuses of Pars with Vollard as he adjusted to his new home city as a painter, celebrating culture in all its forms.

Quoting the artist's writings, Sotheby's published Chagall as saying:

"It's a magic world, the circus, an age-old game that is danced, and in which tears and smiles, the play of arms and legs take the form of great art...The circus is the performance that seems to me the most tragic. Throughout the centuries, it has been man's most piercing cry in his search for entertainment and joy."

Melodramatic, perhaps, to suggest that Rybolovlev's decision to purchase his first painting was a "most piercing cry in his search for entertainment and joy," but undoubtedly the investment in art was one of both financial and emotive power. Of all the artworks to acquire at the dawn of a new passage in one's life, in the move from Russian to Francophone territory following a revolution, the similarities made for a meaningful assertation of his evolution.

Another critical inclusion in the circus motif was audience. Performances were defined in these compositions as much by their whimsy as the people bearing witness. In a time of development and discovery, being seen on a scene was just as critical to moving forward.

In Rybolovlev's case, it wasn't enough to just have Rappo; they needed to make a name for themselves in society on their own.

He settled on his first art purchase of Chagall's *Le Grand Cirque* (1968). The artist was 81 the year it was painted, continuing his self-expression with the same childlike wonder long into his rich life of creativity. In 2003, Rappo facilitated the sale. She told *Monaco Matin*:

> "With the game of intermediaries, the painting, which was valued at 5 million at the start, was going to be sold to him for 8 million. Through my contacts, I learned who the best sellers were, and I presented these people directly to Rybolovlev. I therefore economized 3 million euros. And that was the single, exceptional time where there was a direct monetary exchange between him and me. He sent me back 50,000 euros. But it is important to note as well that some time later, he resold the work for 12 million euros!"

Meanwhile, Rybolovlev was paranoid. There was no authenticity certificate for the work, and he wasn't sure who had helped on the deal.

Rappo, it turned out, was only able to barely finagle the first major sale, with assistance. She had fumbled around her social circles to procure the type of masterpiece Rybolovlev was looking for. She needed to find someone with far more access.

That was how Rappo met Yves Bouvier.

At first, he felt like a saving grace. Rappo and Rybolovlev went to the Geneva Freeport together to work on Chagall business. It was Rappo's first time there, after living in Geneva for almost 15 years. She was not a billionaire art collector, and had no need for a freeport. She had not even realized such a business existed. When Bouvier saw them both for the first time, he echoed their sentiment of unfamiliarity.

"Even though Tania lived in Geneva, I'd never seen her in my life," Bouvier said.

They were concerned because while Rybolovlev had already paid for the piece, he wanted a certificate of authenticity. It was on exhibit in Israel and they were unable to get the paperwork.

"I calmed him down," Bouvier explained.

As he previously paraphrased to Knight, "I will find the certificate for you, and I will be quiet."

This was ideal to Rybolovlev, who perceived him as discreet and sound. "I would not call him a great personality," Rybolovlev said in the same piece, "But he was calm, discreet, and intelligent."

He turned to Rappo and said, "That's exactly the kind of person we need."

Bouvier dutifully called the previous owner, obtained the proper provenance and insurance documentation, and returned with it to Rappo. From there, he moved swiftly.

He called Rappo shortly after the first introduction. Rappo recalled the conversation in detail.

"Madame," Bouvier said, "Can we have a coffee?"

She agreed.

Once in person, Bouvier explained his intentions. "From what they said, I understand your friends who bought the Chagall want to buy more paintings. I have a lot of paintings for sale."

Then Bouvier asked Rappo a question that would change her life forever.

"Would you organize a business meeting with Rybolovlev for me?"

In return, Rappo asked, "Why don't you just go to him directly?"

"First of all, I don't have his telephone number," Bouvier explained to her. "I don't know how to get to him. And I would never do it, if you didn't organize the meeting."

Rybolovlev was almost impossibly inaccessible, and going through Tania Rappo was a more deferential approach.

Then he added, "'If you arrange that meeting for me and I sell something…there will be something for you."

She did not believe him. Many money makers made false promises when it came to remunerations. But at first, it was a means to an end. After all, Rybolovlev was eager to build his collection.

"He was asking me all the time for services. All the time. For everything," she later said. "You know, I was like a sort of conciergerie. And I was doing it with pleasure. But funnily enough, I did it more for Dmitry than for Bouvier."

So she indulged in one of her networking habits—picking up her phone immediately, in front of the person who needed the introduction. In that moment, she was relieved someone else would be handling the art investment, not to mention one of the family's many requests.

She got Rybolovlev on the phone.

"That guy we met, he wants to have a business meeting with you, because he has paintings to sell," she said.

Rybolovlev responded that he wanted to meet.

"Immediately."

Within hours, Bouvier met with the Rybolovlevs at home in Cologny, offering information about the freeport and his suite of art consulting services.

Rappo was there at the beginning of the first deal, but left early. Her son had karate.

From there, Bouvier took control of Rybolovlev's art collection.

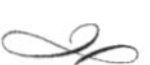

"Natural Le Coultre is convinced that behind the diversity of objects collected by individuals as well as institutions lies an unquenchable thirst for knowledge, enterprise and discovery. Together, an extraordinary journey begins."
-   Natural Le Coultre Presentation, 2014[40]

Yves Charles Edgar Bouvier was born on September 8th, 1963 in Geneva, Switzerland. He was raised in Avully, a very small town in the Swiss countryside of less than 1800 people, about 20 minutes from Geneva by car. With its rolling green hills and convenient locale, it was a hometown aligned with a childhood typical of a nondescript Swiss man, raised in the quiet calm.

For all intents and purposes, Bouvier was born and raised entrenched in a world of Swiss discretion, and built a name for himself to that end. He appeared at first glance to be a nondescript, middle-aged European gentleman, with tufty blonde hair, a receding hairline offsetting a slightly weathered physiognomy, and the standard business trademark of a crisp blue shirt. His upbringing had been upper-class and secure, and his childhood friends surrounded him well into his fifties. After high school (Collège en Suisse), he was studying economics when he decided to drop out of school and ski as much as he could.

But upon further examination, there was something wild about Yves Bouvier. The laconic, withdrawn cultural cues had given way to a near-maniacal twinkle in his very light blue eyes and a perpetual half-smirk, as he relished in tales of adventure, hidden opportunities, and the chance to size up the person in front of him with an unwavering and discerning stare. It was a stare defiant enough to impress a Russian billionaire, looking for security in the gaze of a leader.

It seemed Bouvier had always been this way: a man born well-to-do with a seemingly insatiable appetite for hedonistic pursuits, and the ability to dodge the danger he instinctively sought. As a feckless teen, he raced go-karts on the dark Swiss roads and pushed his athleticism to the brink. Tempting fate.

"I'm someone who has never been afraid in my life." He deadpanned.

A loyal associate beside him muttered in agreement as he continued, alluding to memories of snowboarding.

Bouvier was undeterred.

"Not of anyone."

Where Rybolovlev, with his childhood heart condition, had been hyper-cautious, Bouvier was an adrenaline junkie, pushing himself to the brink in physical activities and sports. Where Rybolovlev stiffened around new people, wary of their potential threat, Bouvier thrived on party culture and loved to connect and push boundaries, and was easy to access and happy to chat with staff at all levels. Where Rybolovlev had been the studious doctor who abandoned the family medical business for investments in a difficult political climate, Bouvier dropped out of college and joined his family at work, infusing a safe environment with his special appetite for risk.

When Rybolovlev sought to destroy his reputation with one fell swoop of Russian power and a polished international media team, Bouvier rose to the challenge with his subtler Swiss confidence, using a network of whisperers and trusted associates who extolled his personality and justified his behavior. But that came much later.

Bouvier got his start working for his father. Like in any family, the Bouviers had private joys and tragedies. His handicapped sister died young, but they rarely spoke of it. He hired childhood friends in so many facets of the business later on that he was accused of nepotism.

At first, the business venture was to earn pocket money for his passionate ski habit, but he soon became fascinated with the company's potential. This excited energy led him to become the media's tag of "The Freeport King," when he took over Natural Le Coultre from his father, Jean-Jacques Bouvier, at 34. He was the scion of a shipping empire – not quite a Grecian magnate from the blue chip set, but of the locally revered freeports.

The family business had been a key player in the tight-lipped world of tax-free storage in Geneva for generations, as one of the illustrious fixtures of Swiss legislation for nearly 200 years. By the time Rybolovlev and Bouvier collaborated, it was the largest art storage and transport operation within the government-approved Geneva Freeport, whose overall goods totaled approximately 100 billion across multiple currencies.[41]

Loyalty, discretion, and trust constituted the key criteria for success with Rybolovlev, and Yves Bouvier seemed to possess all of them. His demeanor was as discreet and polished as anyone expected from a well-connected Swiss man, intertwined with the European elite, as he delicately presented art to the oligarch by way of Tania Rappo, careful not to oversell.

Discretion around massive wealth had been long-ingrained in Swiss culture. As early as 1713, the Grand Council of Geneva outlawed sharing banking information with anyone but the owner of the account. *Livemint* author Venkant Ananth cited French philosopher Voltaire, who wrote in 1794, "If you see a Swiss banker jumping out of a window, follow him, for there is sure to be a profit in it."[42]

By 1934, the Swiss Federal Banking Act heightened these regulations. Revealing a client's identity was punishable by imprisonment. This was much to the dismay of those outside the system.

The Swiss were fiercely defensive about their suspect reputation. With the advent of 21st century regulation, Swiss business experts insisted, financials were not as secretive as they had been in the past.

"Now more and more, we're moving into a world where we have open registers, and registers of beneficial owners in Europe," explained David Wallace Wilson, an expert in trust law, "…In Switzerland, if you open a bank account, after 50 years of Form A, we have to put who the beneficial owner is…The bank knows who the people are around this."

The same could be said for the freeports.

American laws had begun to change for Swiss banks during the 2008 financial crisis, right around when Rybolovlev started to move his liquidity into paintings with Bouvier. Not only was there typically a $1 million minimum in investments to accommodate bank fees, but the Foreign Account Tax Compliance Act was designed to reveal some of the American citizen information locked in Swiss banks. The Swiss institutions would have had to give information to the American government, previously unknown and protected.[43]

Freeports, on the other hand, maintained the security of the old school banking structure. They were safe.

Geneva Freeport manager Andre Decrausaz expressed his frustration with the media's portrayal of Swiss freeport security, ensuring its ethical compass. "Honestly, if you have something to hide, there are other freeports in the world that are less responsible with customs," he said, "But I don't think that you could do it here."

Prior to the freeport evolution, Swiss bankers had maintained a reputation as wealth managers since the Roman Empire. Switzerland's geographic proximity to many other countries by way of mountains, rivers and lakes allowed it to become a market of transit. But its lack of proximity to the sea necessitated an understanding of overnight storage.

The first freeport was inaugurated in Switzerland in 1899, the same year the Eiffel Tower was constructed. The word in French was "porte franc," with "franc" the same word as the Swiss currency. With the advent of increased industrialization, a necessity for short-term storage warehouses of all manner of cargo arose, though it had initially begun with grain and wheat. When Jean-Jacques Bouvier started at Natural Le Coultre as an apprentice in 1953 (taking over the company 30 years later) the company still had stables available to store horses en route.[44]

By then, the freeport had already evolved to be more than just a quick fix. Tax law elongated the permissible storage duration in "bonded" warehouses to be highly favorable, and all manner of elite collector was able to take advantage across industries. The Bouvier's company, Natural Le Coultre, was at the center of this storied heritage.

Privileged classes had been privy to the freeports since the inception of Natural Le Coultre. The company name was actually eponymous, the result of a merger between Albert-Maurice Natural and Emile-Etienne Le Coultre to found a "travel division," designed for the needs of this enterprising purgatory. Le Coultre's pedigree was exceptional enough to be the subject of a book in his lifetime, celebrating the achievements of ancestors dating back to the 16th century. [45] They were so synonymous with the city that legend had it the company transported stones at the bottom of Lake Geneva, and the boat still floated in the water into 2018.

But while Natural Le Coultre reveled in the past, adaptability also moved innovation forward. During the First World War, the freeport followed a mandate from the Red Cross to supply released prisoners of war with provisions. According to an in-house presentation document, Allied Forces members released in Germany were thusly provided with nearly 100 million pounds of bread. Where there was a market, they assured, they had always facilitated.

On the surface, it was drab and grey, but inside, the bolted doors gave way to incredible collections of just about anything. Decrausaz reported their 150,000 square meters of space had over 3 million bottles of Grand Crus, with 200-year-old wine collections worth €800,000. Cars gave way to luxury cars, Amsterdam diamond merchants gave way to over-the-top jewelry lines, and the freeports quickly became more than storage warehouses. They were treasure troves.

Once the client paid for their storage unit, almost everything was acceptable. But not absolutely everything.

"Here, we have clients, all sorts of clients," Decrausaz explained. "We have insurance providers, we have private companies, we have banks, we have art collectors, we have art galleries who are here. We don't ask what they do. When they open a space here, they pay. And it's done. Upon entry there is customs, upon exit there is customs—they can't do whatever they want, there are obligations in terms of food production, not to sell weapons, or things like that—but otherwise, if they say, 'I work in the painting market,' ok, you work in the painting market."

He was referring to Article 184 of the Swiss Customs Regulations, which formally asked for the name and address of the person in charge of the freeport goods. Skeptics pointed to the evasiveness of this practice, in that the official name might not be the acting owner of whatever was hidden in the vaults. However, the freeport teams insisted that customs could—and did—occasionally launch criminal investigations. And that their legal awareness prevented them from accepting anyone who seemed capable of criminal activity.

The Swiss freeport turned away suspicious activities in the world of questionable investments. Decrausaz said corrupt requests came up around three times a year, but with their full list of blue-chip clients, there was no need to take the risk.

Within this legality, Bouvier was at liberty to manage his freeport space as he saw fit.

"Mr. Bouvier is an important client, but, the way it functions, his companies are just within the warehouses," Decrausaz said.

As the client, Bouvier maintained strong ties to customs and the freeport security team despite the scandal, which spoke of his efficiency as much as his personality.

"…He's a person who never cheated with customs, which is important. He never cheated us in our affairs." Decrausaz said on behalf of the freeport, "So for us, really, this affair he had with the Russian person, it's really between the two of them. We don't look at that. I think if he bought some piece and he sold it for 20, it's their problem. Us, we're not there in the middle."

To be sure, Bouvier's freeport was not the only art storage client maneuvering in Geneva. A network of companies within the complex of state-approved Geneva Free Ports & Warehouses Ltd.[46] provided protection to many a wealthy art collector, with five well-known holdings offering storage opportunities. Decrausaz reported that the state of Switzerland owned 86% of the freeports in Geneva, and only 14% of that was privately held. Bouvier held 4-5% of the total—making him the largest holder in the port, holding nearly one third. Art dealers storing works comprised yet another subsection of the freeport ecosystem, and trade among them was common.

Art often changed hands within the freeports without ever leaving the facilities. The pricing was able to fluctuate, and the paperwork could all be handled internally. However, the state-supported freeport was not in charge of that. It was the dealers within.

"[The freeport] does not buy artworks. We don't sell artworks. We do not have direct clients to do that. We are not equipped for that," said Decrausaz. "We are really like a location agency."

But in terms of the art world, Bouvier outdid his predecessors. The company extolled the full suite of services his oversight had offered, catering to art clientele. After Bouvier's father took over Natural Le Coultre in the 1980s, they Fine Art Transports Natural Le Coultre SA, specifically for paintings, sculptures, and other fine art objects.

And he was truly in love with the excitement around artworks. Large and small, old and new, anything beautiful that needed protecting passed through his hands. Without books or art historical education, he discovered things by touch and day-to-day proceedings. Pricing or historical period had little effect on his tastes.

"I am not partial," he said in French, "The beautiful is what pleases me."

As Bouvier explained to *LeParisien* with bright eyes back in 2014, "The privilege of this position is to see these things very very often," He opened his palms for emphasis. "To be able to come into contact with the merchandise here. It's something else, with these works of art, that could be large, small, ancient, contemporary. This variety, it's really a delight."

Bouvier had his own tastes. There were some Van Goghs he liked more than others; some Picassos he found ugly or beautiful…it was a complete passion project for him, unadulterated by expectations.

Rybolovlev too reviewed a slew of artworks from various cannons. He purchased a Van Gogh (*paysage avec Olivier et montagnes en arrière plan—Landscape with Olive Trees and Mountains in the Foreground*—for €18 million in 2009), but did not like all of the works he had seen by the world-famous painter of *The Starry Night*.

Speaking broadly about art investment irrespective of Rybolovlev, Evan Beard compared the process of buying art to an addiction: "You need to be addicted to the drug before you take the medication."

The Rybolovlevs may have had a reputation as uncultured, but Bouvier was impressed to find that they already had a sizeable knowledge of the arts (possibly gleaned from years frequenting museums in Perm) and a robust library of art books.

"It was not me who gave him the virus," Bouvier said, referring to the love of art, "He had already bought some important paintings before he met me."

Nevertheless, Bouvier would reach out and offer the latest works.

He would typically present a piece to Rybolovlev (and his friend Rappo) in the freeport, where buyer and advisor would both offer opinions. Rybolovlev would express his approval or otherwise. If he liked the piece, Bouvier would coordinate with his large team to get the sales, shipments, and other documentation in order.

Across the art world, among the papers was often a certification of authenticity. Authenticity was essential—not just from a cultural value, but for financial. If a work turned out to be fake, the value went to zero.

Though Rybolovlev did acquire an impressive 37 pieces in total, Bouvier presented him closer to 100 works, and he had not liked all of them. The client had his own tastes, too. He was not interested in Dalí or Cézanne; he rejected Berninis and other Picasso pieces. So Bouvier was there mainly to source and procure works as a representative in the art market. the perfect middle-man in a world of Swiss security.

Bouvier positioned himself as a merchant rather than a consultant. His pitch was always some version of, "I have a painting for sale." It was only later that he enlisted specialists and experts to supplement the offerings.

The setup was ideal. As one representative for the Russian said, "A lot of wealthy people want to keep themselves alive, and want to keep themselves private."

To someone like Bouvier, the wealth of knowledge behind closed doors was as rich as it was empowering. Agreeing to store art confidentially while simultaneously seeking art Rybolovlev could buy, meant that Bouvier had dual access in realms where both parties were typically deliberately inconspicuous.

"If nobody knows you, you take all the information," Bouvier told Knight. "It is to be like an octopus."

Marketing materials boasted that the "Fine Art Protectors" maintained "maximal safety," coupled with prestige, guaranteeing 24-hour surveillance, humidity and temperature controls. As one tagline underscored, it was, "a proven expertise offering peace of mind."

The word protector was loaded. It was a term often used in trust law to put very rich people at ease. Not only were the objects protected, but the person who relinquished them and the warehouse head were in control, shrouded by state-mandated secrecy.

The art world's discretion grew from this shared deep need for security, and ultimately, great secrecy. What lurked behind each locked chamber, shrouded in various security measures, continues to remain relatively unknown beyond company walls. Private sales were even more shrouded in confidentiality than auctions, and buyers in both spheres are often unidentified. This raised many a question around legalities, particularly in the realms of money laundering and fraud.

It was not an entirely new problem. During World War II, the freeports housed Nazi art looted from exterminated Jewish families, which was treated as stolen property after the war.

Decrausaz was candid about the complex history.

"The Swiss helped the Jews, they helped the Germans, they helped everyone. It was basically the bank—the piggy bank—of the world."

The word for piggy bank in French was *tire-lire*. It did not translate to piggy bank. After a good laugh when Decrausaz learned the English word, he did a play on words with the word 'pig'—also used to be derogatory.

"Switzerland was the pig of the war."

It was a question of law.

"…If in the 1960s they brought some ivory into the freeport, today, if you bring it out, we're going to say, 'scandal.'" He said, "But at the time, it was not a scandal. So, you must arrive at determining what is scandalous and what was purchased during the period because the market accepted it. You really have to separate those two things. And that is very, very complicated because not all countries are under the same ports."

At the heart of these complexities, Bouvier was straddling art worlds around the globe. With his growing base of Russian clients, he realized the possibilities for two markets, Russian and Swiss, utilizing his coffers of exceptional art masterpieces.

It was important to note that Bouvier and Rybolovlev rarely created sales contracts, especially after the early collaborations of 2003 through 2006. Instead, they generated two invoices, and left the suggestion of a 2 percent commission. The matter was almost never discussed, and business continued.

In 2004, one year after Rybolovlev had purchased his first major Chagall, Bouvier coordinated the first Moscow World Fine Art Fair.

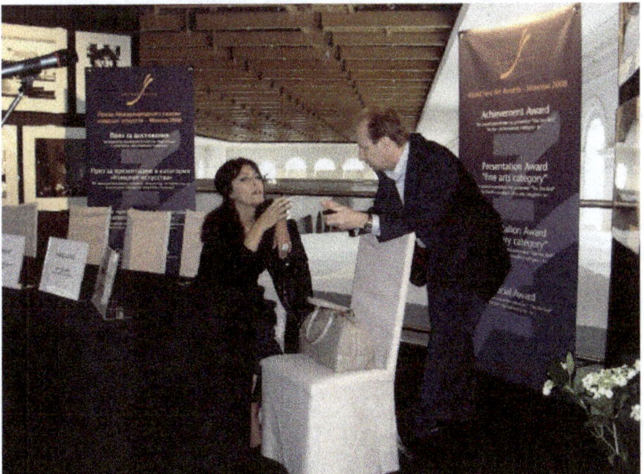

Tania Rappo and Yves Bouvier at the Moscow World Fine Art Fair

Rybolovlev was impressed. "The fair was like a brushstroke to his portrait," he recounted to Knight, "It demonstrated that he had connections."

After their fateful meeting, Bouvier enlisted Tania Rappo to be the fair's Vice President. She was salaried through the company. Elena was on the honorary committee.

"Things with Rybolovlev were going perfectly." Bouvier said.

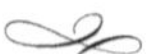

Sixtine Crutchfield was instrumental in operations as well. She was working for Swiss art dealer Jan Krugier at the time, returning to the team from a long stint in Australia. She had an air of grace with her chin-length hair and artistic sensibilities, not to mention a reputation for efficiency, and a global perspective that made her a fantastic fit for Bouvier's needs. When Krugier decided to participate in the Moscow fair, Bouvier poached Crutchfield to come help him run it. She in turn relied on her assistant, native Russian speaker Vera Voitenkova, to translate documents and coordinate with elites. Voitenkova later facilitated translation for the Rybolovlev collection.

From 2004 onward, Crutchfield was a secret weapon—a crutch, if you will—in his discreet arsenal for almost a decade, placing the right calls and advising wherever she was needed on art, media, and anything else Bouvier might need in the interim. To be sure, she was not the impetus behind Rybolovlev's buying power or his curatorial choices, but she was available as a resource when the time was right. In the midst of the scandal, she later described herself as "Team Bouvier."

The idea had arisen from two realizations: one, that the 18th century wares and furniture markets were running down and devaluing in Europe, and two, that newly minted Russians were hungry for cultural capital. After the oligarchs seized their wealth during the Yeltsin years, they were eager to make their mark on art. Although many became some of the foremost contemporary collectors, they also had a strong sense of history from their excellent education and museums. It was the perfect pairing.

"Yves had the idea…He said, 'We're going to try and rejuvenate this,'" Crutchfield remembered. "(For the fair to be a success for the organizer, the exhibitor and for the visitors to be in awe, which they were), it needs to be accessible by truck, it needs to have wealthy people, and it needs to have people who understand what the 18th century actually means culturally. So, well, it was Russia. Because they have the education, you could reach it by land, and they had money.

"Everybody told him, 'Impossible.'

And he said, 'Don't tell me impossible. If everybody tells me impossible, I can do it.'"

And that's exactly what he did.

He revived an old Swiss company called Art Culture Studios, founded in 1927, to focus on the fair, and set about scouting locations in Moscow.

A stone's throw from the historic Red Square in the heart of the city, the Manezh (pronounced Manège) was an important government building, designated to begin construction in 1817 to mark the victory over Napoleonic France after the War of 1812, though construction ended up taking almost a decade.[47]

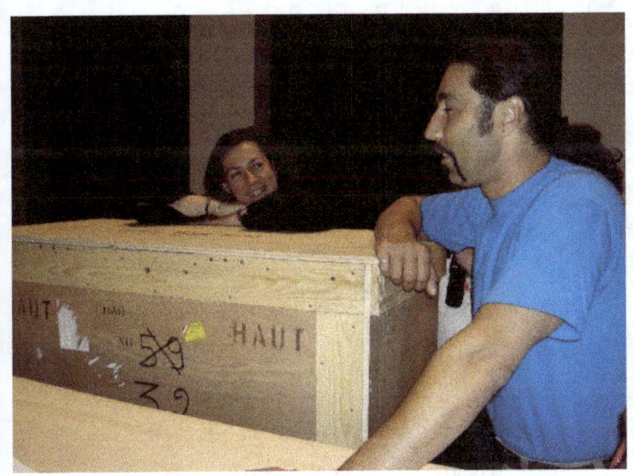

Sixtene Crutchfield overseeing coordination of the Moscow World Fine Art Fair, beside an unnamed art handler

It had been designed with the intention for military pomp, its wide stages to accommodate large crowds had also proved suitable to the worlds of art and design. Composer Hector Berlioz gave his first-ever Moscow concert there in 1868, with an estimated 12,600 audience members.[48]

The Manezh was later used by Khrushchev as a government building after the Revolution, and in March 2004, was burned down[49] in what was secretly deemed an arson attack by the contracting company, owned by the mayor's sister, who was poised to renovate the building.

Looking at the ruins, Bouvier said to Crutchfield, "That's where I want to do the fair. This is it."

She said OK, of course, alongside Tania Rappo. "But we didn't know what it was going to be."

Vladimir Putin insisted on opening the Manezh first with a military celebration, and the art fair followed suit in May 2005.

Over the next five years, the fair was a resounding success.

"It started with 27 galleries who followed [Bouvier]," Crutchfield explained, "To the following year we were at already double that, and then in the end we were 122. In five years."

They built an entire cultural cadre from the ground up. Scenography and lighting design with wood board and plaster, a full suite of security and logistics, all of it was handled by Bouvier's teams for a fair that lasted just four days.

She estimated 17 semi-trailers brought a €31 billion value in artwork (and jewelry) from Switzerland to Moscow.

Luxury brands like Bulgari and Harry Winston breached their non-compete contracts in Russia for a chance to entice the newly minted millionaires with their baubles.

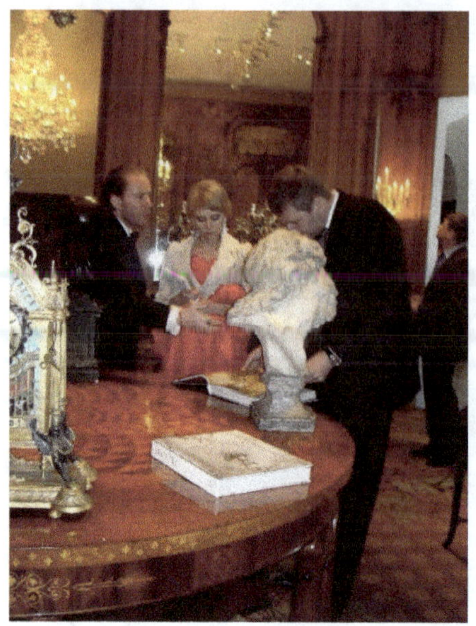

Elena Rybolovleva and Dmitry Rybolovlev at the Moscow World Fine Art Fair

It was important to note that luxury branding and art went hand-in-hand. The most obvious example of this was a company called Louvre, which distributed high-fashion marks around Russia. Many of the pictures from the fair in 2008 showed its name in all caps, in front of a catwalk where fashion shows went on, with Christian Dior gowns.

A concert featuring four Stradivarius violins, a dance performance by the Bolshoi Ballet, a radio broadcast, and a lecture series all capped off the event.

The VIP status was so well-known that the VIP cards were being scalped in the city metros.

Crutchfield remembered with a laugh. "I took the metro or was in the street they'd say, 'Do you want to buy a VIP card?' not knowing who I was. But I was hanging around there like, 'Actually, how much are you selling the VIP cards for?'"

Ultimately, "It was the must-see place to be during that week that we were there," she said. "The Russians loved it. Nothing was done like that before, and nothing's been done since."

More than a decade later, she still spoke from memory about the bulleted facts. "We had 12,000 people at the opening. We had 50,000 people in five days."

The crowds proved that each day was an excitement. It was a spectacular event. Unlike the Western Europeans who came to art fairs in jeans, the Moscow set wore floor-length gowns and diamonds, marveling at their ability to be able to purchase antiques they'd only ever seen in museums.

Everyone was there—from the eager culture-mongers who queued outside in their best to the richest people in Russia.

Dasha Zhukova, Roman Abramovich's wife, was on the scene. Her husband was worth $11.4 billion[50] in 2018, and Zhukova had set about building Garage, a contemporary art space in Moscow with a corresponding magazine, in 2008. The publication was later purchased by Vice.[51]

Leonid Mikhelson, ranked the #3 richest man in the country, enlisted his curator, Italian Teresa Mavika, to scout the fair for possible art to add to his contemporary art museum in a former power plant during the privatization mayhem. Mikhelson was apparently working as an engineer when he sold his car to buy shares in a pipeline construction company. From there, he built the largest natural gas provider in private hands, and garnered a net worth of $18.7 billion. His museum cost $30 million to renovate, with the enlistment of the architect Renzo Piano, who did the Centre Pompidou in Paris as well. Unlike Rybolovlev's classical tastes of Impressionist and Expressionist works, Mikhelson was known to collect works by Christopher Wool and Gerhard Richter.[52] The latter's work was sold at auction for upwards of $30 million, making him the most expensive living artist.

Viktor Vekselberg, the #9 richest, also had an advisor on site. He made headlines in the art world for purchasing nine of the 42 Fabergé eggs ever made, purchased at $100 million the year before the fair. The only collection larger than his own was the Kremlin Armory Museum.

But the Moscow World Fine Art Fair had ties to the Kremlin as well. Tania Rappo was able to finagle the first-ever private art event inside the Kremlin itself.

She had a connection.

Artists, actors, coffee importers, German PR representatives, British writers— the star-studded list went on and on. Crutchfield looked at the photos of the event and named them all expertly. She remarked on the authenticity of the Russian people she met, who were quick to remember her name and fiercely loyal once they built trust.

And in terms of art and cultural collecting, she said, "The Russians are very quick learners."

The world of art professionals was a little more complex. One day a gallerist would be celebrated, the next he would be rumored to sell fakes and end up in jail. Various middle-men worked the room trying to get commissions on sales around them as well. It wasn't uncommon.

"They do that at every art fair in the world," Crutchfield said defiantly, referring to Art Basel Miami Beach and FIAC (Foire international d'art contemporain) in Paris, France:

"I mean, if you walk around Miami, there are so many brokers around…like one time, this is when we were with Krugier at the FIAC in Paris, and Madonna came on the stand. She came with her crowd, her entourage and everything, and she bought something. I saw it; she bought a drawing. Then, like a half-an-hour later, all these people that were in her entourage, like bodyguards and whatever, they all said, 'She came to your stand because of us! So you need to give us commission.'

We just said 'Sorry, this needs to be arranged ahead of time.'"

With this kind of cutthroat competition in mind, the galleries solicited for the event were only the best, regardless of category. They reached out to Impressionist dealers, Picasso dealers, Chinese and Japanese, and people from around Europe. But the Perestroika galleries, focused on Russian art from the Gorbachev era of the 1970s and 80s, could come for free.

Everyone was welcome to dine at the Michelin-starred restaurant on the premises as well, though its origins were less glamorous than comical.

Crutchfield remembered:

"The first year, in 2005, I got the runs like after day two. We were in a meeting and I said, 'Sorry guys I'm gonna have to go, I'm having digestive problems.' And everybody said, 'You too? We've all been doing that!'

So I went to see the managing director of Bulka, the Manezh restaurant. She said, 'Well I don't understand, because we spray the food every night.'

And I'm like, 'You what?'

'Yeah, every night we spray the food so it lasts three days and we don't need to put it in the fridge.'

And I'm like, 'Do not do that please. We're not used to sprayed food.'

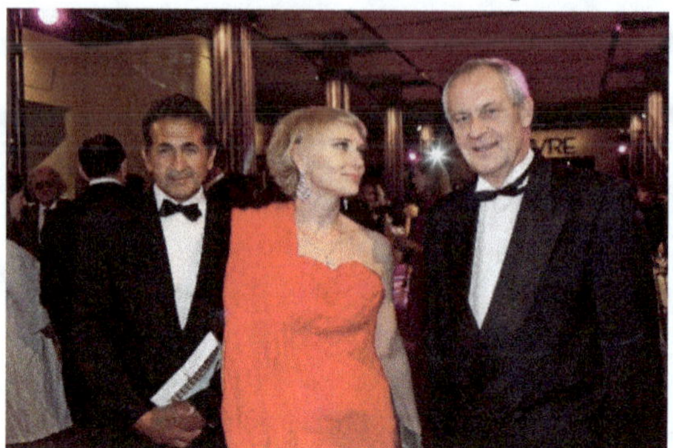

Elena Rybolovleva at the Moscow World Fine Art Fair between unnamed men

Anyway, so we decided to bring our own French chefs. Michelin-starred chefs…It became known that you could come and eat Michelin-starred food so the restaurant was always full. Even people who didn't like art would come and eat there."

She still beamed with pride remembering the fanfare. "Yves really did something quite amazing," she said.

There was no denying it was a fantastic party. One gallery dressed his art consultants as Napoleons, and they got so drunk they had to be escorted out of the building. Once again, the French were defeated.

Damning pictures of the team drunk and goofy-eyed in front of the Kremlin alongside customs authorities drove home the idea that it was a happy, festive time.

On top of it all, Bouvier was confident, connected, and a demonstrated success—and the Rybolovevs approved. Elena Rybolovleva participated in the Moscow fair as a member of the Honorary Committee. In 2008, Bouvier's final year overseeing the fair before he sold it to French event managers, Elena wore her hair tied back with a bright red dress, a white fur stole, and chandelier earrings.

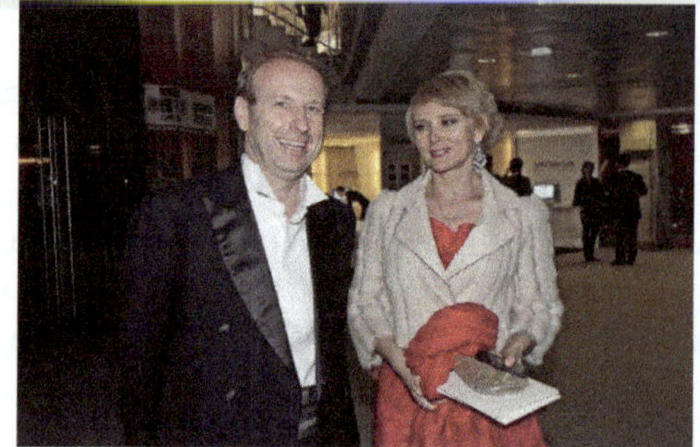

Elena Rybolovleva and Yves Bovuier at the Moscow World Fine Art Fair

But per the photos and her best efforts to fit in, she was still standoffish, standing mostly with her architect for the Petit Trianon—presumably shopping for art for the new space. Elena quietly perused the art beside her husband, a stark contrast to the loud and joyful Russians eager to ring in a new era of art collecting.

Bouvier was attentive to her needs. After all, her husband was a new and important client. 2005, the year of the first art fair, was also when they bought their first painting exclusively with him.

It was Pablo Picasso's *Les Noces de Pierrette*.

9

THE HAPPINESS WHICH PASSES

"THE MYSTERY of a Masterwork" was the title of an article by noted art critic Judd Tully in 1990, following the auction that revealed this Picasso after its long life in the shadows. Ironically, that was the last time it was brought to market in a public way. Ever since, it was back in private collections, largely unknown and maybe even forgotten by the general public. On went the mystery.

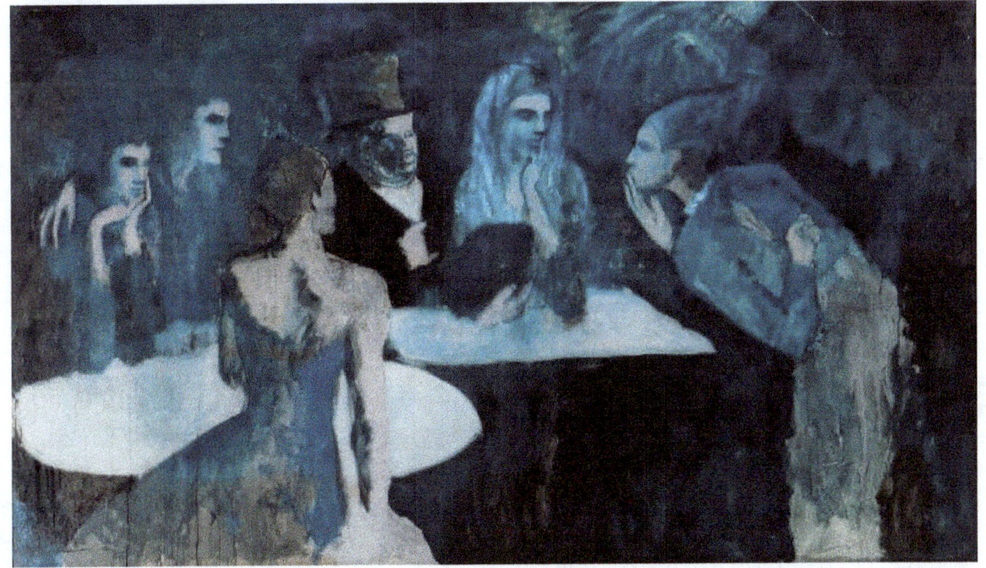

Pablo Picasso (1881-1973)
Les Noces de Pierrette (The Wedding of Pierrette), 1905, 115 x 195 cm
© 2019 Estate of Pablo Picasso / Artists Rights Society (ARS), New York

For art historical reference, *Les Noces de Pierrette* translates to *The Marriage of Pierrette*, but the direct translation of 'les noces' is 'the wedding'. This slight adjustment for clarification was suggestive, in that the marriage itself was derivative of the depicted ceremony.

The painting was made in 1905, at the tail end of Picasso's Blue Period (often listed as 1901-1904). The use of somber, cool tones sought to evoke his pain at the loss of a friend to suicide—by gunshot, at a dinner party in Paris. One exceptionally depressive piece from this period was *La Celestina*, featuring dejected fringe figures to polite society. Beyond his early art classes, Picasso had always been preoccupied by the world around him: he drew inspiration from brothels, studying beggars, gypsies and prostitutes as much as the models in the atelier.

For the wedding scene, the dark palette adds a haunting element to a typically happy milestone. The faces of the bride, groom, and surrounding guests are painted with obscured eyes and ghostly faces. Hands and chins have long, spindly fingers. The bride looks downward at the clown at the right of the composition, whose hand position, though similar to the guests on his left, blows a kiss to the newlywed lady, to the dismay of a pompous groom. Depicted with a top hat and a black coat, he appears to face his bride as she turns away. Although his exact expression is difficult to decipher with its long block of shadow, he is undoubtedly displeased.

A 1989 article in United Press International capitalizing on the hype surrounding the pending auction cited the catalogue essayist, celebrated Catalan art historian Josep Palau i Fabre. A Picasso expert, he explained that the clown in the painting may have been a reference to Picasso himself, as well as a homage to a dejected clown in the 1899 Catalonian play, *The Happiness Which Passes*.

The bride at his side symbolized women allegedly seek power and stability from wealthy men, whereas the woman with her back to the canvas referred to a lover of whom Picasso allegedly thought ill.[53]

At the time of painting in 1905, Picasso was still a very young man, but later in life, would come to be known for a slew of passionate, tempestuous relationships that aligned with this type of thinking. When his liaison with the young and beautiful Francoise Gilot ended in the 1940s, he reportedly shouted at her that she was doomed to obscurity. No one would ever have more than a passing curiosity, he was sure, in a woman who had touched his life of genius so

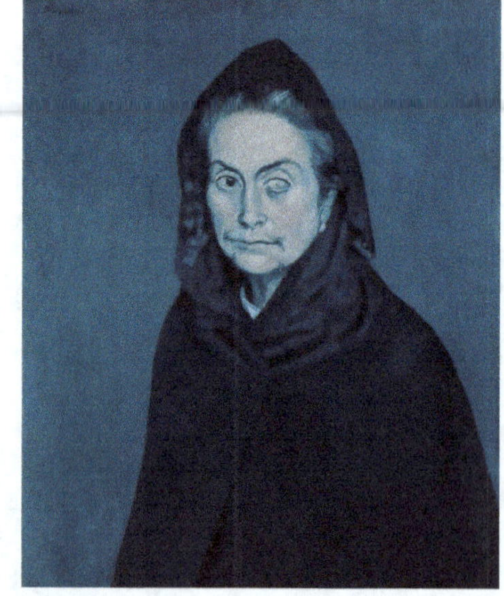

Pablo Picasso (1881-1973)
La Celestina (Carlota Valdivia), ca. 1903-1904, oil on canvas, 81 x 61 cm © 2019 Estate of Pablo Picasso / Artists Rights Society (ARS), New York

intimately.[54] The artist was proven wrong: Gilot went on to live well into her nineties as a moderately, but surely independent, successful artist. She later remarried Jonas Salk, who invented the polio vaccine.[55]

One of the early owners of the "Pierrette" was Hugo Perls. Speaking to his son Klaus, Judd Tully explained that Hugo had purchased the painting in Paris in the 1920s from Picasso's dealer, Daniel-Henry Kahnweiler, keeping it in Berlin. Enraptured with the macabre, it was lost in 1931 when the Hugo and his wife divorced.

Les Noces de Pierrette resurfaced in October 1989 at the small French auction house, Binoche and Godeau at Druot Montaigne, by way of a Stockholm-based man named Frederick Ross. Like the later da Vinci sale, it was exhibited alongside contemporary artworks, in this case, by Andy Warhol. The innovative TV monitors served a similar purpose to the future internet bidding, allowing prospective collectors to place bids in multiple sales. Beyond Paris, it was displayed in New York and Tokyo.

The estimate was $46 million (300 million francs), and a Japanese buyer named Tomonori Tsurumaki paid $51.7 million. At the time, it was the second-most expensive painting ever sold. He had wanted to display it at the racetrack.

But the original buyer lost his money, and 15 years later, Rybolovlev paid $43.8 million to Yves Bouvier for the work. To the public, the painting maintained its staggering value, but in secrecy, it netted a quiet loss at Acquavella Galleries…and a substantial bargain.

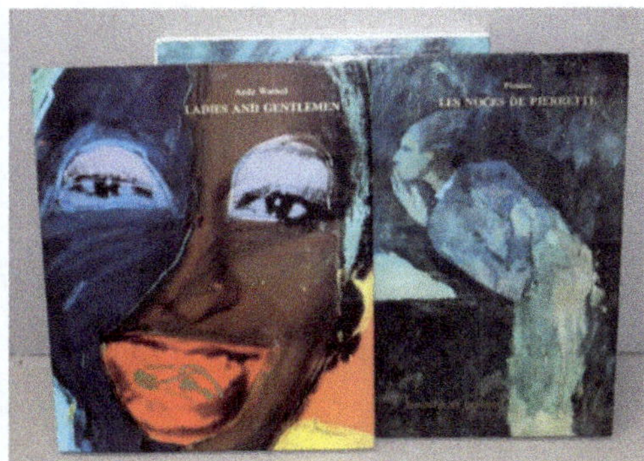
Catalogue from *Les Noces de Pierette* sale in 1989

Though the reports later diverged, Rybolovlev claimed to have agreed to provide Bouvier with a two percent commission exclusively. Instead, according to the legal documents, Bouvier took the difference between his price and Rybolovlev's as well, and went on to provide Tania Rappo with her own remunerations. He paid Rappo about $500,000.

Later, both Rappo and Bouvier would claim Rybolovlev knew about that Bouvier was making more than the two percent, even when the Russian client came to say he had no idea. Either way, there was art to be bought, and for a while there was no explicit discussion of Bouvier's profit.

In 2005, the year the Rybolovlevs bought the Picasso and of the first Moscow World Fine Art Fair, Dmitry presented Elena with what the Geneva legal system referred to as "contrat de marriage"—simply, a contract of marriage.

The term was deliberately vague because it was retroactively filed. When the couple married, young and in love as college students on equal footing, there was no need for a prenup. Then Dmitry went to jail while the family was relocating to Switzerland, and his wife assumed they would be together forever. Speculatively speaking, a prenup was probably the last thing on their minds.

From a legal standpoint, it was somewhat haphazardly assembled. With all the millions accrued and the years traveling, it was strange that he filed something as preventative as a standard document after a decade together. His assets had thus far gone unprotected.

Therefore, the Rybolovlevs were living in semi-community property, known as an 'accrued gains regime.' Whatever was accrued during the marriage as gains for each spouse was divided, presumably, equally among them. Only inheritance or pre-marriage income was separate.

But by then they had been in Geneva for 10 years, and their marriage was fraying. Though Elena's lawyers declined to comment for this project, she reflected in the Swiss publication *Bilan,* addressing her intense desire to become a part of society in the region. Her eagerness to learn languages, collect art, and blend in with her cultural neighbors may have been a point of contention.

"With hindsight, I can see that my integration into Swiss life perhaps dealt the death blow to our relationship…," Elena told the Swiss press. "He never participated in the social or cultural life of the city. We were no longer part of the same world."

From her husband's perspective, Geneva was one of the best places in the world to devise this kind of divorce document. The Geneva court had a three-part system for marital contracts, divided by inheritance, income earned during the marriage, and their own assets altogether. It was so complicated, it was easy: a full suite of services.

"Switzerland is very flexible. You can do up-down-left, you can even contract to do your own à la carte marriage regime if you want to." David Wallace Wilson said, "It can have this, but only this, or that. You can do whatever. It's completely flexible and liberal, which is good."

Because Rybolovlev's marital contract was filed long after the marriage in an entirely different country, it was essentially a 'postnup,' designed to protect the assets he earned at Uralkali. The postnup determined that everything was separate property, starting from day one of the marriage.

The document was undoubtedly designed with an eye towards divorce, as opposed to the default of joint or semi-community property, in which the marital assets were shared. If and when someone decided to begin divorce proceedings, that spouse would not be entitled to half of the other's—and with Rybolovlev already worth well over a billion in 2005, the imbalance was clear.

It was as close to a separation agreement as possible without filing for separation. More than a line in the sand, it was a brick wall.

Elena was not sure what to do. She sought advice from her close friend, Tania Rappo.

Rappo, herself on her second marriage, told Elena that if she were in her shoes, she would not sign anything without enlisting a lawyer. Elena, considered by many to be the smarter of the couple, took her friend's advice.

She refused to sign the contract.

Less than a month later, Dmitry Rybolovlev created his Cypriot trusts. They were called Virgo and Aries, named after the astrological signs of his daughters, and had them each listed as primary and secondary beneficiaries on their respective accounts. He transferred the shares of his preexisting companies, and his latest paintings, into these trusts for their protection. Trusts were commonly used in dynastic planning—planning for your current children, any future children, and any descendants thereafter. But by placing all the assets in his daughters' names, they were also kept out of reach of his wife.

In later documents, Elena said, "I am convinced that Dmitry did not include me as a beneficiary of the trust in a deliberate manner."

Trusts were seemingly simple as well, in that they took shares and valuable assets and placed them out of reach for anyone looking to seize assets in Rybolovlev's own name. But technically, placing assets in a trust rendered them the responsibility of the trustees, and the asset of the beneficiary. If Rybolovlev was neither, he was therefore relinquishing power. He was placing complete 'trust' in the trustees.

"But look at the background from where they come," Wilson said, referring to Russia. "They trust no one."

The way to circumvent the possibility of missteps was to name himself the "protector" of the trusts.

"A protector is not a necessary figure of a trust," he clarified, "You can have a trust without a protector."

Nevertheless, he said, the protector feature was becoming increasingly standard. It was a way to maintain control to hire and fire trustees, and to add in any special stipulations. In other words, overriding powers.

"Once the settler puts in the assets, this is irrevocable. This is out. This is gone. There is no more control there," He said in his trademark mile-a-minute style. "So for you to come back in through the window to say 'I want to control this,' typically that's by special company provisions and other elements."

The word protector had been used in Bouvier's businesses to ensure that assets were stored safely. It was interesting that both the trusts and storage units used this same wording.

"The U.S, usually, they tend to use the term enforcer," Wilson continued. "It's the same thing. Because technically protector, curator, enforcer, it's the same idea of kind of the supervisor, OK?"

Tsar. King. Commander-in-Chief.

Rybolovev had taken all his assets out of his name and placed them in somewhere they were protected—by trustees for him, and by him for his children. The threat of his wife's seizure was significantly diminished.

As Rybolovlev went on collecting with Bouvier, all 37 works were in two companies: first Xitrans, then Accent Delight, which were both moved into the Virgo trust. Like Salvator Mundi LLC, each painting was its own company safely stowed within.

Elena and Dmitry continued to shop for art together after the 2005 creation of the Cypriot trusts, but the marriage was self-destructing. Even as they were seen together at the Moscow World Fine Art Fair in May 2008, where Elena was on the honorary committee of the Moscow fair even three years later, they were on the brink of collapse.

Rybolovlev was traveling more and more. In December 2007, he warned his wife about upcoming bills at Prada of upwards of $10,000 in the U.S.—women's clothes, and not for her. In March 2008, just months before the couple went to the Moscow art fair, he rented a room during a week in Courchevel for his mistress in the same hotel as the family. The mistress was dropped at the airport at 11am.; his wife and child were dropped four hours later.

Elena confronted her husband in October about his constant infidelities. Her husband said he was not going to change his lifestyle, and, in her words, "that he was free to satisfy his libido as he had been doing, and that [she] would have to accept this or ask for the divorce."

In the meantime, he told his family they might not have "any more money to live on." He reduced the family allowance from 900,000 to 10,000 Swiss Francs per trimester, and informed his wife she needed to fire all the house staff (except the children's nanny) for financial reasons, exerting still further pressure for her to manage her own liquidity with loans.

Then, for two days in December 2008, he took his mistress for a weekend in the presidential suite at the George V Hotel in Paris. The flight and room alone cost 500,000 Swiss Francs.

Elena finally hit breaking point.

On December 22nd, 2008, exactly one month after her husband's 42nd birthday and 10 days after his most recent mistress extravagance, Elena filed for divorce. He left the family home on Christmas Eve.

It was a strain on the whole family. Elena was prone to bouts of severe anxiety, and her daughter, Ekaterina, was plagued by depression for being placed in the middle of the financial and emotional battlefield, privy to her father's indiscretions. The couple was hot and cold, rich and frugal—and ultimately, utterly unhappy.

One day they would absolutely hate each other, the next they would go out for drinks. One scorned lawyer (and there were many in the wake of the divorce as Rybolovlev sought the right person) compared it to the Cold War. There was no way of knowing how they would react to one another, or how the financial war would play out. They would go months without talking, and then be completely fine.

During the ensuing proceedings, there were two things in play: Firstly, that she never signed the postnup, and secondly, that her husband's assets were tucked away in trusts and vaults around the world. She sought to seize them from Cyprus to Singapore, the Cayman Islands and Saint Tropez. So the divorce proceedings in Geneva became twofold as well. What was she entitled to, and where could they find it?

Elena hired Swiss celebrity lawyer Marc Bonnant, a renowned orator celebrated for generations for his legal acumen. She also enlisted private investigators, who sought to trace Rybolovev's assets for seizure. Nearly a decade after the Uralkali share controversy and imprisonment for murder, Rybolovlev was literally under siege once again: this time, by the woman closest to him for more than half his life.

He explained in the divorce filings, "Elena knew that the reason for the displacement of the artworks was due to my fear that anything considered as being connected to me would have been at risk."

Meanwhile, her Petit Trianon project languished in an ill-fated construction pit, with heaps of dirt and a large crane upsetting the civilized neighbors. Elena attempted to freeze her husband's assets, but her own dream of a retreat at home stood frozen as well. Rumors in Geneva claimed her architect was never paid, and as they could see passing along the lake in their boats, the home was never built.

This became the ultimate sticking point in the divorce. It wasn't a question of money, but of pride. There would be no poolside parties and no place for the Impressionist paintings Elena had been vying for. All that hard work to fit in was being undone. That was the true upset.

The sad, empty pit was an unfortunate metaphor for the family's time spent in Geneva. After everything they'd been through, it still never quite felt like home.

Rybolovlev was forced to find the right people to trust, and he believed unequivocally in Yves Bouvier. Though the dealings seemed OK at first, many around them had reservations.

Given the newly created trusts, Bouvier's role was suspect from the get-go. Managing personal assets was one thing, but technically speaking, trust and trustee law was something quite different. Under the protector rules, Rybolovlev had more than a personal authority over his art storer and dealer. He had legal authority. He could mandate Bouvier to do as he pleased if need be. But this unto itself posed liability questions for Bouvier, especially as the scandal unfolded later on.

Wilson said it best. "Is he a broker, is he an advisor, is he an employee, what the hell is his relation?"

Even Bouvier's camp had reservations. Speaking of Rybolovlev, freeport manager Andre Decrausaz openly disapproved.

"If you took off my freeport hat, I am a friend of Yves'," Decrausaz said candidly. "So, for me, it stays there. I think it was imprudent to work with this person. But it wasn't my decision. He decides."

In the meantime, the relationship between the Russian oligarch and the Swiss art dealer was no holds barred, and the collection spoke to that astounding partnership.

❧

Over the course of his continued relationship with Bouvier, Rybolovlev would go on to collect an astounding six additional works by Picasso from a range of periods in his prolific lifetime in a seemingly erratic chronological order: *Mousquetaires à la pipe* (musketeer with pipe), 1968; *La soeur de l'artiste* (the artist's sister), 1899; *Joueur de flûte et femme nue* (flute player and nude woman), 1970; *Homme assis au verre* (man sitting at the mirror), 1914; *Tête de femme, profil* (head of a woman in profile), 1905; and *Espagnole à l'éventail* (Spanish woman with fan), ca. 1920-1925.

They were all highly museum-worthy, and deeply significant in Picasso's long history. From the Spanish themes of his autobiography to his fascination with women, to his love of smoking and his troubled marriages, the collection could easily have been its own exhibition as a teaching method for the artist's life and various stylizations over an astounding career.

Yet despite this staggering number of works, trouble was already brewing.

The two later works that Rybolovlev purchased from Bouvier, *Espagnole à l'eventail* and *Femme se coiffant*, (at €27 million for the pair in 2013) were inspired depictions of Picasso's last wife, Jacqueline Roque in 1957.

The couple met in 1953, when Roque was 27 and Picasso was 69. At the time, he was living with his mistress Francoise Gilot and their two children, but she left him by 1955. Soon Roque became the sole object of Picasso's artistic fixation: one year, he painted 70 portraits of her.[56] Following the death of his wife Olga,[57] they married in 1961 and purchased a home in Cannes, the beachside town along the French Côte d'Azur,[58] and spent 20 years together.

Roque was small and dark, with smooth high cheekbones and sharp black brows. Picasso's fascination with her "oriental features" was hyperbolized through the exotic subject matters, and *Espagnole à l'eventail* was a particularly strong example of this imaginative depiction. Her features were amplified, chiseled and stunning, offset by the shape of the fan and the flat backdrop, all in grays and blacks, like an old photograph.

But because she came into Picasso's circle so late his life, the complexities of his mistress and children were enduringly problematic. Francoise Gilot published a tell-all book called *Life With Picasso* that portrayed Roque as a conniving, evil stepmother, who prevented two of Picasso's children from attending his funeral. The latest biography by Pepita DuPont, *La Verité sur Jacqueline Picasso* (The Truth about Jacqueline Picasso) was so badly received by Picasso's granddaughter Marina and her stepsister Catherine Hutin-Blay that they filed a lawsuit against the author for defamation.

Still more legal instability was to come. *Artnet* pulled together the full narrative.

Hutin-Blay was the original owner of both the paintings Rybolovlev acquired by way of Bouvier. The Swiss art dealer had taken them from a gallerist he knew at the freeport named Olivier Thomas. Thomas had them restored by conservator Flavio Capitulino, a Brazilian restorer based in Paris, who had cleaned up other masterworks by artists known to be in Bouvier's arsenal for Rybolovlev—among them, Chagall and da Vinci[59]. According to Capitulino, however, the Picassos were then hung at Natural Le Coultre to be viewed by the Russian oligarch.

The restoration of the two paintings in question, however, was apparently highly confidential.
Because of Capitulino's preexisting relationship with Hutin-Blay, he asked her directly in a casual conversation — had she really sold the two portraits of her mother, Jacqueline?

Her answer was no.

Catherine Huntin-Blay believed that Olivier Thomas had sold her paintings (including a third Rembrandt work, *Man In A Gold Helmet* from 1656) without her consent.[60] She latently realized they were taken from her home in Mougins, Picasso's final residence, when Thomas was doing an inventory report on the way to a storage warehouse (not Natural Le Coultre).

Thomas then cut off Hutin-Blay's access to her own storage space, at his base in France, Art Transit. She threatened to call the police and had the locks changed. Whether they were already gone she couldn't be sure.

Investigation for "abuse of trust, fraud, concealment, and laundering," opened against Thomas in both 2015 and 2016, but it was eventually closed out.

It turned out that Hutin-Blay had "forgotten," she sold Thomas the piece. Paperwork turned up during the lawsuit that she had used an account in Lichtenstein.

While it was not uncommon to use the term "Private Collection" liberally, Hutin's name was explicitly mentioned in the provenance pages of the Rybolovlev catalogue. The need for privacy among high-net worth collections had served to Hutin-Blay's detriment with Thomas, but Bouvier's record-keeping was nevertheless accurate.

Instead, the assault turned to her character. Rumor had it she drank three bottles of champagne a day, plus medications.

In the interest of both pride and transparency, Hutin-Blay paid off a cumbersome inheritance tax and planned a *Musée Jacqueline* in a renovated former convent in Aix-en-Provence, set to open in 2021. She had inherited 2,000 Picasso pieces when her mother died in 1986, all made between 1952 and 1973. The museum was expected to house 1,000 paintings alone,[61] alongside ephemera, drawings and mixed media works.[62]

Bouvier eventually claimed he had no knowledge that the paintings may have been unlawfully obtained, and certainly at the time of sale, Rybolovlev had no idea. In their mutual ignorance, the oligarch's rich collection continued to grow.

After all, though Rybolovlev was a wealthy man when he acquired his first two masterworks in 2004, he was about to get much richer. And like the heaps of the Petit Trianon, there was another large pit on the way.

10

FLOATING

FROM GENEVA, Rybolovlev continued to oversee Uralkali's operations, maintaining his post as Chairman of the Board. His family and company both prospered in the early 2000s. A leadership style characterized by determination, decisiveness, and quiet but exacting tactics, maintained order. The company flourished and diversified. Where Bouvier was nicknamed 'The Freeport King' in Switzerland, Rybolovlev was known at home in Russian media as 'The Potash Tsar'.

Potash was a common abbreviation for potassium fertilizer. It had always widely occurred naturally in soil and could be harvested directly, but the term also derived from pot-ash—quite literally, ash of the pot. In the early days of its use (at the turn of the 18th century),[63] potash was the process in which ash from burnt wood was soaked in pots, culling the potassium from the wet mash.[64]

When soil was used for farming, the natural potassium deposits were removed and needed to be replaced. Food waste transplanted potassium back into the earth… even via waterways as humans digested potassium-rich plants and foods. 21st century innovation and cultivation allowed potash to be widely accepted as a successful way to increase crop yields and correct farmland imbalances. Nitrates, sulfates, and chlorides were all suitable means of potash modification production.[65] In its various forms, 95% of industrial potash was used for agricultural means by 2018. [66]

For optimal impact, the chemicals necessary for people and plants were extracted and redistributed as salts to agricultural outposts around the world, often as potassium chloride or potassium hydroxide in the form of sparkling ores. Potash was then exported, perfect for emerging markets seeking to sustain populations (and dietary intakes) on the rise. As such, potash markets consistently correlated to population booms, and it was a promising industry. 80% of potash was exported globally.

Moreover, only 12 countries in the world extracted potash, rendering the Ural region of Russia uniquely positioned to export to more than 100 countries worldwide. In India, for example, a Saskatchewan-based Canadian potash company reported that 100% of potash was imported, compared to 90% in Brazil and 70% in China.

Uralkali added magnesium salt production, and significantly opened up export to all BRIC markets to great acclaim. In 2006, 90% of Uralkali's potash was exported outside Russia, and provided 10% of the world's global supply singlehandedly.[67] Ramsay's biography cited 16,000 employees under Rybolovlev, including the 50% stake in the Belarusian Potash Company (BPC, or BKK – Belaruskaya Kalijnaya Kompaniya) acquired in 2005.[68]

By 2018, the company website claimed the Uralkali accounted for 20% of the world's potash production, including 50% of the BPC volume. Along with those involved in the supply chain process from mining to export, Uralkali estimated 11,000 people in their main production unit alone. These criteria proved Urakali was the world's fifth largest potassium company.[69] As of 2018, the company website claimed it ranked third.

Under Rybolovlev's purview, Uralkali greatly capitalized on its existing resources. The price of potash imports in China and Brazil increased for favorable circumstances on the Russian company's terms, and the Baltic Bulk Terminal (BBT) launched in Saint Petersburg, constructed in 2001 to facilitate transport. Journalist John Helmer noted that in 2007, the price of potash export to Brazil was raised six times, for a total increase of over 90%.

Regardless, Russian potash had sustained a rich history before Rybolovlev. After salt deposits were first discovered in the Ural region in 1925, the USSR State Planning Committee established ordinances to develop Soviet potash as a state-approved industry the following year, constructing the first mining center shortly thereafter in Solikamsk, a small town in Perm. Berezniki was the seat of the second potash mining complex (Berezniki 2), constructed in 1930, and it was soon linked to Solikamsk by 1935.[70] A third Berezniki mine (Berezniki 3), was constructed 30 years later, in 1965—the year before Rybolovlev was born.

Uralkali's Berezniki region suffered its first sinkhole at Berezniki 3 in 1986. Believed to arise due to tectonic fractures, sinkhole conditions are exacerbated by erosion of concrete underground as a reaction to brine over time. Long-term mining has been proven to create these scenarios, and the consequences are disastrous. Repeated sinkholes cause the responsible mining tunnels to collapse underground, and hundreds of earthquakes have been recorded in response.

Although mismanagement in the 1950s and 60s was considered a factor in the sinkhole situation of the 1980s, their somewhat regular occurrence suggested that it was not unique to Uralkali. Beyond Russia, sinkholes had also sprung up at 80 mines around the world, among them, in South Africa, Israel, China, the United Kingdom, the United States, Mexico and Belize.

While mining had been a common aggravator of terrain, it was not always the exclusive cause. Any irritation causing fractures could result in sinkholes, even air holes underground in areas like Florida, where the earth should typically have remained filled with humidity and rain. During droughts, these air holes have been known to cause similar fractures (and sinking) to mining. For example, during his tenure as President of the United States, Donald Trump's residences at Mar-a-Lago and the White House both had sinkholes on the premises. Strangely, they each occurred on May 22nd in 2017 and 2018 respectively.[71]

The Trump sinkholes were of a significantly lesser impact than those the Russian mines were facing; as was often the case, the range of these environmental events varied in severity. Sinkholes generally occurred both suddenly and gradually, with the latter ultimately much more terrifying.[72]

Fortunately for Uralkali, in the aftermath of the abrupt 1986 sinkhole crisis, Berezniki came out stronger. Berezniki 4, a newly constructed mine at the time, was utilized in advance of initial plans. Berezniki 4 rescued mining output when Berezniki 3 was incapacitated. By capitalizing on this impetus, Berezniki 4 maintained production and became the company's largest mine into present day.

But more than 30 years later, the company was challenged again.

On October 17th, 2006, the earth sank quickly at the Berezniki 1 mine, the oldest on the premises. Water rushed through the flooding tunnels, and miners frantically fled in the darkness. It was something known as a "cover-collapse" sinkhole, and the team at Uralkali was understandably extremely concerned. Attempts made to stagger the influx of aggravating brine from the flood proved mostly futile.

Vladislav Baumgertner, then-CEO of Uralkali, called Rybolovlev to bear the bad news in Perm.

"I offered to fly out immediately," Rybolovlev explained in a Russian documentary film from 2008,[73]

"And I was already in Berezniki the next day."

Once he arrived, he looked at the aftermath alongside the governor, the mayor, and Rybolovlev. They descended into the mines themselves to see the site of the initial accident, evaluating the situation in tandem with expert environmentalist opinions, sourced from mining specialists flown in from around the world.

Tools to measure toxic gas output were brought in right away. Blinking lights on their hardhats were automated to notify teams when to evacuate. It was the most effective way to spread information, so far underground that radios would be

rendered null and void, and often tuned out regardless by the shrill sound of
the drills.

"We went down; we looked around," Rybolovlev recollected, "And I
remember having this feeling that this would not be the last time something like this
would happen."

Senior leadership and laborers alike stayed in the trenches, literally attending to
the situation down at the scene of the accident, and figuratively working tirelessly to
remedy the issue without mounting complications. In waist-deep salt water, workers
used their machinery to frantically try to drain the mounting water. When the
machinery pipes broke down, they repaired them on site and kept pumping.
Through the ebbs and flows of the flood, plans were made to evacuate the workers
and halt production in the event of further complications.

The workers were especially concerned about their livelihoods. There was a
long culture of hardworking miners, which had evolved over nearly 100 years and
been celebrated during the communist era. The old-time concept of a determined
proletariat was evidenced by the ethics of those coping with the sinkhole's
complications.

"We were all ready to stay for a second shift," affirmed Igor Goroshko, Chief
of the Section on site, nodding eagerly, "We understood that this was our work, and
lives were on the line." Footage from the event confirmed Goroshko's willpower, as
he turned the wheel of the pump and gestured to his crew to motivate them.

Rybolovlev's intuition proved spot-on. Despite their best efforts to stop the
flooding, toxic hydrogen sulfide gas soon released into the mine. Low doses caused
eye, head, lung, and stomach irritation, and high doses could have proven instantly
fatal.[74] 10 days after the first sinkhole, on October 27th, the floods continued to
grow more severe, and the risk of explosion more catastrophic.

Rybolovlev called Sergei Dyakov, Deputy to the General Director.

"Don't you think it's time to get our people out of there?" Rybolovlev asked.

"I don't know where that feeling came from," Dyakov said on camera, "But he
had it. It's the truth."
Dyakov assured him they would bring workers out of the mine, and the Chairman
was instantly relieved.

Every 30 minutes, an update on the status of the workers was released to the
team. The headlights were blinking to notify 471 people it was time to evacuate, and
support from neighboring cities was called in. Within an hour, 471 dropped by less
than half to 219. The last 100 workers were rescued less than two hours after the
first warning. Citizens of the town were soon relocated, and a $270 million rail
bypass was offered as a solution to avoid the danger zone.

Rybolovlev was proactive to the point of relentlessness throughout the crisis
management, dissatisfied until the project reached completion.

"A feeling of calm did not return to me until the last man got out of the mine,"
Rybolovlev told the documentarian.

The zone was restricted and blocked off in the aftermath, much to the dismay of locals in the region, as a preventative measure.

Uralkali suffered no casualties.

⸎

"The most important thing is preserving human life," reiterated Rybolovlev in the film, "But when a company's market capitalization falls by a billion dollars, you start to look at things a little bit differently."

The sinkhole catastrophe was not covered by insurance, and the costs were deeply problematic. Damages alone totaled an estimated $7 million.

But the economic fall-out could have been much worse.

In September 2006, Uralkali publicized the decision to place shares—from Rybolovlev's majority stake via a company called Madura Holdings[75]—on the London Stock Exchange. Though they were already trading in Russia, the global implications of the much larger exchange rippled through international markets as investors and competitors anticipated strong results.

In finance, this was referred to as floating the IPO (the initial public offering). More than going public, it referred to a specific number of shares being made available.

On October 10th, 2006, exactly one week before the first sinkhole appeared on the 17th, the company had a change of heart. They decided to pull out, publicizing that they had not received a desirable enough share price from investors.

The speculation as to why was immense, but no one could say for sure. Strategists weighed in that perhaps there were too many Russian listings due to market.

Had the company proceeded as planned, the aftermath of the mining accidents may have led the securities to collapse, with shares reduced to all-time lows. Instead, they held off until October 2007 and had massive success: their order book was 23 times oversubscribed. Journalist John Helmer reported[76] that UBS calculated a 116% increase share price compared to the beginning of 2007.

Uralkali gained over $1 billion.

The following year, in 2008, ongoing investigation into the scientific realities of the Berezniki sinkholes deemed them unavoidable. Governor of the Perm Region Yuri Trutnev issued a formal statement to that end, relinquishing responsibility from the company. At the time of the IPO, Trutnev was also Natural Resources Minister, appointed in 2004. Previously, he had been Mayor of Perm—elected in 1996, the same year Rybolovlev was released from jail for murder charges. Yuri Trutnev eventually went to work as Vladimir Putin's Deputy Prime Minister.

Naysayers against Rybolovlev's business practice claimed that the crisis arose from his relationship with Yuri Trutnev. He had been appointed Natural Resources specifically because of his ties to Rybolovlev, and had actively shortcutted environmental regulations to speed up production for Uralkali on the brink of the IPO. According to this theory, Trutnev and Rybolovlev had mishandled the business practice, with a disregard for human life.

Skepticism provoked additional review following Trutnev's conclusion that the company was not responsible for the accidents, led by Igor Sechin. The sinkholes were blamed on negligence. As a consequence, shares plummeted 92% from a summer high. Values did eventually rise, but never to their former boom.

In 2010, after more than 15 years at the helm and a prison sentence, Rybolovlev was finally successfully pressured to divide his majority stake at Uralkali among three lesser oligarchs: Suleyman Kerimov (25%), Filaret Galchev (15%), and Alexander Nesis (13.2%).[77]

It was a favorable agreement, to say the least. Thanks to the buy-out, Rybolovlev's net worth soared with an additional $6.5 billion.

For a time, it seemed that business at Uralkali stabilized. Ernst & Young awarded CEO Vladislav Baumgertner an award for "Best IPO" at the Young Entrepreneur Awards in 2012.[78]

Then drama began again. In July 2013, Baumgertner pulled out of the Belarusian Potash Company trade agreement Rybolovlev had fostered in 2005. The decision resulted from claims of undocumented sales in both countries to the detriment of the other. Come August, Baumgertner was briefly detained in Minsk, Belarus, extradited home to Moscow, and placed under house arrest as he awaited criminal charges for abuse of power.[79] The ongoing battle plunged Uralkali shares, and Sechin considered placing a bid for the company in 2013.[80]

In the end, Sechin did not purchase the company. Charges against Baumgertner were dropped as of February 2015, and Uralkali was approved to delist from the London Stock Exchange that November.[81]

By then, Rybolovlev was long gone from Uralkali disputes, but he remained cognizant of the dangers of share seizure. Given everything he had been through—prison, tense meetings with state representatives—he was not going to risk losing it all.

So he made some very glamorous financial moves: most importantly, the decision to buy more art than ever. When he fully liquidated the last 10% of his shares in 2011, he had purchased the Uralkali company planes, moved to Monaco, and, distrustful of the Swiss government's possible collaboration with Russian enemies, was gradually moving his artwork out of Geneva.

The need to hide assets had gone far beyond the divorce. Rybolovlev explained in the 2008 proceedings:

> "Elena knew pertinently that the transfer of these artworks and furniture were
> caused by the desire to ensure the security of this property against the certain

instability associated with Russia. I have in no case tried to move matrimonial property outside of Switzerland without her consent with a goal of 'reducing the mass of matrimonial property'…

…Elena also expressly admitted that I had explained to Mr. Bouvier that the reason for the need for a transfer away from Geneva was the result of the risks and the situation which had occurred in Uralkali in Russia."

The art was going to Hong Kong, and to London, where he was preparing in case he needed to move the family:

"Following the considerations of which most notably related to the risks characterizing the legal system developing in Russia, I had to take necessary measures with a view to eventual emigration with my family to England if it ever became indispensable, as well as those related to transfer… the most part of which were favorably held in two trusts constituted under the auspices of Cypriot law."

In addition to the divorce and tensions in Russia, there was another pertinent Swiss regulation that went into effect in May 2009. Simon Hewitt, an art journalist well-known in Geneva and a regular attendee at the Moscow art fair, covered the plan to make Swiss customs, "Euro-compatible." While the freeports still functioned as tax free hubs for the objects, some on-site services were taxed. Secondly, the privacy laws that changed at the banks had caught up to the freeports:

"All artworks stored at the Freeport must now be recorded by storage companies in an inventory listing each item's description, value, size, date and place of storage, country of origin, and the name and address of 'the person with the right of disposal' over it. The inventory must be kept on a computer database in storage companies' offices, and be readily available for inspection by Customs. The information must be kept for five years."

Bouvier's business in Geneva continued, but 2009 was the year he became a Singapore resident.

Rybolovlev relied on Bouvier in the event that either his wife or the Russian government could seize his artwork. Beyond Hong Kong and London, his art was mostly going to Bouvier's latest marvel: his brand new Singapore Freeport.

11

THE SAFEST PLACE

FOLLOWING THE IPO, Rybolovlev steadily and aggressively purchased new work in full force. He dealt exclusively with Bouvier, who took advantage of the rapid influx of business (and funds, approved of or otherwise), opening his Natural Le Coultre freeport offshoot in the Asian city-state in 2010.

The move to Singapore would have been strategic regardless of the profits from Rybolovlev's payments. Singapore had a well-earned reputation as a place where the ease of doing business was incredibly fluid, most favorably as it extended to regulation and the creation of new companies. This made it an ideal place to use various company names to conduct operations. Bouvier was a shareholder in 24 companies in Singapore alone, many of which were used on behalf of his warehouses.

In addition to making Singapore his business hub, Bouvier exported the capabilities of Natural Le Coultre in the Geneva Freeport to Hong Kong and Luxembourg, maintaining shareholder responsibilities across jurisdictions. This was Bouvier's crown jewel: he had set his sights on the region in 2005, around the time of the first Moscow Art Fair, and built the structure at a cost of $100 million.

Many in the art world, including those closest to Bouvier, only speculated about the source of the investment. In the world of Swiss discretion, certain questions would always go unasked—or at the very least, unanswered.

Bouvier loved the complexities of these wildest high-level art transactions, reminiscing about his years as a reckless athlete. "In the mountains, it was the same," he said to Knight, "I go to the place which is the most complicated, the most risky place."

Each of these autonomous territories in Bouvier's arsenal had been regulated to allow freeport businesses to serve the locality. Bouvier, the Freeport King, had far surpassed his family's legacy for one of the premier storage facilities in Geneva and gone global with the profit and expansion.

As of 2018, Singaporean operations were run by his longtime loyal friend Yves Meyer, who had known him for decades before the time came to relocate to the Asia Pacific region. Meyer was middle-aged, friendly, and very careful in his dealings with top clients and members of the press, but very jovial with his trusted team. The team included Mathieu Foschia,[82] an up-and-coming art expert who joined Natural Le Coultre in 2012 and rose to be Logistics Manager. When the recorder switched off, Meyer reminisced about his younger years in the Bahamas and the future of his new Singaporean home, while Foschia affectionately cracked jokes about Meyer's weight.

The Singapore Freeport was previously run by Tony Reynard, Bouvier's childhood friend. He had moved to Singapore when his wife found work in the area, and Bouvier offered him the position. He eventually left the company, staying in the city.

One thing everyone could be sure of was that Singapore was intensely agreeable for the Swiss businessmen: clean, controlled, safe and sunny.

Together they transplanted employees from Geneva to the brand-new, state-of-the-art location.

With its history of iron-clad security and an ever-growing list of billionaires per capita, Singapore was an ideal choice for a freeport in Asia. Natural Le Coultre collaborated with the Singaporean government to declare their designated warehouse free of GST (Goods and Service Tax). This collaboration was so explicit, in fact, that the freeport was attached directly to the Changi Airport, and incoming luxury items were vetted by the same staffers as the border patrol. Each loading bay was equipped with a scanner, surveillanced by these auxiliary police, with one large enough to scan an entire aircraft dock.

In Singapore, the police were the only citizens permitted to own and carry guns. It was a culture of rule-following and harsh penalties, so the likelihood of robbery or invasion was exceptionally low. In the nine years since the freeport had opened, as of 2018 there had never been an attempted theft. As Meyer's associate Foschia said simply, "We are in Singapore."

Furthermore, the clientele was ideal for tax-free storage of luxury goods. The booming restaurant scene in one of the richest nations in the world, coupled with an effusive culture of generosity, meant that alcohol and jewelry distributors had an ideal jumping-off point to transport around Asia, and in the locality. At the right price, there was no reason to pay taxes on the storage of back-stocked luxury goods.

This held particularly true for Chinese investors, motivated by the historical plague of instability in their home country.

"What's interesting about Singapore is the Chinese," Decrausaz said from Switzerland. "Because if the Chinese buy things today, and they bring them to

China, you know, there could be a change in government in two minutes. Fine, if I'm Chinese, and I buy a painting, I would never put it in China. I'd store it…and if ever I have an issue with the regime?"

He snapped his fingers.

"I leave China, with a place to recuperate what I've bought."

It was a matter of security.

"That's not to say that I bought something wrong or something criminal," he said protectively, "It's just that I put it in the bank. Everyone has their methods if the future doesn't go as planned. I'm going for lunch today at noon, but I brought a sandwich with me, just in case I don't go to the restaurant."

Unlike the Swiss port, the Singaporean structure was custom designed start to finish, and as a result, felt as close to impossible as anything to pass illicit items through its doors. The entrance to the building involved two gated vehicle checkpoints and a revolving door with a security key code before allowing the visitor to pass through the main door, a circular glass entrance that locked on both sides before letting the visitor enter to the main lobby. There, identification was immediately confiscated, and radiation-driven metal detectors searched the visitor, who raised both their hands. Once through the four tests, the visitor finally put a guest pass around his or her neck like an Olympic medal. They had survived, and graduated to a land the lanyard called in bold red letters: 'The Safest Place.'

Nevertheless, the whims of the ultra-rich were outlandish. One Indonesian billionaire had cherries flown in for a party and kept them stored in Singapore. Another client had customized furniture built just for his showroom, shipping in referred craftsmen from Australia.

In the meantime, an expat community of about 4,000 Swiss meant meetings with Ambassadors and a gateway to the world of East-meets-West, all with the benefits of extreme accommodation and emphasis on regulation.

It was Bouvier's signature appetite for the extreme. Everything was tailored with flourish, and brand new.

Inside, the first feeling was the gust of a blustery chill—an odd sensation for the sticky heat of Southeast Asia. Maintaining the approved museum-grade regulation for the warehouse was no easy feat in a region where the temperature averaged a high of 87 degrees Fahrenheit daily. From the extreme heat outdoors to the extreme cold indoors, none of the plants the landscapers had envisioned were able to survive. They dried out and all had to be removed, much to the chagrin of the perfectionists on site. At export garages on the premises, the doors slid shut within seconds to prevent the cold air from escaping. The doors made a loud thud as they rapidly shuttered down.

The slamming doors and clicking heels on linoleum were the only sounds in the empty, highly secured hallways. A stunning geometric sculpture by Israeli-born artist Ron Arad (b. 1951) featuring prominently in the main hall best summed up the message. It had been disassembled following an exhibition at the Museum of Modern Art in New York and custom-installed to fit the slightly smaller

Singaporean warehouse hall. The piece was called *La Cage Sans Frontières*: the cage without borders.[83]

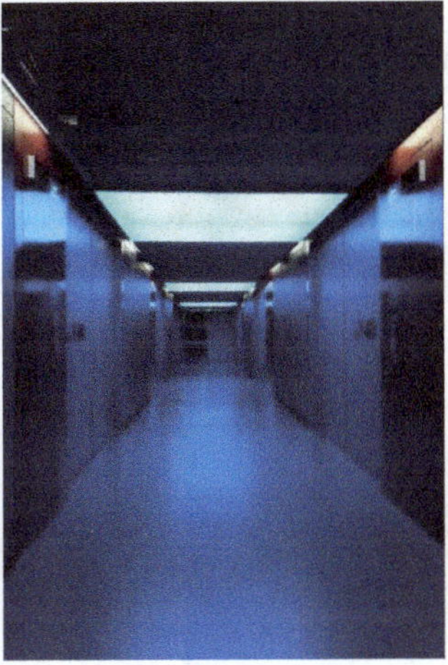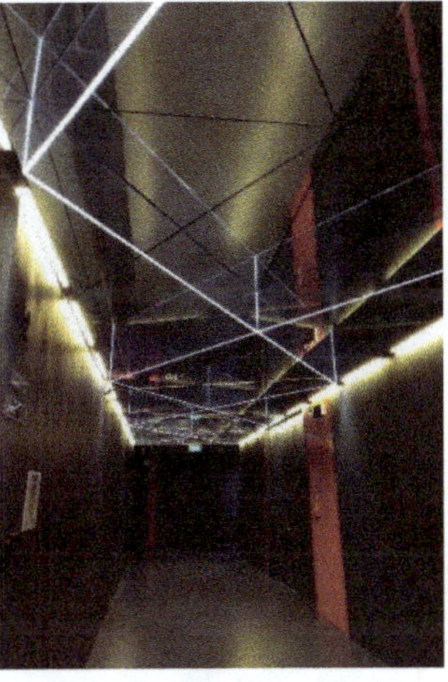

Inisde the Singapore Freeport, taken by Alexandra Bregman

In this attention to detail, the warehouse was spectacularly contemporary. Lighting was custom created by American designer Joanna Grawunder (b. 1961), whose crisscross silver lines and blue and green casts on the corridors rivaled any Sci-Fi movie about lasers and protection. Being inside the Singapore Freeport was like being transported into the ultra-sleek future, where safety and security trumped all else. Grawunder's eerie colors alluded to the complexities of who and what lurked behind closed doors.

The journey into storage began with customs, who were equipped with loading bays and scanners of all sizes, including one allegedly large enough to search an entire plane. Then, an inventory report was created, and finally, the items were ushered into the client's storage unit of choice.

Beyond the inventory report, the freeport mangers were completely beholden to the client's discretions. Meyer echoed Decrausaz in terms of regulation.

"If you're a freeport," Meyer explained, "You don't know really what is inside. You don't know what is in the crate."

Realizing how dangerous the words were, he quickly corrected. Just because the client called the shots did not mean that illicit activities occurred. The responsibility sat with the VIPs, but it did exist.

"You don't hide things in the freeport," Meyer insisted, "Because customs can check anytime."

Singaporean customs came often to inspect the inventory, cross-checking the log numbers and the inventory reports against specific units.

"They say, 'I want to check this lot, this lot, this lot,' and they come and check." Meyer said with a lilt.

Yet the mystery of the freeport had led to salacious storytelling around what lurked behind the doors, and Meyer walked on eggshells during media outreach.

"Never trust a journalist," Meyer said some time later, "Because you tell them a story, and in the news, it's a totally different story."

He continued, his Swiss French accent thick with frustration:

"Because they don't like nice stories. When you tell them, 'You don't hide stuff here because you have police who check what comes in and out, you have customs, (and we had maybe two or three inspections by customs already this year), you have an inventory…' They don't listen. They write, 'Ooh, they hide art pieces.' We don't hide anything!"

True to form, former American FBI investigator and art book author Robert K. Wittman explained that this was not enough. As an article in the *New York Times* explained:

"All of the objects stored at these facilities are insured by their owners, and insurance companies 'are not required to report to the F.B.I. or to Interpol' if a policyholder is insuring a stolen object. They have no law enforcement purview."

The rationale behind the intense amounts of secrecy had always been asset protection.

"It's like a bank," Meyer said. "You don't want to tell anyone that you have an account with Citi or BNP[84] or UBS. It doesn't concern anyone."

Foschia qualified. "Insurance knows, the lawyers know…you have some people you can trust who know. Customs know. But not the world."

Meyer then described various scenarios as to why someone would choose not to publicize their assets. Family feuds could be caused by articles detailing private collections as each member coveted a prized work of art. Maybe announcing the ownership of a valuable item would encourage kidnappers, he offered, waiting outside the building to kidnap you, "every time they see you with a box."

"It's normal that people want to keep their secrets." Meyer said earnestly.

The intimate understanding of a variety of threats allowed the team at Natural Le Coultre to grant a substantial amount of autonomy to the private clients. Inside the private rooms, clients were even permitted to install their own cameras, so long as they didn't tamper with existing security.

The client called the shots.

"We say what we are authorized to say," Meyer said.

And how much was that?

"It's like a Swiss banker," Foschia reiterated. "You don't say anything."

They continued to insist defensively that basic client privilege necessitated a sense of discretion, and the policies at Natural Le Coultre were like at any other warehouse. All the while, they expertly navigated the dark wide halls, de-activating and reactivating multiple alarms along the way with authoritative, high-pitched beeps.

The typical client had a storage room, marked ST, and showroom, marked SR. Each required a special security card. Depending on the VIP, there were increasingly elevated levels of security.

The most elite option was a private suite. A brightly lit gray room featured an industrial side table against a small wall with a chair on the left, and on the right, a massive, locked safe. The client would take the room and place metals and jewels inside the compartment, treating it like an office.

Entry was a two-key system contingent on both the client and the manager. The manager escorted the client through the building with their employee code, and then only the client had the final key to their room and safe. Only the staff had access to the main door, and only the client had access to their belongings. And if for some reason, the client lost the key…

"Boom, kaboom!" said Meyer, motioning with his hands to show how the team would crack the safe, "And then they pay for it."

This extreme situation had allegedly never happened. It would certainly be out of character to risk damaging the items, especially considering that even the fire extinguishers were gas-only, to avoid any water damage in the event of emergency.

Sometimes, the client did volunteer to share access to the suite, granting the staff equal footing for these kinds of scenarios. One alternative was presenting the staff with a specially sealed envelope that required being broken to use, kept in a safe place on their behalf. But mostly, the final judgment call was with the VIP.

The Singapore team was proud that their lavish operation was very different than the humble discretion back home in Geneva. To them, Geneva was old and sleepy, and this was state-of-the-art. And to be sure, Bouvier was able to maintain his strong presence in Singapore into 2018, even after his relationship with Rybolovlev, and his reputation, suffered deeply in Europe.

After all, he believed the accusations to come were false.

"They said I stole from the vaults of my clients," Bouvier said, "That's totally crazy…I didn't have the key."

IV. The Floating World

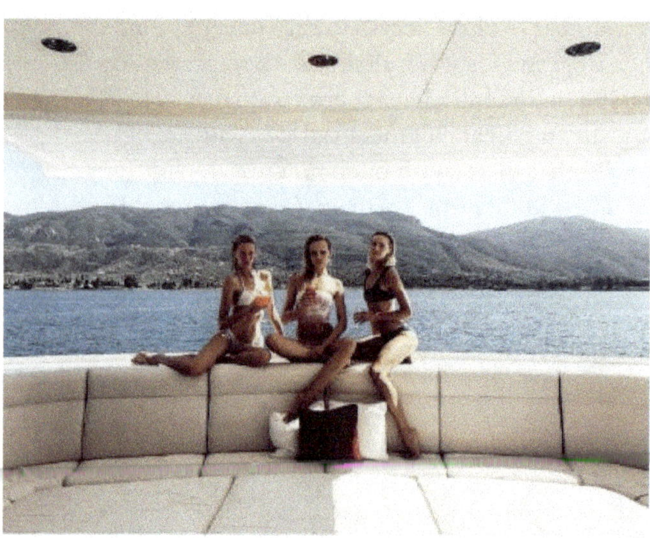

12

BOYS' TOYS

With his valuables safely stowed in Singapore and troubles in Geneva and Russia behind him, Rybolovlev was thriving after his latest move to Monaco. Effectively separated from his wife, he had formally relocated in 2010, where the principality was as glamorous as it was financially and personally beneficial. Rybolovlev's friend Vadim Vasiliyev introduced him to the region, and Tania Rappo and her husband were already there much of the year. Later, Rybolovlev had his parents relocate to the Riviera as well, and they finally sold the apartment in Perm that had been his childhood home.

Monaco was a place for contradiction. It was a principality, a country, and a city all at once…a place where tradition had always been at odds with the nouveau riche, where cars went fast but time passed slowly. In the warmer months, it was a place to relax in a gentle bustle of quiet clinking glasses and loud whirring engines…and while it was always a place for great wealth and safety, it was earning a reputation for implacable and immutable danger.

Moving to Monaco, as opposed to the French territory, was an astute financial decision. Simply put, the sovereign state was a tax-free zone. To be a citizen of Monaco came with enormous tax privileges, some of which a resident could enjoy by buying real estate or opening a business. The true coup for Monegasque financial gains was to become a citizen, with its coveted passport.

Although the passport holders were prevented from playing in the illustrious Monte Carlo Casino, the capacity for financial gain was exceptional. Because it was so desirable, obtaining the passport was notoriously challenging. Wealthy hopefuls in-the-know all clamored to obtain one, and the waitlist for approval was purported to be as long as 40 years. In order to be approved, or possibly even to jump the list, new ruler Prince Albert of Monaco had to grant his blessing.

Like Geneva, Monaco had a long history as a place of refuge—especially for unsavory characters. François Grimaldi was the first ruler of the Monaco settlement in the 13th century, named Il Malizia in Italian, or François the Malicious, for having seized the territory through brute force and deception. In order to enter the region, he had worn a monk's robes and invited himself to the sanctuary of the monastery and asked to stay the night. When the keepers of the monastery obliged, he revealed his sword beneath the costume, and mass murdered the monks to ensure his conquest. Forever afterwards, the Monegasque coat of arms featured a monk with a hidden weapon. It was a place for enemies disguised as friends.[85]

Then, Prince Rainier I kidnapped and raped a beautiful maiden. Local legend suggested she used witchcraft to cast a curse on the family, dooming the Grimaldis to an inability to succeed in love.[86]

Later, author W. Somerset Maugham coined the term, "Sunny place, shady people," in the late 1800s, which became a commonplace description of the French Riviera among everyone from African financiers and award-winning authors to whispering waitresses enduring into present day.

In spite of, or perhaps precisely because of this lore of instability, Monaco maintained a long tradition of wealth and cultural prosperity. The tax-free principality attracted some of the world's wealthiest people, including Russians: Tsars and aristocrats took advantage of the neighboring South of France coastline until the fall of the monarchy, and in contemporary times, the French Riviera hosted fellow Russian oligarchs Roman Abramovich and Suleiman Kerimov in nearby Cap d'Antibes.

With an estimated net worth of $6 billion, Kerimov also made his fortune by way of his looser stake in Uralkali. In 2017, Kerimov was suspected of cheating the French government out of €700 million by buying five homes in Antibes under a fake name,[87] but he was released on bail. In 2018, Abramovich was forced to pay out taxes for undervaluing his home in the area as well.[88] In addition to his ties to Boris Yeltsin, residences in France, and superyachts, Abramovich became well-known as the owner of the Chelsea football team in England, which he had purchased in 2003.

In 2011, Rybolovlev purchased a majority stake (66.67%, just like at Uralkali…the same number as the year he was born) in Monaco's renowned Association sportive de Monaco football club. In English, the team was called AS Monaco. The minority owner was Prince Albert himself.

Aside from the emergence of at least two illegitimate children, at least in the public sphere Prince Albert had managed to stay relatively unscathed by scandal. He was a graduate of the prestigious Amherst College in Massachusetts, and an instrumental member of Monegasque society who undoubtedly wielded incredible power, the majority of which was for good.

The year before Rybolovlev purchased AS Monaco, Albert and his old friend and fellow Amherst classmate, Paris-born Jérôme de Bontin, invited the Amherst soccer team on a tour of the region where they played the pros throughout France, culminating in a match against AS Monaco and a stay at the royal palace. The impetus for the choice was that de Bontin's son Nicolas had recently started on the team.

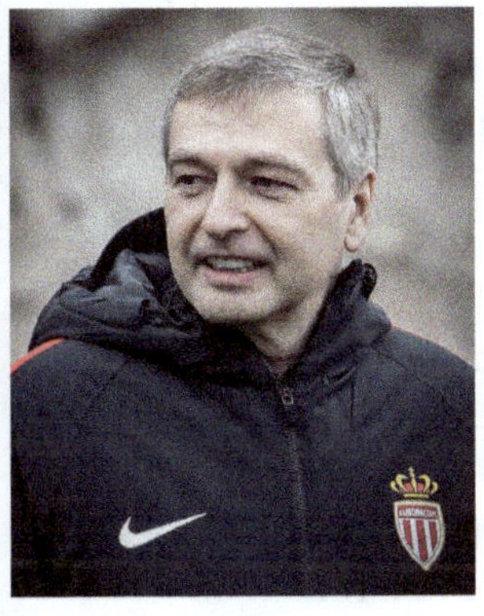

Photo AS Monaco / Stéphane Senaux

Rybolovlev's decision to buy AS Monaco was indisputably an investment in the location as much as the community. Like the more high-profile pastimes of racing yachts and cars, football was at the core of Monaco's leisure culture, and "Rybo," as the local football fans and friends at the club called him, had inserted himself into a big part of the way that citizens could connect.

The club room was not just for fraternizing; it was a place of business. Rybo and the Prince hobnobbed in the presidential lodge, the government lodge, and the saloon in-between during games, with an exclusive members group of around 60 to 70 people in the room at any given time.

In a later series of investigations, *MediaPart* did an expose on suspect behavior in the football club. Namely, Vasilyev and other members of the football team organization were recruiting players underage, drawing up contracts as early as age 12, even though they were officially supposed to wait until the players turned 18.

In one particularly controversial email, Adjunct General Director Nicolas Holveck explained to Vasilyev about a player born in 2004:

"Vadim,

See attached for a proposal for the young player from Paris that I was talking about before vacation. All the recruiters say that he's the best of his generation…he wants to play in Monaco. [Director] N. Weber knows his mom really well, he already helped her during a very difficult situation. This would cost us around 200,000 Euros, but spread out over 5 seasons. I think we should really do it. Are you O.K. that we move ahead on this quickly. We must have your advance approval."

It was a full suite of services to cater to the talented underage player and his family. They were even on the case to find his mother employment in the area.

Vasilyev had asked an agent, Pierre Philip, about the legality of this practice five years earlier, in 2013.

He wrote via email, "Can we bring under-18s to Monaco? How does that work?"

To which the agent answered, "Most clubs sign a pre-contract when the player is less than 18…it's not a perfectly sure situation, but if the club waits until he's 18, it's often too late."

So it continued.

After all, it was big business. MediaPart estimated Vasilyev's cut of AS Monaco's gross total over the 2013-2018 period as €41 million, a mere 10% of the 410 million over the last five years. He also gleaned revenue cuts from the marketing, ticketing, and sponsorship opportunities, with a package of 1% of 50 million until 2016, after which he negotiated his salary from €750,000 to €1.25 million.

But for all the revenues around the game, Prince Albert never offered Rybo the passport he sought.

There was also talk that Bouvier and Rybolovlev wanted to open a freeport in Monaco, and that the project had been vetoed—or deliberately overlooked—by Albert himself.

Just like Geneva, Rybolovlev wasn't quite fitting in. Those who interacted with him remained respectful and deferential to the point of uncertainty.

"We weren't close," said one AS Monaco club member, "I'd see him around and say hi because he is the owner of team. That's it."

Even Rappo doubted Rybolovlev's ability to speak with the common man. "Besides his lawyer and his hairdresser," she told Knight, "I don't think he sees normal people at all."

Or as Thomas Seydoux told him, "Nobody really knew who had access to him."

It was not by accident that regular people did not interact with the Russian oligarch. It was a security measure.

Rybolovlev had panic rooms and bulletproof glass windows installed in his homes. He would not drink a water that was handed to him unless he opened the sealed bottle himself. He leaned deep into his plate at mealtime, shoveling food in, causing raised eyebrows. He was wary of new people, because he felt he had reason to be afraid.

Often seen along with Rybolovlev at the games was Vasilyev, his newly appointed club Vice President, his lawyer, Tetiana Bersheda, and a young blonde who appeared to be his elder daughter, Ekaterina. Ekaterina was the namesake of Rybolovlev's first major trust. Anna, his second daughter, was used for another. It was the Ekaterina trust that Rybolovlev used to purchase his stake in AS Monaco.

Like the football club, the artwork purchases were made through the trusts, by way of multiple companies. Accent Delight International and Xitrans Financial were the primary companies involved, though they were listed as entities incorporated in the British Virgin Islands. There was also Rigamora Holdings, the company name for the family office, based in Monaco with about 50 employees, and Madura Holdings, another family company based in Cyprus. The latter had a team of about 12 people reviewing acquisitions under the trust's names.

The word Rigamora sounded suspiciously like rigamarole, defined by Merriam Webster as "confused or meaningless talk," or "a complex and sometimes ritualistic procedure." By 2010, the trust structure was certainly excessively complicated.

"It's just a galaxy of companies…" Wilson said, "There are zillions of them out there."

If the companies were a galaxy, the trust structure was a satellite. It launched the items into outer space, and from there, each SPV, special purpose vehicle, held a specific thing.

"Typically you have moving parts: you have an aircraft, you have a yacht…you have crew, you have payroll," Wilson clarified. "It's easier just to put them in a company and manage it like a company."

These categories were referred to in the private client industry as 'boys' toys.' Rybolovlev's world definitely fit that description. With every new acquisition, he was becoming a formidable playboy in the world of ultra-rich Russians, and distancing himself ever further from his soon-to-be-ex-wife.

Elena Rybolovleva was still actively trying to trace the locations and values of these assets in court. But even then, the question was not where the assets were, but how they were taken from her. If she was trying to reach them, her best strategy was to question the offshoring process, rather than their safe and elaborate storage. Meanwhile, Dmitry Rybolovlev was buying more art than ever through his trustees.

When the number of art items escalated, communications with Bouvier about each piece were overseen by the head of the trust, Mikhail Sazonov. Sazonov was based in Geneva at a family office called Barrhorn SA, with a storied history in investment banking. With his knowledge of French and Russian, it was Sazonov who facilitated all correspondence with Bouvier on Rybolovlev's behalf, brokering deals and negotiating before the oligarch would view the artwork. He even met Bouvier personally on more than one occasion, since he was fluent in French and lived nearby.

A Cyprus-based spokesman for Rybolovlev laughed when asked which artwork was Rybolovlev's favorite. It appeared to be a ridiculous question. The trustees were the ultimate owners of the art collection, but the loyal team at the trust offices provided materials before the final judgment calls, strictly adhering to the designated budget and deferring to their protector.

To know what Rybolovlev was thinking when he looked at a painting therefore remained a mystery. Instead, the trustees continued to approve anything that came under their purview.

One of their biggest purchases was La Belle Epoque.

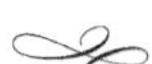

The beautiful blue waters, open skies, and French joie de vivre of 'the Cote d'Azur,' instantly felt like home to Rybolovlev. When he decided to move, he purchased the $400 million apartment on Monaco's Avenue d'Ostende, above the centrally located banks. It was called La Belle Epoque, so named for the historical period between 1890-1914. The 'beautiful era' was marked by idealism and the lavish whims of the wealthy in France and England before the grim realities of the 20th century's war and revolutions took hold.

As of 2018, the La Belle Epoque transaction remained the most expensive apartment sale in the world. It had beautiful black bookshelves in the two-storey library, a spa with a jacuzzi, breathtaking waterfront views featuring a pool and trees on a terrace, and even its own customized Monopoly set which included the name of the property on the board in metallic letters.[89]

The apartment had been previously owned by Edmund Safra. The Jewish-Lebanese billionaire descended from the important Safra banking family, and his brother Joseph Safra spearheaded investments around the globe. Among them were Banco Safra in Brazil, the nation's 8th largest bank, and J. Safra Sarasin in Geneva. Joseph Safra even owned a 50% stake in Chiquita Brands, home to the infamous Chiquita banana.[90]

Edmund also culled many investments around the world, but made just as many enemies. He was found dead at home in La Belle Epoque under mysterious circumstances in 1999.

Two scenarios circulated. One suggested that Safra's collaboration with the American FBI to expose a Russian money laundering operation through his company, Hermitage Capital with Bill Browder, led to a break-in and shooting at the home, with violent intimidation that forced his staff to confess to arson. The other version was that one of Safra's nurses, American Ted Maher, accidentally set fire to the apartment, in an ill-fated effort to curry favor with the master of the house through a doomed heroic attempt to save him. As the latter was considered the most likely in Monaco, it resulted in Maher's consequential imprisonment for murder, since Safra asphyxiated to death.

Maher's culpability was consequently heavily disputed, most notably by his wife, Heidi, in an expose by Dominick Dunne, even as Maher received a 10-year prison sentence for the crime.[91] After a failed prison break in 2003, Maher was eventually released two years early. Dunne called the story, "one of the most fascinating cases of [his] career."[92]

Safra's wife's lawyer during the investigation was Marc Bonnant, the same man who went on to represent Elena Rybolovleva, Dmitry's wife, nearly a decade after Safra's death.

Safra was a cousin of another noted Syrian Jewish family, the Nahmads. They had garnered a well-earned reputation as purveyors of some of the most important 20th century art known to history, best for Picasso and Modigliani, thanks to strategic ties with Picasso's dealer David-Henry Kahnweiler at the tail end of Picasso's career. The paintings had floated them through difficult periods, financial and political. Like Rybolovlev, they were known to store art in the Geneva Freeport (though not with Bouvier), and no one was able to gage the true value and quantity in their collection. The Nahmad family has never been confirmed as facilitating sales with the Rybolovlevs on the Picasso works, but the artistic and financial connections between the collections were undeniable.

Brothers David and Ezra Nahmad, and their sons, both named Helly, had many similarities to Rybolovlev. Their gallery was among the first to show regularly at the Moscow World Fine Art Fair, and they were residents in Monaco. They were reported to have art stored in Geneva as well, although they worked with Rodolphe Haller and its head Christian Aegerter, not Yves Bouvier. As *Forbes* reported in 2007, "Their treasures take up 15,000 square feet of a duty-free building next to the airport in Geneva. What's inside?

"'It's a secret,' says David Nahmad."

Rybolovlev had secrets, too.

13

WATER SERPENTS

THE CULTURAL connection to the French Rivera was mutually beneficial to the artists who visited the region. They cherished the sea, and the residents cherished their paintings. Both the artists of his first two major works, Chagall and Picasso, had major ties to the area. The Musée National Marc Chagall was in nearby Nice, created with 17 later paintings[93] dedicated by the artist's will,[94] and a Musée Picasso was in Antibes.

Rybolovlev had also subsequently acquired two *Water Lilies* by Claude Monet: *Nymphéas* (1897-1898), and *Nymphéas* (1914-1917), purchased in 2008 after the Uralkali IPO for €46.5 million and €42 million respectively.

Like the Russian oligarchs, aristocrats, and 20th century painters, Claude Monet had a lifelong love affair with the Cote d'Azur. When his friend Pierre-Auguste Renoir invited him to visit Paul Cézanne in Monaco in 1883, he returned on his own over and over. Inspiration took hold, and Monet reportedly painted nearly 100 paintings along the vibrant blue coastline.[95] In one painting from the era, *The Mediterranean (Cap d'Antibes)* from 1888, the impressionistic style of the gestural waters was innovative in its day, but the lapping waves of the clear waters seemed almost realistic in their evocation of serenity.

More importantly, though, were the waterlily paintings. Monet's waterlilies were international icons on permanent display in New York at the Museum of Modern Art and the Musée de l'Orangerie in Paris, and conceived of at Monet's permanent beloved residence, Giverny, outside Paris. It was an idyllic paradise designed by Claude Monet from the ground up. He fostered the preexistence of marine botanicals and added his own, finding joy in the tweaks and the natural world, studying the blooms in different swathes of light. His garden sourced flowers far and wide, and the home was later opened to the public as a museum, a living testament of what the flower paintings captured in perpetuity.

The waterlilies were some of the most treasured paintings in French history, with rooms devoted to them at both the Paris and New York museums. Rybolovlev's acquisitions came by way of private collections, but the earlier water lily work had at one time been gifted and exhibited at the Art Institute of Chicago by its original American collectors, the Morris family. The second work was originally purchased by Russian-born art dealer Katia Granoff, an important part of the Impressionist art world until her death in 1989.

Monet made almost 300 waterlily paintings—40 on a grand scale.[96] The Rybolovlev catalogue quoted Monet as saying, "Everything I have earned has gone into these gardens. I do not deny that I am proud of [them]."

Once again, the subtlety of the title in translation suggested attitudes towards women: the word "nymphéas" derived from nymphs, goddesses in mythology. There were multiple Greek stories surrounding the mysterious creatures and the lure they held over men from their mythological place in the water: some said that the flower was born out of an unrequited love for Hercules, others said it was the gods taking pity on the abandoned water nymph scorned by Apollo, God of the Sun.[97] In both cases, the undercurrent was explicit. Women as beautiful as flowers were beholden to the water, left behind and betrayed by men in power long after their attempted seduction.

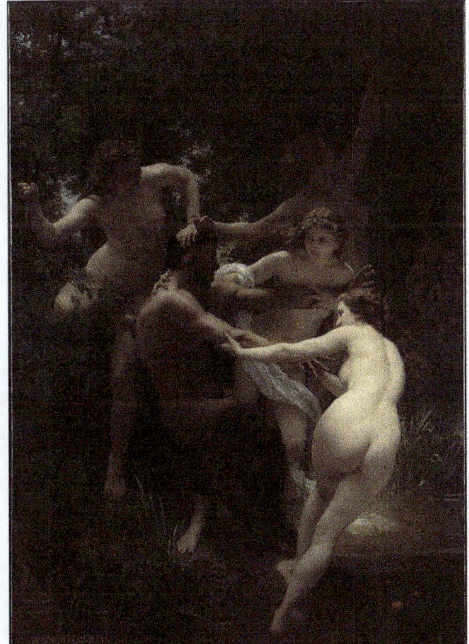

William Adolphe Bouguereau (1825-1905)
Nymphes and Satyr (1873), oil on canvas, 260.4 x 182.9 cm

During the period that Impressionism was taking hold, a drastically different Neo-Realist movement was also taking shape in France. The overt use of classical subjects underscored these same narrative morays much more forcefully. One strong example was William Adolphe Bouguereau's *Nymphes and Satyr* from 1873, in which four nude, comely nymphs coaxed a Satyr into the water despite the fact he could not swim. Though the satyr appeared beguiled, the tension between the male and female figures was pronounced in expression and form.

In 2018, Bouguereau did not maintain his place in the highly coveted art historical canon, nor the art market. His work was not on par with the likes of Monet in terms of investment, and thus faded into relative obscurity for the general public. Neo-Classicists were collected in the United States during their prime, where many continued to be on view at university collections, such as Clark University and Smith College, both in Massachusetts.[98]

Rybolovev did not collect Neo-Classical paintings, but he did purchase *La Méditerranée* by Aristide Maillol (1861-1944). In a dark, glistening bronze, the figure of a woman in a crown braid raised an art to her face, reclining forward with a downcast gaze. For an undisclosed sum, he acquired the work from Dina Vierny (1919-2009) in 2003. She was indisputably the artist's muse, maintaining a museum in Maillol's name to uphold his legacy, and becoming world renowned as an important art collector in her own right.

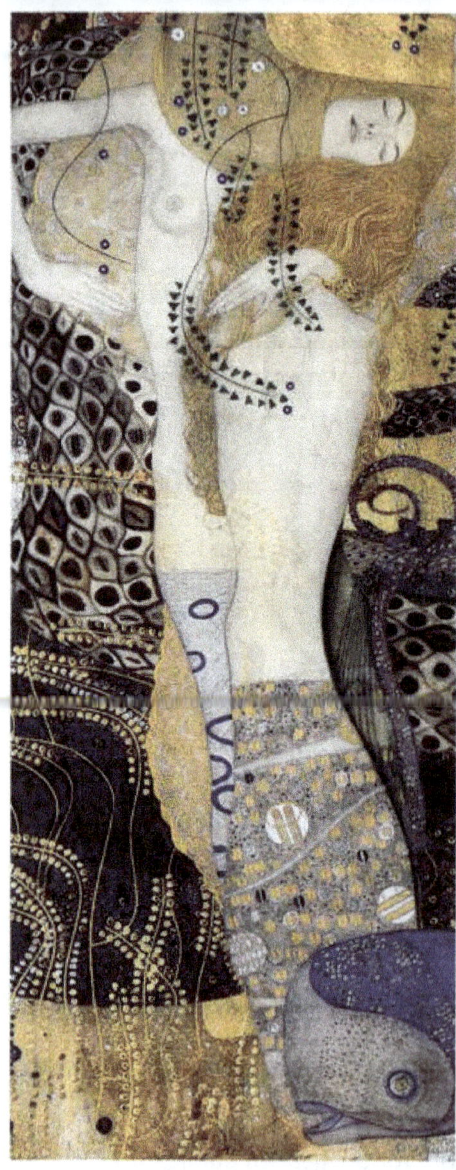

Gustav Klimt (1862-1918)
Wasserschlangen I, 1904-1907, pencil on parchment with watercolor and body color, heightened with silver, gilt, bronze gilt, and gold, 50 x 20 cm

As her biography *Dina Vierny: Histoire de ma vie racontée à Alain Jaubert* explained, Vierny was the daughter of a Russian Jewish dissident. Vierny's father, Jacques Aibinder, was first arrested in Russia at the age of 15, when he filled his pockets full of chocolate from an arriving ship and was stopped by the Cossacks, a local ethnic group known for their attacks against Jews in the region. He refused to back down and was sent to a Tsarist prison.

"One lived very well in Russia as a merchant," Vierny later told her biographer, "When one was selling, one was buying. But when one was thinking, they were finished!"

This was the era within which Chagall was also struggling. Vierny's family of Ukrainian Jews were not just combatting the whims and complexities of the Russian state, but also deep-seated prejudice. But Vierny's defiant father made many connections with the socialist revolutionaries while he was in jail, and emerged even more indomitable five years later than he had been at 15. As a socialist enemy of the state, he was tried again, and was set to spend six years in Western Siberia before the revolutionary coup released him early.

The Aibinder family eventually moved to Paris, very much the Grand Circus Chagall had described to their eyes. Paris had become a place where Russian émigrés all found work—even fallen aristocrats were taxi drivers. People were "singing in the streets."

Vierny loved to sing as well, and grew up fast, beautiful in her strength. She was unafraid of her body, posing nude for photographer Pierre Jamet as she developed.

It wasn't long before Vierny caught the attention of the Parisian art community, and her beauty was shared and celebrated by artists forever after. One of her earliest experiences was when she paid a visit to the studio of celebrated artist Aristide Maillol. He wrote her a letter inviting her to his studio in 1934. Like her father when he went to Russian prison, she was just 15 years old.

She went to the atelier, looking for the oldest man in the room. When she approached who she thought was the elderly artist, it turned out she was mistaken. It was another old man. Everyone laughed, but it wasn't long before the collaboration between artist and muse became a reciprocal admiration.

"I hadn't thought to pose particularly, but I was quickly seduced by the power of entering into his creation," she later explained in the book.

Though *La Meditérranée* had proceeded their working relationship, dating four years before Vierny was born in 1905, it was Vierny's form that inspired Maillol, at 63, to return to sculpture. Unlike his inspiration, Auguste Rodin, Maillol worked alone, studying and scrutinizing in intellectual solitude. But Vierny awoke his new burst of passion for artistic discovery.

"Maillol, don't be afraid to ask me to remove my clothes," she told him, "…Nudity is purity."

He echoed her sentiments. Vierny spoke of a story Maillol recounted to her, which served to inspire him for the rest of his artistic career.

At the turn of the century, Maillol was very close with his sister, Marie, who was often found in his company:

"One day, she takes off her boots, she enters into the sea laughing, barefoot and arms raising up her skirts, laughing open-mouthed, strutting. This movement had him completely bothered. It was furtive, but it was nothing at all. Very quickly, she came out of the water and they never spoke of it again. But for him, all his life, this movement, he looked to render it in sculpture. All his life!

And to all his models who posed for him, he said, 'Ah, what a young girl walking in the water you could be!'"

Perhaps the most important purchase Rybolovlev ever made, aside from the *Salvator Mundi*, was a critical investment in this same thematic vein — *Wasserschlangen II* (in French, *Serpents d'eau*, in English, Water Serpents or Snakes) by Gustav Klimt (1862-1918) from 1904-1907. Klimt's work came out of a completely different art historical moment from both the Neo-Classicists and the Impressionists. He was the from Vienna, Austria, the seat of the Jugendstil movement from the late 1800s to early 1900s.

In Vienna, the period was marked by a strong interest in decorative art and design. For Klimt, son of an engraver, this manifested with a clear preoccupation with orientalist geometric influences, wherein he collaborated with his friend and partner, Emilie Flöge, to procure fabrics and motifs from the Far East.

Rybolovlev purchased *Wasserchlagen II* in 2012. As was common by 2012, Bouvier facilitated Rybolovlev's purchase through Sotheby's. Sotheby's, in turn, corresponded with the current owners, who were able to trace the painting back to the heirs despite its confiscation during the Holocaust.

Klimt's paintings in particular were implicated in unjust seizures during World War II. Because he was instrumental in the Jugendstil (translated as Young Style, or Art Nouveau, New Art, in French) his work came to typify the apex of tension between the Viennese literati and the neo-conservatism at the onset of Nazism. Some of Klimt's best benefactors were Jewish women from prominent banking families.

The better-known stories surrounding Holocaust restitution in Gustav Klimt's canon pertain largely to two major portraits of Jewish women: *Portrait of Elisabeth Lederer* (1914-16) and *Portrait of Adele Bloch-Bauer* (1907)—better known as *Woman in Gold*.[99]

The Lederers were very close with Gustav Klimt. Elisabeth's mother, Szerena, was also the subject of one of the artist's portraits, and invited him to dine at her table very often. She asked Klimt to paint a second portrait of her, but he declined, preferring her young daughter as a subject instead. Elisabeth later married a gentile aristocrat.

When World War II broke out, Jews were targeted by the Nazi party and sent to death camps. Elisabeth thought she had found safety in her Christian marriage, but her husband abandoned her out of fear. Frantic, Szerena created documentation that said her daughter was the illegitimate child of the artist. This was not impossible, as the Rybolovlev catalogue essay by Joachim Pissarro estimated that Klimt had as many as 14 untraced descendants, but his best-known biological son with a prostitute became a Nazi-endorsed filmmaker. Elisabeth was saved from extermination, but later died prematurely of illness regardless.

Klimt did not paint Szerena twice, because he almost never created portraits of the same woman more than once. The only exception was Adele. Her husband Ferdinand, a Czech sugar magnate, commissioned the works. The artist made many sketches of his wife in return, culminating in the golden painting.

Waifish and fragile, she glowed in the *Woman in Gold* portrait. During the war, the painting was confiscated from the family along with all their business assets. Adele had no children, but her niece Maria Altmann later sought to retrieve it from her new home in California in 1999. She went head-to-head with *Republic of Austria v. Altmann*, in a groundbreaking legal battle.[100] Altman was granted the painting back as the rightful heir in 2004, selling it to the Neue Galerie in New York for an astounding $135 million in 2006.[101]

This set a precedent for all Holocaust art, so in the case of *Wasserschlangen II*, Sotheby's was careful to seek approval for the sale from the heirs of the painting's original owners in Austria. Like the woman in gold, the water serpents had been confiscated during Nazi takeover. They ensured that the profit from the transaction was divided equally between the current seller and heritage owners.

Rybolovlev first viewed the painting on September 3rd, 2012, followed by a meeting on the 11th in Paris where Bouvier's representative, Jean-Marc Peretti, offered to buy the painting. At $183.8 million, it was one of the most expensive paintings of all time. For reference, Klimt's *Bauerngarten* (Flower Garden) sold at Sotheby's London for £47.9 million ($59.3 million) five years later in March 2017, and it was considered the third-most expensive painting in European history.[102]

But of course, Yves Bouvier only paid $112 million.

"They're holding back for 180 and are at the breaking point," Bouvier emailed Mikhail Sazonov, "I think they are ready at 190. But I should be able to twist them to reach 185 with the payment of a deposit and the balance in 30 days. What should we do???"

With the stakes so high, the trustees authorized a maximum of $185 million. A deal was reached in a fabricated compromise: $183.8 million.

Bouvier received more than $3.6 million, and Rappo, $4.78 million. Rybolovlev claimed he still had no idea Rappo was receiving anything.

Bouvier later had Sotheby's provide insurance documentation for the piece, confirming its value at $180 million for Rybolovlev's records.

It took Bouvier four years to get the work to Rybolovlev, and as of 2018, remained the most important work by Gustav Klimt still in private hands.

It was Bouvier's favorite piece in the Rybolovlev collection.

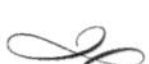

The Rybolovlev catalogue asserted that Klimt made 131 separate studies for *Wasserschlangen II*, and that it was so important, it was exhibited multiple times before it was completed to the delight of 13 critics. While *Wasserchlangen I* featured two women awash in gold, black and blue, *Wasserschlangen II* was a crowning work, with three fully nude blondes stretched out across the canvas in splashes of orange, green, blue, purple and gold. One critic the catalogue quoted was Ludwig Hevesi. He wrote:

> "Sea serpents. Scarlet, sprinkled with gold shimmering in bronze, patterned with colorful scales like a mosaic. Moving in languorous curves through the crystal deep. Above shimmering shingle, in which pale and dark gemstones polish each other. Intermingled with nymph-like figures, mermaids forms that also do nothing but surge and undulate in flowing curves, in swimming

hues…Here the tide is just ebbing. The watery women have lowered their eyelids; they float gently with the current, which swells their loose manes of hair."

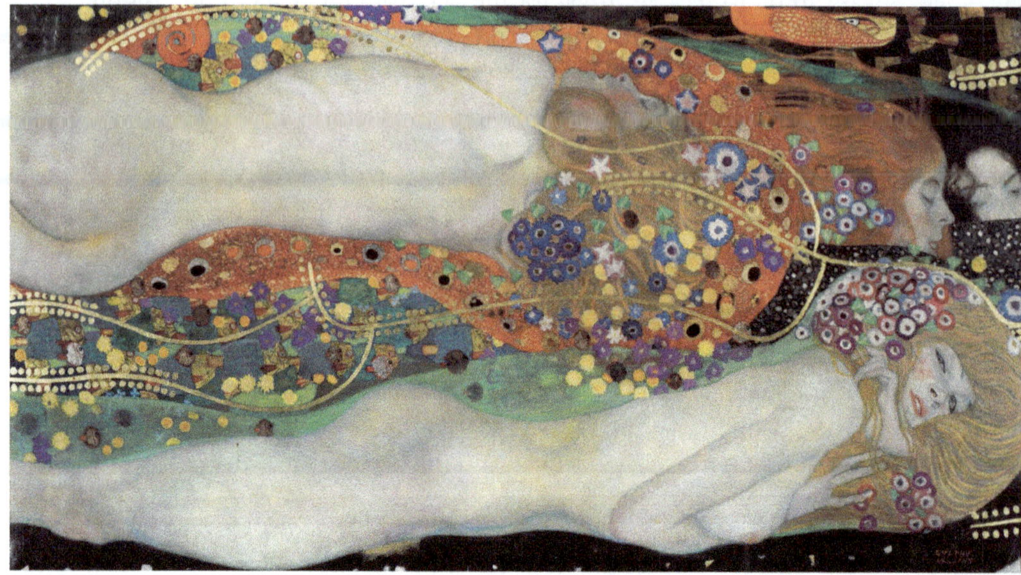

Gustav Klimt (1862-1918)
Wasserschlangen II (Water Serpents II), painted in 1904 and 1906-07, oil on canvas, 80 x 145 cm
Exhibitions and literature 196-197

The essayist compared the speckles of gold throughout the painting to coins.
Though the subject matter was the same as in the Bouguereau work, the Art Nouveau approach placed the women in positions that defied typical conceptions of depth, and the result was immersive and intoxicating. A notorious if passionate womanizer, it was noteworthy that the women were blonde, redheaded, and brunette, because many of Klimt's better-known works feature dark-haired maidens…usually, his more pious patrons from the Viennese elite, fully clothed.

The clothing was secondary to him, simply a means of communicating geometric expertise while he fixated on capturing the flush—and flash—of erotic pleasure. He made a significant number of gestural studies of women masturbating from many angles, and reveled in the slender flesh of the female form. Klimt sought to capture not just the beauty of women, but their enigmatic prowess as femme fatales.

Much was made of Klimt's fascination with the female form. It has been the subject of feminist discourse, as historians pondered whether his interest in womanly wiles was chauvinistic or celebratory—and if it could be both. In their mysterious expressions, the suggestive slender forms, and the surrounding myth of the man who created them, the sirens took on a multi-layered quality that made them prized the world over for their great beauty and guile.

Therefore, the paintings were not so unlike the beautiful women who inspired them.

The work was sold at a $10.3 million loss, for $170 million, to an undisclosed buyer.

Before formally moving to Monaco and buying the AS Monaco Football team, Rybolovlev celebrated his Uralkali IPO with the construction of *My Anna* in 2007. Though the word "my" was affectionate when put before his younger daughter's name, it was actually "MY," or "M/Y," a known abbreviation for Motor Yacht. [103] The 220-foot superyacht had 22 crew in nine cabins to serve up to 17 guests[104] in six cabins, and the boat was valued a $111 million the year it was built. After the construction of the smaller 110-foot yacht in 2017, also named *Anna*, the first became better known as *Anna 1*.

This first *My Anna* was designed by Michael Leach Design with Feadship De Voogt Naval Architects. The former had a series of famous quotes on their website, leaving most everything else to the imagination. Quips like, "I have the simplest of tastes. I am always satisfied with the best," by Oscar Wilde really said it all as they flashed across the screen.

Rybolovlev's yacht was designated as a Cayman Islands yacht with its flag, to grant the boat special tax and customs exemptions as non-EU.

As of 2018, the renamed *Anna 1* was for sale, with an asking price of €65 million, as Rybolovlev had completed the second *Anna* with the same design team. Multiple advertisements for *Anna 1* detailed the cushioned seating on the main deck, the entertainment center with its 50-inch Panasonic television screen, and the disco-ready "Kaleidescape" with a DJ mix deck table and a working smoke machine.[105]

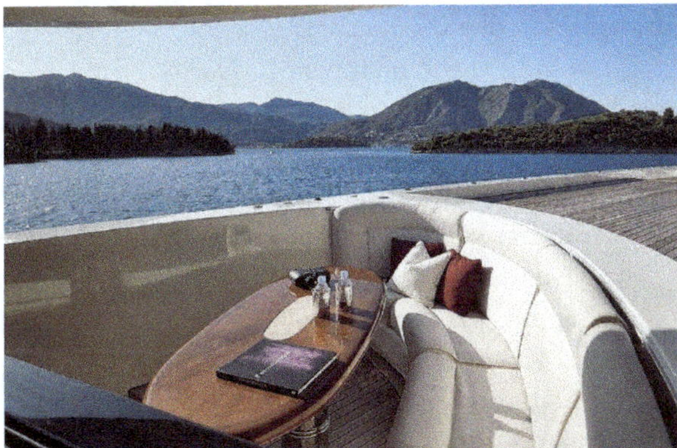

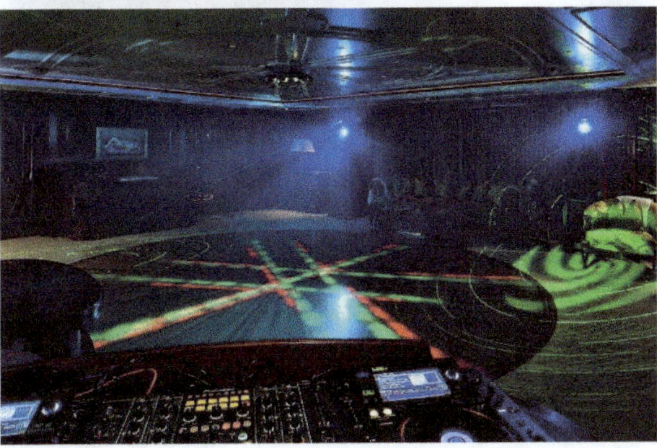

The nightclub inside M/Y Anna, from the for-sale listing. Images from Boat International

In the party room, a flat painting of a nude on a blue cushion was barely visible behind the disco lights. A classically-inspired observation lounge and multiple dining areas alfresco completed the party boat in an over-the-top amalgamation of all things glamorous and festive.[106]

Apart from publicizing the capabilities of the construction for sale and leasing purposes ($581,000 per week in the summer and a discounted $500,000 in the winter) details of *My Anna*'s wild parties were deliberately mysterious.

"You and I will never know what happened on that boat," said one contact with a winsome look, staring off into space at the bar—perhaps longing to join the party, or remembering one he could not discuss.

The off-the-record source did mention that guests on *My Anna* included fellow oligarch Roman Abramovich, whose yacht, *Eclipse*, was more than double the size of Rybolovlev's at 533 ft. Bouvier himself had three yachts as of 2018, including one with rare and elegant wood paneling. Abramovich had much in common with Rybolovlev, including owning his own football team, Chelsea Football Club in England and a slew of other investments so extravagant the *Wall Street Journal* nicknamed them "the Roman Empire." But like Rybolovlev, his beginnings in business started very small, even if they were always lucrative. In 1988, he and his first wife Olga ran a side business making dolls that was wildly successful—until his infidelities broke them apart.[107]

Looking at the pictures of *My Anna* for sale, one could easily imagine doll-faced sirens draping themselves like accessories across the long round sofas, waking up with stretched lanky legs on the clean beds, or plunging into the sea off the coast of a remote and beautiful island.

And thanks to Instagram, now you don't have to wonder.

In August of 2018, Russian supermodels Daria Strokous, 27, her best friend Ginta Lapina, 29, and Valentina Zelyaeva, 36, hopped onto Rybolovlev's superyacht. The girls were close friends, working with the same modeling agency for many years.

Though they were all lanky, fair-skinned blondes with piercing blue eyes (the

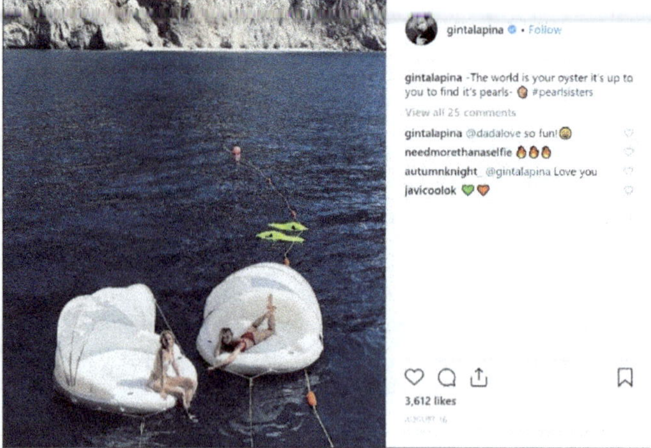

same coloring as Dmitry's wife, Elena, and the central blonde figure in the Klimt painting), they had slightly different personalities. Zelyaeva became a wellness columnist for *ELLE Russia*, Lapina was a happy-go-lucky Latvian, and Strokous was more serious—even somber.

They documented many aspects of the trip, from waking up in the morning to fun water sports. It was a week of girlhood, of friendship, and of undeniable sex appeal. With prolific captions like, "Heyyyyyy baaaaabe," and "All the girls wanna play Baywatch [peace-sign hand emoji]," the carefree weekend on Rybolovlev's boat was as stunning as it was comical. The Russian oligarch was not pictured.

"The world is your oyster it's up to you to find it's pearls - [seashell emoji]" Lapina wrote on August 16th. She received 3,612 likes for the phrase and its corresponding image, Lapina and Strokous looking at the camera from the deep blue water from blow-up oyster floats. It was likely that they were in the Greek isles, seeing as Rybolovlev had conveniently purchased the private island of Skorpios from Aristotle Onassis in 2013. Technically, the island was bought and owned by his daughter Ekaterina through the trust. Born in 1989, Ekaterina was just one year older than Daria Strokous. Like Klimt's water serpents, the blondes were playful, beguiling, and at home in the water in their barely-there bikinis.

"Woke up like this [gold heart emoji]," wrote Ginta Lapina, looking up at the mirror from her bed in a bikini and a crop top, legs, hair and arms splayed. The antique patina on the mirror in the golden light bore reference to Klimt's use of

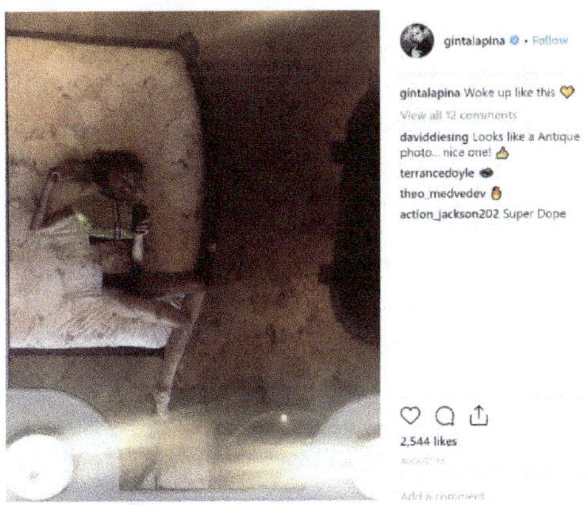

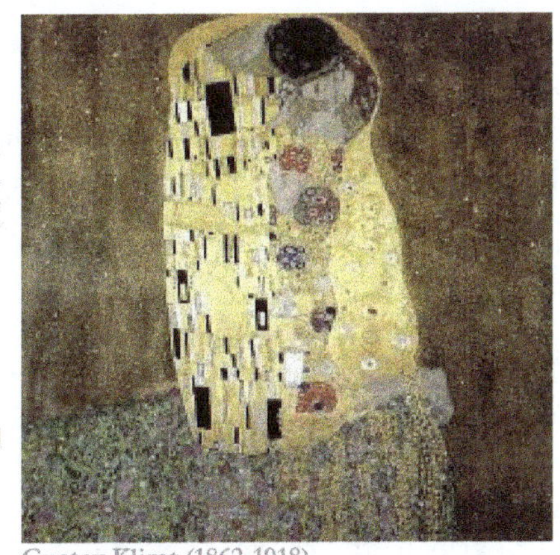

Gustav Klimt (1862-1918)
The Kiss (Der Kuss), Oil on canvas (1907-1908).
Overall size 180 x 180 cm.

gold leaf in paintings—not as effusively in the Rybolovlev acquisition of *Serpents d'eau*, but to great fanfare in the infamous painting, *Woman in Gold – Portrait of Adele Bloch-Bauer* (1907), as well as *The Kiss* (1907), and *Fulfillment* (1909). One commenter, a lighting designer named David Diesing, commented astutely, "Looks like a Antique photo…nice one! [thumbs up emoji]". [108] She received 2,544 likes.

"Tea o'clock [alarm clock emoji]" wrote Valentina Zelyaeva, posing adorably in her miniskirt with a teacup and saucer. She faced the sun, with rolling hills behind her and the bright blue water, presumably having walked out of the dining room with her tea. 2,152 likes.

For those knowledgeable in the world of yacht parties, however, Rybolovlev's was not as fun as it looked. 'Tea o'clock' was in fact regimented, with visitors saying the boat ran more like a military operation than a fun party. Breakfast, lunch, dinner, and all activities were planned to a T. Even the menu was set.

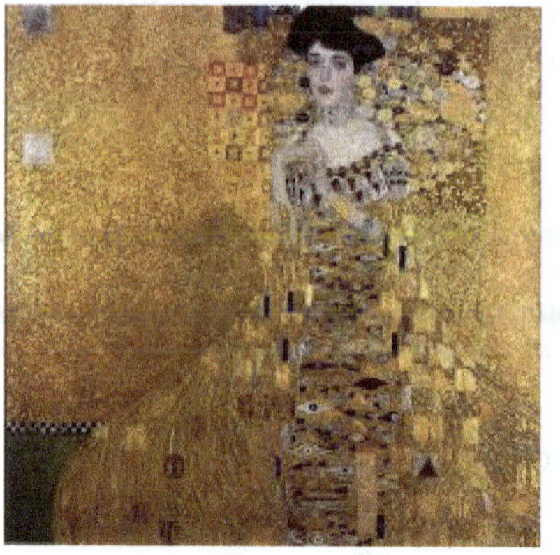

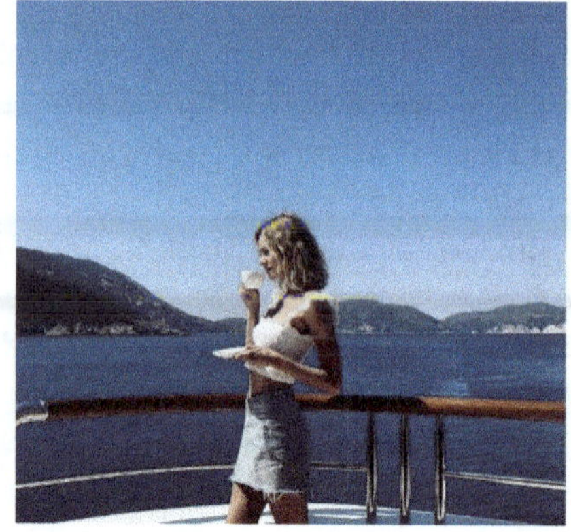

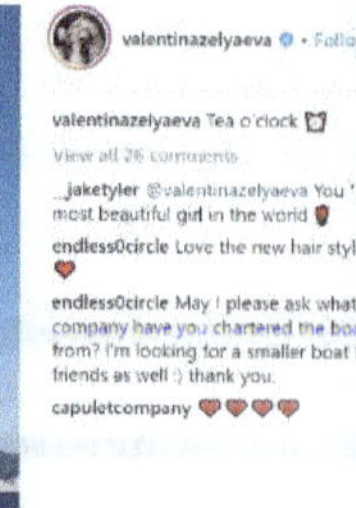

Gustav Klimt (1862-1918)
Portrait of Adele Bloch-Bauer I (Woman in Gold), Oil, silver, and gold on canvas (1907), Overall size 138 x 138 cm,

Though less sensual than the other poses, 'Tea o'clock' evoked *Jeune filles au bord de l'eau* (young girls at the water's edge) by Pierre-Auguste Renoir, which had also made its way into Rybolovlev's collection. The Rybolovlev catalogue referred to Renoir as "the painter of happiness," and noted his ability to depict the free time of the growing class of bourgeoisie. Furthermore, Renoir's first job was working as a porcelain maker. As Zelyaeva held her dainty teacup, it evoked a glimpse into the world of delicacy and leisure. Unlike many of the other artists Rybolovlev later collected, Renoir had a stable love life and a healthy business sense, selling artworks for francs in the thousands in his own lifetime.

The Instagram unwittingly referenced this tableau, in which two women with their backs to the canvas looked out onto the water, perched comfortably on furtively stroked strands of grass.

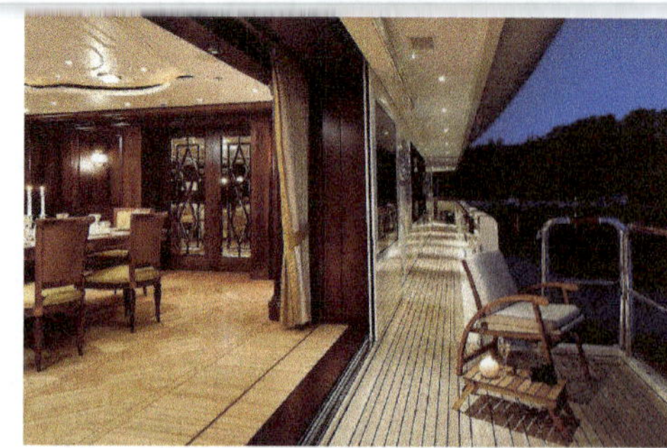

The deck on M/Y Anna, Image from Boat International

As Renoir also had an eye towards eroticism, featuring innocent blonde bathers and harem girls alike in compositions not unlike the water serpents Klimt later created. Just as in Rybolovlev's world, depictions of both leisure and women went hand in hand. He was studying the Neo-Classicists, but increasingly moving into his own distinct style.

According to his catalogue provenance documents, it appeared that Rybolovlev acquired the Renoir in 2010 for $45 million from Steve Wynn, the Las Vegas-based art collector known for once accidently destroying a Picasso at home by splicing his elbow through the canvas.[109] Dealing with this level of collector was placing him in a new category. With every passing year, the number of astounding works in his collection, corresponding to their valuations, was rising.

But his personal life was falling apart.

14

ETERNAL SPRING

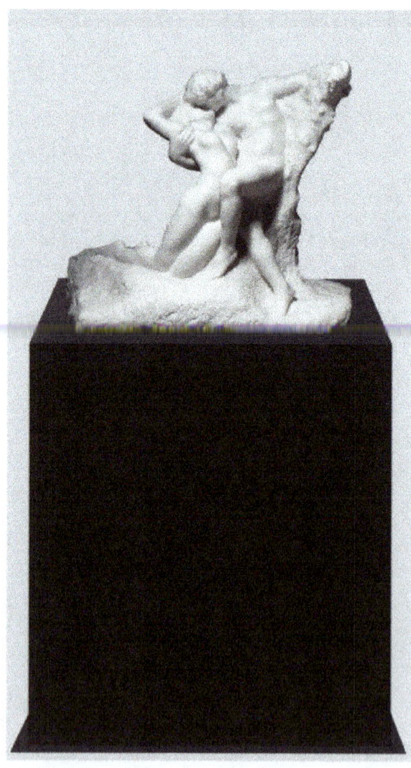

Auguste Rodin (1840-1917)
Eternal Spring, 1901-1902, white marble, 65.8 cm,

THE FORCEFULLY SENSUAL embrace of August Rodin's *Eternel printemps (Eternal Spring)* was so overwhelming when it was first presented in 1884 that viewers found it practically pornographic. Man and woman intertwined in the sculpture with their faces obscured by the material. Melded from the same block, they appeared to be melting into one another, bodies glinting with the marble's white patina, unable to escape the barriers of their passion.

The woman's legs stretched outward, but her back arched toward her lover as he pulled her inward with a single arm, hand above her breast. Whereas the woman's feet were immovable on the thick cast base, the man dipped his right arm and foot outward, tempting the viewer with his freedom and his strength, challenging the confines of the artistic space.

The daring effect of this Rodin sculpture was at once polarizing and intoxicating. One biographer Ruth Butler saw *Eternal Spring* as pools of mystery, like the works featuring water elsewhere in Rybolovlev's collection. "Rodin's models were analogous to

Monet's lily ponds and poplars – they were his nature, his leaves, his shimmering movements of watery surface." She wrote, "They held unfathomable secrets."[110]

But while some historians saw secrecy, others saw unabashed transparency—a lust superseding conventions of respectability.

"He invented a new and very modern visual language, creating figures that seemed almost real," Valérie Hess, head of the *Impressionist and Modern Art* sale at Christie's in Paris, explained in promotional materials for the work. "That's what he was so often criticized for when his works were exhibited, and what was almost disturbing for a contemporary viewer. He's not hiding anything."[111]

Such was the nature of love versus lust: electrifying in its open eroticism, yet mystifying in its layers of uncertainty and pain. Hiding in plain sight.

Rybolovlev purchased three Rodin works: a marble *Eternal Spring* at £30 million ($48.1 million), a bronze *Le Baiser (the Kiss)* at €7.5 million, and *Eve*, at $26.25 million. The last work was the only one that stood alone—no man, just the haphazardly discovered, unfinished woman on her own. Rodin had to stop work on it because his model had become pregnant.

Rappo and Bouvier received their own respective millions, with the full amounts still unknown to Mr. Rybolovlev.[112]

Bouvier's lawyer Daniel Levy drove home that this was common business practice.

"When you walk into a store and purchase an item, you rarely know how much a shopkeeper paid to acquire the item and can only assume the shopkeeper's acquisition price is less than the sales price to you," he reiterated.

What art historians most definitely agreed on was the autobiographical nature of Rodin's lustful sculptures, particularly *Eternal Spring's* influence from his relationship with Camille Claudel, the tempestuous young apprentice.

In 1882, shortly before he began the piece, 42-year-old Rodin met 18-year-old Claudel. Bold and self-assured to the point of defiance, Claudel's youthful vitality and eagerness to learn entranced the celebrated genius, and they began an affair almost instantaneously. Photographs from the era show Claudel unencumbered by vanity, with an unadulterated and direct stare that allowed the light to catch in her sparkling eyes.

Rodin was also intrigued by Claudel's career, and her financial difficulties as a struggling sculptress.

Art historian Rachel Corbett cited a survey from Claudel's teen years which perfectly captured her confrontational flirting style.

"Your favorite qualities in man?" asked the survey.

"To obey his wife." Claudel wrote.

"Your favorite qualities in woman?"

"To make her husband fret."

That being said, Corbett was quick to note Claudel's hesitation. She was a young girl focused on her career, disinterested in kowtowing—not just to Rodin, who was widely admired by colleagues and prospective lovers alike—but to anyone.

Rodin begged her. "Have pity, mean girl," he wrote in 1883, "I can't go on. I can't go another day without seeing you."

But Rodin was never monogamous, nor was he hesitant. In one particularly aggressive story, art historian Martin Gayford described Rodin's passion for conquest through the memories of famous dancer Isadora Duncan's studio visit.

Strolling around the figures with Duncan, "He showed his works with the simplicity of the very great. Sometimes he murmured the names of his statues, but one felt that names meant little to him…He ran his hands over them and caressed them."

Overcome, Rodin soon began breathing heavily. He picked up small bits of clay and pressed them tightly into his hands; he enjoyed leaving his fingerprints in the sculptures as well. When he opened his palms, he had shaped what Duncan described as "a woman's breast, that palpitated beneath his fingers".[113]

They went directly to Duncan's studio thereafter, where she gave him a private performance. Rodin lost his last shred of self-control, and immediately moved towards her, caressing her the same way as the sculptures he had shown hours before.

Duncan said, "He began to knead my whole body as if it were clay."

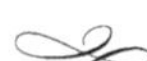

When Camille Claudel finally succumbed to Rodin's advances, the art suggests the collaboration was fantastic. Historians assert that the sheer bliss of *Eternal Spring* stemmed directly from the bubbling passion of their furtive love. In the meantime, Claudel remained the dutiful apprentice in her role, providing skill and insight in the subservient position accordingly. As evidenced by the works, their professional collaboration took on a fruitful rhythm.

Eternal Spring was intended as a subset of a larger work, *Gates of Hell*, commissioned in 1880. It was intended to be a monumental homage to

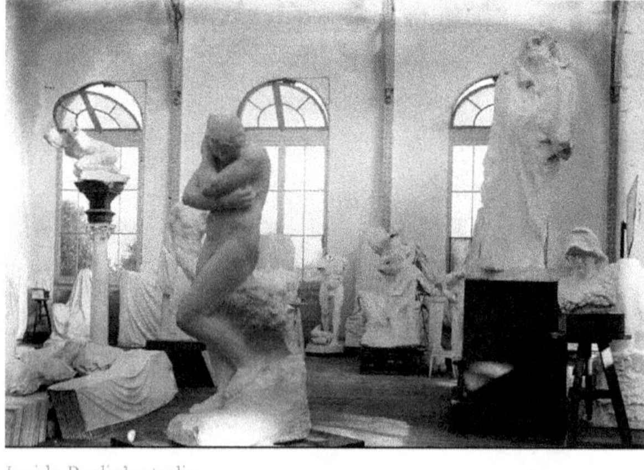

Inside Rodin's studio.

Dante's *Inferno*, commissioned by and for a decorative arts museum. The *Eternal Spring* piece did not find its way into the *Gates of Hell* doors, on which he worked scrupulously for 40 years until his death. But it was never completed. The piece just kept growing, and it was never good enough.

The souls Rodin created over and over languished, waiting for their place on the gates to hell, until he died.

Instead, *Eternal Spring* stood alone. It remained an encapsulated testament to a happier moment shared between the two lovers.[114]

The same could be said for *The Kiss*—another bronze purchase of Rybolovlev's from 2011, acquired by way of the Rodin Museum for just €7.5 million. Like *Eternal Spring*, the sculpted kiss told the story of equal partners in lust. The woman pulled the man towards her, leaning her head forward, in a similarly passionate pairing to the first work. It was originally called *Francesca*, originally intended to tell the story of adultery in Dante's Inferno, in which Francesca falls for her brother-in-law Paolo, and her husband comes to stab them to death[115]. When the work was finished, it was too happy for hell's gates, and was renamed and added to the canon of cheer. Though it encapsulated a moment of bliss, its reality as a tale of infidelity had been the impetus for its creation. The lovers were still doomed.[116]

Claudel assisted on the *Gates of Hell* projects, not just as a sculptress with a fine eye for detail, but as a model. Her family was horrified when they saw one work, the *Age of Maturity* from 1902, recognizing her nude figure in all its impropriety.

Eventually, the gates of hell opened on their personal life.

Rodin continued to be swarmed with attention, and young women flanked him. Despite his protestations that Claudel was his true love, he did nothing to hold back from the younger women, nor to relinquish his ties to his main partner and common-law wife, Rose Beuret.

Beuret and Claudel developed a rivalry so intense that Corbett recalled a story of Claudel spying in the shrubs outside Rodin's house. Beuret caught her outside and threatened her with a gun.

Claudel was incensed at his refusal to leave Beuret. The emotional toll was largely credited as the reason for her descent into madness when she avoided leaving her studio so doggedly that her family grew concerned about the state of filth, and had her committed to an asylum in 1913.

It was largely implied that the artist was not nearly mentally unstable enough to warrant her committal. Nevertheless, she was unable to work again. She died in the institution 30 years later in 1943, far removed from the previous buds of a successful career in obscurity.

At the end of his own life, Rodin eventually legally married Rose Beuret. But she died two weeks after the marriage was official, and he followed suit some months later. [117] Whereas Camille Claudel's work faded into Rodin's canon, his sculptures endured as an essential part of art history for 100 years, still celebrated into present day.

Rybolovlev failed to resell *Eternal Spring* at auction in London; it was bought-in at the lowly £3.8 million. In May 2016, it was purchased at $20.4 million, still half what he had paid originally. The other Rodins remained in his collection.

15

BLACK SWAN

THE PRIVATE DETECTIVE Elena hired provided her with the passport information of the young women on board *My Anna* nearly a decade before Daria, Tinta and Valentina documented their summer getaway weekend. Whether out of fear or legal agreements, these records and communications were later sealed, but the results were so damning that they were acceptable as grounds for divorce proceedings.

The party line from the team was that Dmitry, "was not a model husband."

Arguably the most damning piece of evidence in the divorce proceedings was Rybolovlev's yacht trip to Croatia in June 2008. Young women identified by boat passport records as 19 and 20-year-old students enjoyed parties aboard, as did Rybolovlev's mistress who arrived on the yacht the following week from Moscow, subsequently traveling to Venice, Monaco, Dubai and beyond. A note warned the crew that the next visit to the boat would be Elena.

Elena confronted her husband about the young girls. The divorce filings alleged, "He said that he appreciated only teenage girls, younger than his own daughter."

"All my life I have lived this way," the documents said he told her, "And I will not change."

He openly admitted to sleeping with his butler, his assistant, and the 'students,' and happily "shared" them with fellow oligarchs who came aboard to party.

Elena asked about the risk of sexually transmitted disease from his excessive unprotected sex. After all, she was trained as a doctor.

Not to worry, Rybolovlev was said to have assured her according to the filings. All the young women aboard were virgins. Just to be sure, they were also given blood tests before boarding—apparently a fairly common practice among the ultra-rich in uncharted waters.

Prostitution was rampant among elites around the world, and Monaco was a microcosm for both the ultra-rich and the money-hungry. It was not uncommon to see young girls swarming the clubs and the docks looking for the party. But Monaco residents often insisted that the girls were not for hire.

One AS Monaco Football Club member and Monegasque resident put it best, "They don't have prostitutes in Monaco," adding without pause, "If anyone wants to get prostitutes, they just go to France."

Although the women pictured on Dmitry Rybolovlev's yacht a decade later were notated as past age 18 with legitimate preoccupations and careers, not everyone in his social sphere who threw boat parties was so careful to ensure their 'models' on board were approved and legal.

The best-known case of underage prostitutes on a superyacht was the Turkish *Savarona* scandal of 2010, two years after Elena filed for divorce.

An expose was traced by the Romanian publication *The Black Sea*.

In September 2010, Kazakh businessman Alexander Mashkevitch (also spelled Mashkevich) paid $309,000 to rent the *Savarona* yacht for eight days in Turkish waters.[118] It was built in 1931, much older than the freshly constructed *My Anna*, with sweeping gold-rimmed banisters and black walls evoking a chintzy *Titanic*. Like *My Anna*, the yacht featured a jacuzzi, a mirrored-ceilinged library and TV room, and alfresco dining to guarantee a luxury experience.[119]

Allegedly, the name of the boat derived from a species of African swan. But if that was the case, *Savarona* was an obscure species. The mystery of its origin thus remained lost to time. Swans in Africa were mostly black, and in finance, black swans were known as highly abnormal and unpredictable circumstances. While the name of the boat may have been a mystery, its tie to black swans was soon revealed by a staggering series of events.

It was Mashkevitch's fifth year renting the boat, which he had used most recently that June. Like Rybolovlev, Mashevitch was involved in the mining industry, making investments primarily through the Eurasian Natural Resources Corp (ENRC). In November 2007, one month after the Uralkali IPO, ENRC decided to float their IPO on the London Stock exchange as well.[120] In 2013, fellow Kazhakh-Russian Suleiman Kerimov purchased a 3% stake in Mashevitch's ENRC.[121] Kerimov had also purchased Uralkali shares from Rybolovlev.

Investigate Russia reported that party coordinator and prominent real estate developer Tevfik Arif was acquitted in Turkey in 2012.[122] The scandal had come back into the news cycle in 2016, because Mashkevitch and Arif both had ties to American President Donald Trump.

There were numerous additional Russian investors in Trump properties around the world, including his casinos, dating back to as early as 1984.

Mashkevitch invested with Donald Trump to help him build Trump Soho with real estate developer Tevfik Arif, who acted as a business partner during that deal. Arif's company, Bayrock, had an office in Trump Tower as early as 2001.[123]

The Trump Soho hotel opened in 2007, and Arif was photographed there to celebrate.

The following year, Donald Trump went on the David Letterman Show and said explicitly, "Well I've done a lot of business with the Russians. They're smart, and they're tough, and they're not looking so dumb right now."[124]

2008 was also the year Dmitry Rybolovlev purchased Trump's Palm Beach home for $95 million, more than double the $41 million Trump had paid for it four years earlier.[125] Rybolovlev never lived in the home. Despite comments about the relationship between Rybolovlev and Trump made by liaisons, all connections were later denied. The house was called Maison de L'Amitie – in French, the House of Friendship.

When Mashkevitch planned to have a party with his influential friends and business associates in 2010, it was Tevfik Arif who coordinated the details. Working with middle men named Musa Chelik and Gunduz Akdeniz, ten Russian girls were flown to Istanbul specifically for the event—and specifically to engage in sex acts. When they arrived, Arif inspected them, and sent one of the less attractive girls back to Moscow. They were down to nine prostitutes.

Originally, they had sought girls between 16 and 18, but after a scare with police, decided to look for girls who were officially legal, between 18 and 23, for protection.

This strategy was useless, and the party proved disastrous.

The party was interrupted by a Turkish military helicopter raid. They promptly arrested the nine women, taking them out of suites littered with used condoms. Some of the men were arrested, too.

During subsequent interrogations, Akdeniz and Arif insisted the girls were there as guests, as companions—as anything but women for hire.

Arif countered on trial, "One of my friends came with his wife. One of them came with his girlfriend."

When the women arrived, Akdeniz insisted innocently, they would, "seat them at the table to decorate it, like flowers."

16

FABULOUS OR FALLEN

NUDES in the throes of passion continued to dominate Rybolovlev's collection. Besides the iconic paintings by Klimt and sculptures by Rodin, Rybolovlev acquired two sex scenes by Henri de Toulouse Lautrec, once again called 'The Kiss' (like the Rodin bronze) and later 'The Kiss—in Bed'. The former was purchased in 2008, not long after he floated the Uralkali IPO, and the latter was acquired in 2013.

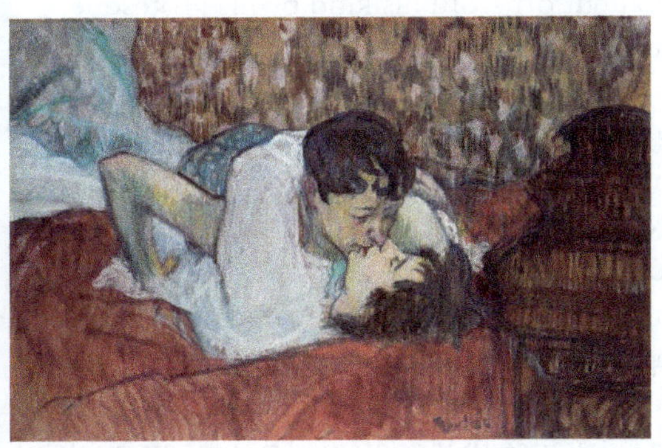

Henri de Toulouse-Lautrec (1864-1901)
Le Baiser, 1892, oil on cardboard, 38 x 58 cm

Bouvier sourced and presented the work to Rybolovlev through the appropriate channels of Mikhail Sazonov and the trustees. When asked how he selected the works for his important patron, Bouvier replied with a few matter-of-fact, succinct answers.

"He likes women," he said. "Like any art dealer, my job is to know my customers' tastes and to respond to them."

The positioning and the titles in the two paintings were indeed literal. Both works featured the same couple, locked in an intimate embrace. But these works differed in that the featured couple were not just prostitutes, but lesbians.

Henri Marie Raymond de Toulouse-Lautrec-Monfa (his full aristocratic name) was fascinated by the secret life of Montmartre's women for hire, the Rybolovlev catalogue explained, fixating on their most intimate moments. In the early hours before the men came to receive their services, Toulouse-Lautrec would sketch them not as a customer, but as a friend.

The artist felt at home among the prostitutes, and the familiarity was evidenced in the works: tucked into one another, the lesbians were free to be unencumbered by expectations or clientele. These unconventional sexual proclivities felt far away from the male gaze of patriarchal art and sex, later codified by Picasso among others. Mutual respect was presented in the gentle, soft glow of the pair, providing them with relief just as much as the artist.

Because Toulouse-Lautrec was no stranger to self-medication. He suffered greatly in his life, debilitated by dwarfism from childhood. As explained in a *Huffington Post* article by Madelaine Dangelo, he descended from three sets of feudal rulers from the Counts of both Toulouse and Lautrec, and the Viscounts of Monfa. This formidable aristocratic heritage was actually due to the fact his parents were first cousins, and he was born in 1864 with a hereditary disease that left his growth stunted and his bones hopelessly fragile. After two accidents at 13, he never grew past his adult height of 5'1.[126]

So despite the warm support of his parents, he could not escape the tragedy of his misfortune. Adulthood was plagued by the physical agony of illness and the mental agony of feeling deeply set apart. His primary source of solace was the underworld of misfits, where he was not judged for the shortcomings that affected him in more elite circles.

It was the demimonde, literally the 'half-world' of fringe figures and degenerates, pursuing bliss at any price to their reputations against the more respectable morays. Dangelo quoted fellow painter Édouard Vuillard, who said crudely, "As a physical freak, an aristocrat cut off from his kind by his grotesque appearance, he found an affinity between his own condition and the moral penury of the prostitute."[127]

In a cross between medical necessity and a love of the festivity, Toulouse-Lautrec became preoccupied with phantasmagoria. He lived in the era known as La Belle Epoque, marked not just by the golden leisure that qualified the name of Rybolovlev's apartment, but by a love of escapism in all its forms. Like fellow artist Vincent Van Gogh and other bohemian characters in the dark corners of Montmartre's party culture, he was a regular absinthe user, which later greatly impacted his work. He even drank it from a hollowed walking stick.[128]

Absinthe was a vivid green, smoky substance that contained potent amounts of alcohol (75%, double the average vodka), as well as the active ingredient, wormwood, which often induced hallucinations and was referred to as 'the green fairy'. While in the case of Van Gogh's mental instability, it may have led to self-harm. For Toulouse-Lautrec, the love of absinthe and unconventional thought evolved into an illustrative quality in the artist's later works, reflective of his rich inner life.

There was no doubt that being different and substance abuse went hand-in-hand in the Parisian art scene well into the early 20th century. Rybolovlev's catalogue quoted Carol Mann's *Modigliani* biography, in which artist Maurice de Vlaminck explained, "The done thing was to be or at least to look abnormal or strange. Everyone smoked opium, consumed hashish…took alcohol and ether."

With Rybolovlev's love scenes, however, the drug use felt far removed from the quiet passions of the women in love. The paintings in Rybolovlev's collection were made rarer in that they were oils, as the artist was widely known for gestural sketches and prints, inspired by the free-spirited nightlife and imbibing. The paintings provided a rare escape.

Toulouse-Lautrec greatly admired Edgar Degas, another artist around the absinthe scene. Beyond the party life, his depictions of dancers both on and off stage were celebrated for their expertise around motion and emotion alike. He infused his paintings of the ballet with the same energy that they carried on stage, with electrifying cool tones and a sense of vibrancy never matched. Like Toulouse-Lautrec, he spent a lot of time behind the scenes, familiarizing himself with the more intimate moments of performers.

One of Rybolovlev's earliest purchases was *La danseuse rose* in 2008 for €25 million. It was a pastel on canvas rather than an oil painting, and the lightness was as electrifying as the sensory sublimations of Toulose-Lautrec's world. It had exceptional provenance, at one time passing through the collection of the Maharani Sita Devi of Baroda, India. Prior to her divorce from the maharaja, she maintained a residence in Monaco and spent much time enjoying the glamor of Paris.

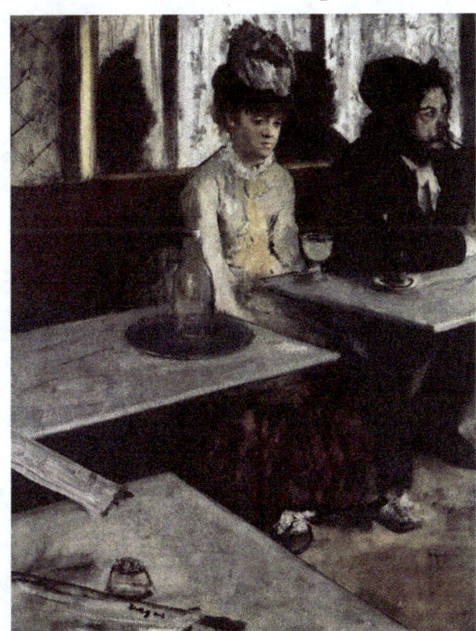

Edgar Degas (1834-1917)
L'Absinthe (Absinthe Drinker, In a Café), 1875-1876, 92 x 68.5 cm, © RMN-Grand Palais (Musée d'Orsay) / Hervé Lewandowski

But clear lifestyle parallel was best evidenced in another work, *L'Absinthe* (alternate titles *Absinthe Drinker* or just *In a Café)*, from 1875-1876. A woman sits beside a man hunched and reflective over her glass of the pale green drink. It was staged: Degas enlisted a model/actress friend to personify the values he was attempting to show—in short, that absinthe and a life of excess could be devastatingly dangerous.[129]

Marianne Engler's essay for MoMA[130] explained about his infamous parties at brothels and cabarets alike in the context of Toulouse-Lautrec. She wrote: "Clad in exotic costumes and mixing up the deadliest concoctions of cocktails (American style) that he served at infamous soirées with hundreds of guests, Toulouse-Lautrec's creative flame burned brightly as he walked (albeit with some difficulty) on the wild side.

At one of the more spectacular of these parties, the 1895 housewarming fête for Alexandre (Thadee) Natanson, editor of *La Revue Blance*, and his wife Misia, the artist outdid himself, serving 300 guests 2,000 cocktails (or so he proudly claimed) mixed in lurid hues of red, pink, yellow, and green, and apparently creating the desired effect, as several guests (including the artists Pierre Bonnard and Édouard Vuillard) left the party horizontally, as they had to be carried off to an impromptu 'triage unit' for the hopelessly inebriated."

In the catalogue essay from its showcase at the Musée d'Orsay, art historians point to Japanese elements of space and line in Degas' work as well, which made for an interesting correlation to Toulouse-Lautrec's love of Japonisme. Toulouse-Lautrec was an avid lover of the Japanese woodblock printing art known as ukiyo-e, which translated most commonly to 'art of the floating world.'

Edo period Japan (1604-1868) ran just prior to La Belle Epoque in France. The woodblock prints were noted for thick block colors and storytelling sensibility, an aesthetic which instantly found its way into French posters as homage. One of the best-known artists of ukiyo-e was Kitagawa Utamaro (1753-1806), whose depictions of concubines made a special impact on Toulouse-Lautrec.[131]

Ronin Gallery, a well-respected Japanese print-seller in New York, expertly juxtaposed Montmartre's world of absinthe drinkers in La Belle Epoque of Paris with the festive abandon of ukiyo-e, even addressing links between the prostitution networks:

> "The floating world revolved around worldly pleasure. The Yoshiwara offered the beautiful, the sensual and the physical, inviting its customers into a fantasy of love or lust. To visit this licensed prostitution district, patrons were required to travel across land and water; ripe with anticipation by the time they arrived. This mysterious and illusory world operated by its own rules, developing its own dialect, festivals, and even conception of time. Upon entering the main gate, visitors could purchase guidebooks to learn the intricacies of each brothel, the roster of *oiran* (elite courtesans), and words of wisdom for this district of perceived femme fatales."[132]

But as the Ronin Gallery essays revealed, the beautiful world of drugs and parties could only exist with the demimonde, the half-world of the grotesque. This too had ties to the East Asian art world.

> Misia Nathanson, the wife mentioned above, once asked, "Tell me, Lautrec, why do you always make your women so ugly?"
> He quickly shot back, "Because they are ugly!"
> "To Lautrec, beauty was found in the grimace," the essayist explained, "In the distinctive features that he inflated to near caricature. His portraits of performers evoke the Japanese *mie*—the exaggerated dramatic pose, often held at a climactic moment in a kabuki production— to create dynamic portraits of recognizable public personas."

And to be sure, Japanese eroticism took many shapes that had parallels with the more grotesque realities of Parisian prostitution. There were many hierarchies of "women of pleasure," as they were traditionally known (asobi-onna). Historian Janet Goodwin quoted a courtier writing a friend, cited by the *Japan Times*. He was eager to encourage his friend to join, saying, "In one evening of delight, we'll forget that we must grow old."

Japan's modernization led to a gradual shift away from Edo-period aesthetics over time, and Toulouse-Lautrec died in his thirties from illnesses related to everything from depression to syphilis. But while Edo Japan held the strongest aesthetic similarity to the inner life of Toulouse Lautrec, it was the opium trade in 19th century British colonial China that drew the strongest parallels to his wild life in Paris.

This was best evidenced by the juxtaposition of a Japanese courtesan image and one by Toulouse-Lautrec called *Reverie d'opium*. Utamaro's *Courtesan Hitomoto from the House of Daimonjiya* dated circa 1805, from the series "Contest of Full Bloom Beauties." [133] The courtesan was drawn in a composition that made use of three-quarters of the space, with her long cigarette stretching across the page in a pale pink to match her elegant robes. Her hair was tied up in a two-pronged bun, and her face turned coyly to the side as her comely legs were exposed.

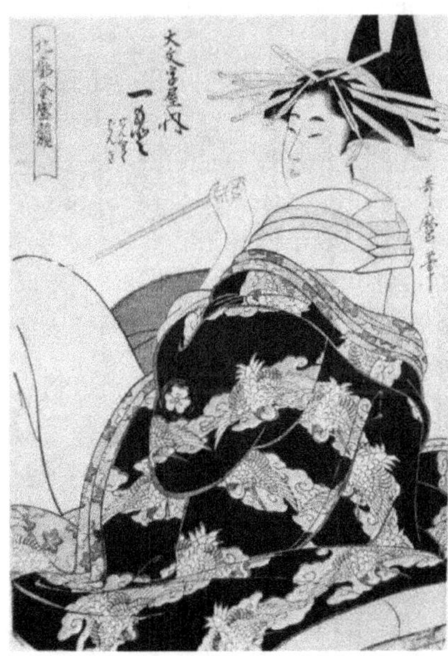

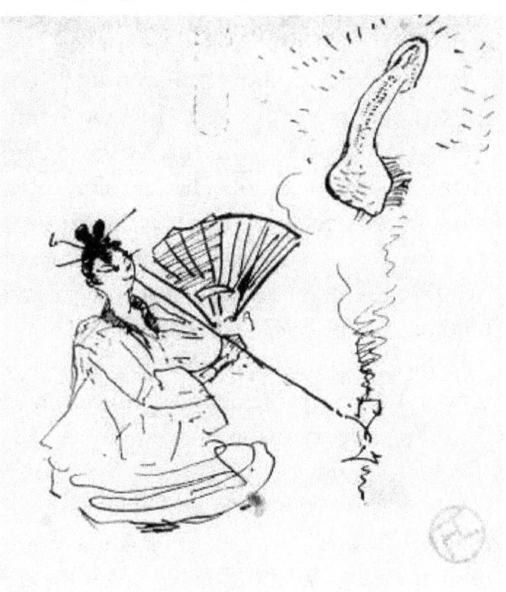

Kitagawa Utamaro (1753-1806)
Courtesan Hitomoto from the House of Daimonjiya
dated circa 1805, from the series "Contest of Full
Bloom Beauties. 36.2 × 26 cm, from Ronin
Gallery

Henri de Toulose-Lautrec (1864-1901)
Reverie d'opium

In Toulouse-Lautrec's *Reverie d'opium*, the composition was surprisingly similar. Although the courtesan was on the left side, she held her long opium pipe in a way that stretched far across the sketch in a similar composition theme. Like the Utamaro, she too had her hair up and her face cast aside.

The biggest difference was that in Toulouse-Lautrec's exploration of Orientalism and drug use, the opium reverie rendering led to a dream. From the smoke of the opium pipe, a shifty, indiscernible figure emerged a phallic surprise!

The apex of the 19th century opium trade was at its height in Hong Kong.

❧

Hong Kong was a slightly smoggy Cantonese city with a complicated history. The British began importing opium to China from India in 1820 as a payment method for Chinese exports to England. It was more cost-effective than silver, which the British also had to source from elsewhere. Tensions quickly escalated in Canton as the medical qualities of opium were imminently outpaced by its addictive properties. By 1839, 20,000 chests of opium were burned in protest. Steps were taken to eventually stop the opium trade altogether.[134]

The Opium Wars led to the takeover and opening of five major Chinese ports in 1842: Canton, Ziamen, Fuzhou, Ningbo and Shanghai. Hong Kong was officially under British control, and thus opium import to the country continued, and they were exporting the prepared substance to China.

By the 1880s, opium trade eventually declined, as the mainland Chinese opium was even more cost effective. The opium trade formally ended in 1917.[135]

After British seizure in the 1880s, it changed hands in 1997 to return to mainland Chinese control. The tumultuous transition drew many to explore the new possibilities of uncharted territory, and it became a city marked as much for its shady party culture as it was for its commercial opportunity.

Although Hong Kong was technically a part of China, its status was set apart throughout the political shifts.

In fact, the entirety of Hong Kong was designated as a freeport zone, making it a fantastic haven for the arts. There was no need for government approval to facilitate freeport status in the warehouse. Every warehouse had opportunities for tax-free art storage.

By the early 2000s, the globalized art scene had found its place in Hong Kong, with noted Western art galleries such as White Cube (seconded only by London, opened in 1993), Opera (opened in 2004), and Gagosian (opened in 2011) all added to the cache. The Central district was host to both art galleries and nightclubs, and VIPs would be entertained in high style by their art dealers. The overlap with big players in the arts was undeniable: when the VIP experience included the company of beautiful women, it was often a means to close the sale…of the paintings, naturally.

Picassos, Chagalls, and many more were discussed in the same settings as the women, and the strong bonds fostered over orgies resulted in million-dollar art investments.

The budding bastion of commerce was also host to a rich and complicated underworld. Under the right lens, Hong Kong was a den of iniquity catering to the most extreme and unconventional of desires. Hong Kong took transactional affairs to new heights—or new lows. Even if they weren't prostitutes, men bestowed tokens of their affection in the form of designer bags, which the women promptly resold to second-hand shops that dotted the Central streets, repaid with the cash.

To say that 21st century Hong Kong was a playground for the party-going Western male would be an understatement. Hedonist underground sex clubs for bondage (Western BDSM and Japanese shibari alike), orgies and full-scale prostitution went hand-in-hand with copious amounts of drug use. Impoverished women from neighboring Asian territories came to Hong Kong for the financial advantages, local women took advantage of financial opportunity, and foreigners explored their wildest fantasies.

In addition to this tacitly condoned patriarchal art market infrastructure, Hong Kong was home to the largest number of French citizens in Asia. Various reports indicated that the number of French people moving to Hong Kong continued to grow at 5% year over year. In 2016, there were an estimated 25,000 French people in the principality—double the number from 2006. They held a combined 800 companies, with a combined reported revenue generation of €14 billion.[136]

Yves Bouvier had a company called MEI Invest in Hong Kong. It was implicated as the primary facilitator of funds during his transactions with Rybolovlev. For each of the payments he gave Tania Rappo, a disproportionate number, at least 26 of the 37 sales, came from this same company.

Swiss investors in the region numbered far fewer than the French, with the majority of Swiss companies preferring Singapore as the seat of business to Hong Kong. It seemed that with MEI Invest, Bouvier, once again spread across worlds.

⊂

When Zahia Dehar was a little girl in Algeria in the early 1990s, she was obsessed with the film stars of Egyptian old Hollywood. The way the dancers moved and captivated their audiences was a source of unfaltering awe, and little Zahia aspired to one day hold the same power over men with her wiles. She studied her own small body, waiting for the time when her womanly curves would finally arrive.

Zahia insisted on wearing bold makeup in the meantime, applying it from the shocking age of three. Passing adults paused in alarm and suggested she take it off. But if anyone tried, she just started crying.

"When we are young, we love stories, we really love the dreamworld and the magic world," she explained to her Francophone documentarian, Paris-based fashion photographer Hugo Lopez. "I think it's much better that way."

Lopez's documentary, *From Z to A*, was a fascinating look at Zahia's inner and outer life, as beautiful as it was insightful. Coupling intimate conversations and daring photoshoot sessions with classical music, he provided a much-needed look at the rise of this captivating and complicated young woman.

Zahia was just 20 years old when the film was made, walking the line between emotional uncertainty and physical confidence.[137] She spoke bemusedly about her childhood, reveling in the delights of her pin-up body and the many facets of her whimsical imagination, but keeping the darker moments shrouded in allure. Throughout her interviews, she batted her lashes and fussed with her hair, but never broke from the gaze of the person who engaged her.

She went on about the Egyptian starlets, lilting to Lopez, "How I watched them, almost, every day. And afterwards, I would do it myself; I would do the same thing. And I loved it.

"I danced and I danced…I found it so beautiful how they were, the Egyptian women from the 1960s. They had a particular charm."

Her family was eventually broken apart in Algeria, and Zahia's mother moved her to Paris with her younger brother when she was 10. By her adolescence, her body began to blossom. Suddenly, she had arrived, "plate on platter."

"I had one sole wish: to grow up," she explained, "As soon as I began to grow up a little bit, it was like, 'Oh, I'm beginning to have a woman's body.' I felt very urgently, from the get-go, that I didn't want to be doing the same activities as the kids my age."

Teenage Zahia was more comfortable around adults who understood her unconventional, creative flair.

"I was very feminine, and afterwards I passed my time with people much older…" She mused, "I never went out with my school friends. I went out more with friends I met elsewhere. I preferred that. I felt better."

Zahia shared the same unusual quality of her Egyptian idols. There was something that instinctually drew men and women alike to her, both lustfully and protectively, and there was also something mournfully, deeply unique that set her apart. She was rapidly morphing into a sex symbol—first discreetly, and then as a full-blown sensation.

Certainly her appearance was a fascinating factor: The jutting curves of her buxom appendages were hoisted atop a tiny, leggy frame, bonded against her with dresses so tight she could only take quick, nimble movements in her spike heels. Her dark doe eyes were thickly lined and set with heavy false eyelashes, starkly offset by what was then a flowing, yellow-blonde mane.

She drew comparisons to many icons. Of course, the Egyptian starlets of her childhood had imparted a unique sense of movement and confidence, with her dark eyes and olive skin evoking something of a faraway place. Her hair and clothing were more like Brigitte Bardot, the French actress celebrated for her miniskirts, headbands, and bold eyeliner. Occasionally, taffeta, tulle, and fairy wings also found their way into the stylings.

The most complex comparison was Marie Antoinette, the French queen publicly beheaded by guillotine for a level of decadence considered vulgar by her constituents. Marie was married to the king at only 14 years old, and plunged head-first into a life defined by fashion, festivity and laughter. She had built her own menageries at the Palais de Versailles, and in her opulent paradise far away from reality, she felt a sense of calm and home.

But the queen was ridiculed by her constituents for misunderstanding them and flouting her resources. The line "let them eat cake," was used to rake her over the coals in the press, even as it became synonymous with the excitement of decadence. Oddly enough, the comparison was also made to Elena Rybolovleva when she was building Le Petit Trianon home in Geneva (see page 29).

With her penchant for pastels and her tendency towards excess, perhaps Zahia was most like the doomed ruler, sent to her death at 37. The woman she came to be—part smoldering Egyptian starlet, part girlish French coquette; part reigning Marie Antoinette, part curious child—was the brainchild of her retro-fab whimsical imagination. But her notoriety was, at first, the byproduct of defamation by others.

Zahia's sexuality had escalated quickly, and by just 16, she was embroiled in what her documentarian politely called "coquetterie": a delicate term for her somewhat-accidental descent into sex work. She spent her nights out at the clubs, then went back to high school in the morning.

By 17, she was the subject of French media frenzy. Her services were sold to two well-known football players, Karim Benzema and Franck Ribery, and she was flown to Ribery's 26th birthday party in Germany as the treat.

Inevitably, this constituted child sex trafficking, and the fame of the football players was cast in various and conflicting lights. Zahia was at once a sex-crazed jezebel and a child who had been victimized and ill-equipped to handle the ensuing scandal. The back-and-forth mirrored Zahia's own questions about self, and charges in the prostitution case were ultimately dropped in 2014 when Zahia told the courts she had misled the players to believe she had been 18.[138]

"It's so complicated to live through that," she told Lopez, "And what's more, I was young!...I had just started my life."

The experience wreaked havoc on her identity, her family, and, most importantly to Zahia, her future.

"I had no understanding of what had happened to me," she recalled to him woefully, "...I said to myself, 'This is horrible. What in the world did I do to deserve this pain and enormous humiliation?... 'What is my life going to be? I don't have a life anymore.'"

She despaired for hours, wondering what to do next.

The answer was to tap into the inner goddess she'd always believed herself to be. She relied on the same escapism as Marie Antoinette to cope, creating her unique brand unfettered by the influence of others. It worked wonders. She was the darling of the fashion world, and eventually became the muse of Karl Lagerfeld at Chanel, who insisted that Zahia had the ethos of an old-world courtesan.

In fact, she had already been envisioning her own clothing line, even at the time of her prostitution scandal. With her continued embrace of her own desire and desirability, fascination surrounding Zahia only mounted.

"I tried to live my life," she decided, "A life that pleased me, where I could be happy."

She amplified all the elements of her charm, creating a fashion line she had always envisioned. There were so many places to find inspiration. She sought joy in the crinkled paper liner of a cupcake, the color pink, the backside dimple just below her hips and the eyes of a fawn. All of it was eagerly funneled into her new life.

"I don't condition myself," she told Lopez of her eclectic tastes, "For me, this is reality."

One symbol that recurred in her fashion photography was the white bunny. It was part Playboy logo, part child, striking the same complicated chord with which Zahia continued to seduce the world. Frolicking in seemingly empty mansions, she had the vibrancy of an enthusiastic young queen, but the lingering tragedy of a melancholy je ne sais quoi. There was still something of the child in makeup about her – enduringly fragile, even in her own new self-assurance. Because the most captivating thing about Zahia's carefully cultivated aesthetic was her surprisingly genuine openness. She remained, through it all, a disarmingly resilient young girl who never truly stopped believing in her own power.

Her pursuit of happiness took on near-manifesto levels.

"We all have things that make us happy, but we are prevented from doing them." She said passionately on camera, speaking faster and faster, "We don't dare, because there are certain conditions and ways of life that are imposed. Are we here to be imposed on, or are we here to move forward by doing things we love?"
She did her own sketching, celebrating her own body and those of others. Her fashion line logo was a Z, which trailed into the curvature of her uniquely shapely body.

"I find the woman's body very beautiful. I am very passionate about it, and by femininity. For me, femininity is an art. I am so happy to be a woman, and to take pleasure in it; to amuse myself with that femininity."

She continued, "Because women are like living works of art."

As the cameras rolled and snapped, Zahia expertly dangled her heels and stretched her form across furniture. She opened her mouth and cocked her head. She leaned forward and back against the plush with agility and prowess, confidently toying with the viewer.

She set about branding herself as something far more than the subject of a tawdry affair, replacing the event with an overt lingerie line anchored in her own suggestive frame. It was funded largely by a mysterious "Hong Kong investor," who found her a new apartment complete with specially-designed furniture customized to her evolved imagination.

The customization felt a bit like a freeport showroom. Pink, rabbits, and beautifully constructed office furniture sat silently waiting for the client, Zahia, to approve. Everything was ready for her to work.

In a *Le Point* article Bouvier later condemned as inaccurate and slanderous, the Swiss art magnate was linked to the French-Algerian lingerie designer, which claimed that Zahia was being funded by him, attending dinners with VIP clients. They even printed photos of the two together.

At the mention of her name, Bouvier uncharacteristically raised his voice in frustration. His private life had nothing to do with the matter at hand. Besides, the photos were doctored, and he suspected they were planted when the Russian sought to destroy both his reputation and practiced discretion. He had them taken down.

Furthermore, in Geneva, Bouvier had an age-appropriate, non-prostitute partner of 25 years with whom he preferred to remain relatively discreet. When the story came out, his well-to-do girlfriend was forced to reset her social life, because people kept approaching her with a mixture of sympathy and horror. She reportedly changed hairdressers out of embarrassment…a big step for a coiffed Genevoise. Whereas the photos with Zahia may have been doctored and shared with the world, ample evidence of the blonde 50-something couple could be found at many local events.

Zahia's mention of Hong Kong seemed innocuous enough, and far enough away from her world in Paris to avoid suspicion. Yet while the official relationship between Zahia and Yves, whatever it was, remained behind closed doors, most of Bouvier's assets during Zahia's heyday were proven to have gone through MEI Invest, his Hong-Kong based company. MEI Invest was the primary culprit accused in Rybolovlev's lawsuits.

Given Hong Kong's long-running seedy underbelly and relatively recent art culture, it made sense that a Hong Kong investor with French artistic proclivities would fund the former prostitute turned fashion-forward Parisienne—Bouvier or not.

By 2015, Zahia assured interviewers that she was financially independent from her Hong Kong backers. Either way, one thing was for sure: Zahia was far more than the light she was cast in as a young prostitute. Perhaps a man like Toulouse Lautrec in the 21st century, a hedonist at home with improbable characters despite his respectable bearings, saw first what no one else had been able to catch.

One particularly poignant essay by Cora Michael addressed the Toulouse-Lautrec's emotional portrayal of the prostitutes, raising an important question about their social status in life. It could also have applied to Zahia.

"The directness and honesty of the picture testify to Lautrec's love of women, whether fabulous or fallen, and demonstrates his generosity and sympathy toward them."[139]

Rather than commodify them in a lustful desire for all of life's pleasure, Toulouse-Lautrec was driven by gratitude for their acceptance of him in all of his imperfections, reflecting that sense of understanding through the reverential depictions of his unlikely muses.

This provided the most interesting overlap between the world of Bouvier and Zahia: a kindred love of art and pleasure.

"I like what is pretty," she said simply, echoing Bouvier's own approach to art history.

Zahia's love of beautiful things, her own sensuality, and her high-power connections all lent themselves to her mystique. This gave way to providing the framework for a number of interesting art renderings.

On a home tour for the film, she paused in front of a David LaChapelle portrait[140] of her, totally nude. It was an electrifying purple, with a phantasmagoric boat styled as a Ganesha elephant, the Hindu god of wealth and remover of obstacles. Zahia's distinct body shape stood in orange and pink water, her pubic area covered by purple flowers. Her arms opened like a bodhisattva, set apart from other women.

"Sometimes I find myself sad," she said, "But then I pass by the painting and all of the sudden, it gives me a bit of joy."

Another piece by Pierre & Giles was a cross between the biblical and pornographic. Zahia stood strong against a floral background, clutching a fruit to conceal only her pubic area. Like the Rodin sculpture *Eve,* the depiction of Zahia was stand-alone and hypnotizing, and the fruit a symbol of a knowledge not yet embittered with the bite of truth.

Above all, however, the sensuality of artistic representations of Zahia evoked nudes by Amedeo Modigliani. The pose of the Pierre & Giles work cast her as something of a Venus, in a three-quarter pose replicated through the centuries, and the reclining nude shots were very much like his oil paintings of the many women he found fascinating.

The deification aspect of the art deeply resonated with Zahia. As she said to Lopez later, "A woman should be treated as something incredible."

Undoubtedly, Zahia's body delighted so many men, and the art created in her likeness was a testament to that. After the paintings, a number of resin casts of her body were created, both for exhibition and personal use.

White, pink, glossy and matte, they celebrated her form for eternity, as art was wont to do.

In her candor, Zahia discussed these replicas in an openness marked by hesitation and fear.

"I'm very scared…that one day, I will be in the middle of looking at the little statuettes, the busts. I have many at the house. I will be looking, and, I'll say to myself, now, that I'm very happy to have them. Because I'm looking at them, I'm looking at my body in the mirror, and I see the same thing.

But I have an image of myself at 80 years old, all alone, with my little bust, in the middle of looking at it,"

She opened her eyes wide.
"Crying."

V. To Possess Her

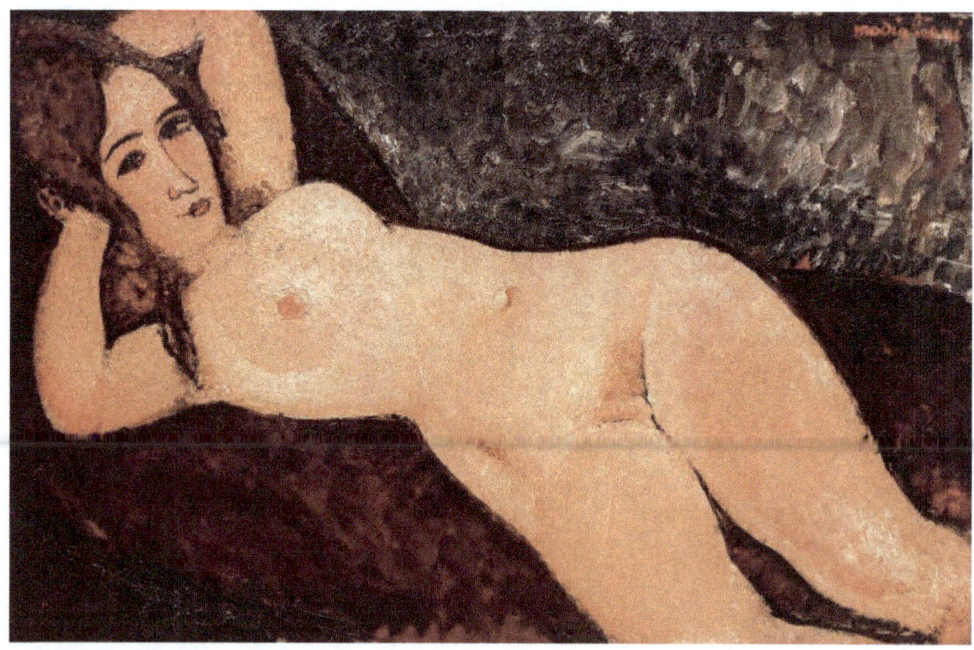

Amedeo Modigliani (1884-1920)
Nu couché aux bras lévés, 1961, Oil on canvas 60 x 92 cm,

17

—

THE MYTH

After the yacht and the Belle Epoque apartment, Rybolovlev invested a 10% stake in the Bank of Cyprus in 2012. As a token of gratitude, the government granted him Cypriot citizenship with something called a "golden visa"—a residency break Monaco's Prince Albert had thus far been unable to provide.[141]

At that point, Rybolovlev was already deep in his divorce battle, as Elena had filed back in 2009. Not only was he clearly profiting from the pristine landscape and sanctity of the Greek isles, but he was investing in the region for his own security. More than Singapore, it was the ultimate safe space for his many assets. The trusts in his daughters' names (and astrological signs), and the trustees, had already been in place for years.

Compared to the regions of Geneva and Monaco, Cyprus was a better business decision and cultural fit for a Russian oligarch.[142] Monaco may have had its fair share of Russian oligarchs with their tax decisions under suspicion, but Cyprus was far better-known for its reputation for Russian intervention. According to a 2013 paper by the National Bureau of Economic Research in Cambridge, Massachusetts, it was estimated that 85% of firms established by investors from Cyprus were registered in Russia.[143-144]

The following year, Rybolovlev purchased the idyllic private island of Skorpios using his daughter Ekaterina's trust for €120 million, a manageable yacht ride away from affairs in his new place of business. Like Zahia had been, the purchase was a birthday present.[145] And like all Rybolovlev's investments, it was a secured sanctuary. Each car on the island was registered as its own company held within the trust—a sophisticated take on his original multiple license plate diversion when he escaped Russia.

Skorpios had previously been owned and revitalized by the family of Greek shipping tycoon Aristotle Onassis. As per boat tracking records, it went onto serve as a major base for the family in the summer months. Most publicly, it was where Dmitry's daughter Ekaterina married her husband Juan Sartori in 2015.[146] In 2018, Juan Sartori announced his candidacy to run for President of his native Uruguay. Those close to the family assumed Rybolovlev was financing him.

"You can buy a president as easily as you can buy a painting," said one off the record source.

To Yves Bouvier, the island was a play as Rybolovlev vied for his daughter's affection in the heat of divorce proceedings. She had new horses every year, access to a jet in her name (called M-KATE), and was, for all intents and purposes:

"Totally manipulated."

Rybolovlev's elder daughter had been keeping secrets of his infidelity since she was 14. In the divorce proceedings from her teens, her father was accused of exerting intense psychological pressure, explaining that the secrecy was the best way to maintain the family.

He made her swear to say nothing of his indiscretions to her mother. Long before the jet, the football team, and the private island, he bought her a €1 million horse as a token of his gratitude—effectively "buying her silence."

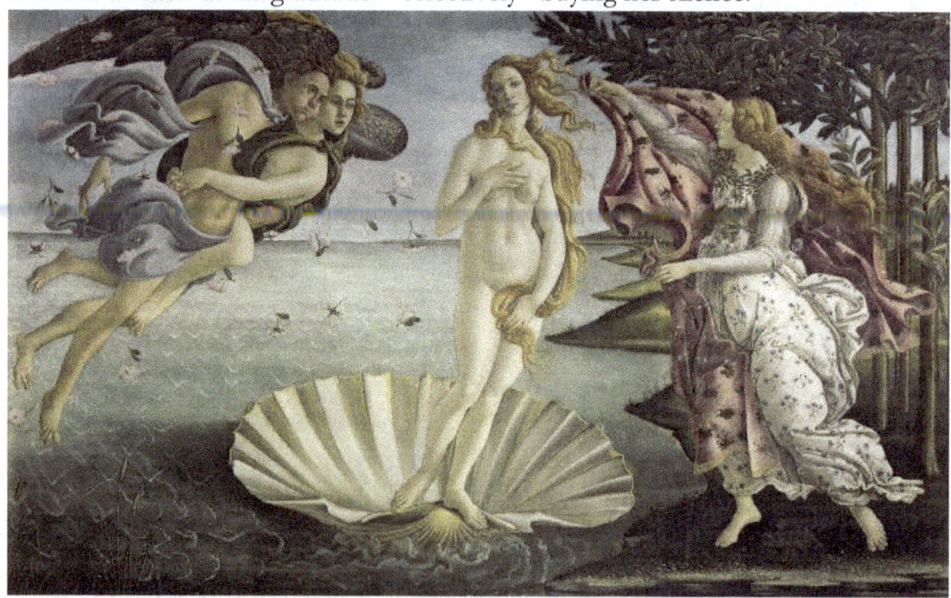

Sandro Boticelli (1445 - 1510)
The Birth of Venus, c. 1485, tempera on canvas, 172.5 x 278.5 cm,

Some years later, Rybolovlev decided to invest in building new villas on the island, and was granted a special permit to do so within the 'Natura' laws protecting the landscape. The permit decision was granted on his 51st birthday.

In statements for *Monaco Matin,* Tania Rappo echoed that the purchases were for control, and as such, that Rybolovlev felt very much at ease in Cyprus. "There are three places in the world where I can do what I want," she paraphrased, "At home in Skorpios, in Cyprus, and in Monaco."

Like Monaco, the region had a reputation as a tax haven in a geographically convenient locale. It had stunning sunny days, pristine aquamarine waters, and a long heritage of art, passion, and danger.

The region was so enduringly beautiful in fact, that it featured heavily in the myth of the goddess Aphrodite. Greek poet Hesiod, active circa 700 B.C., deduced that Aphrodite's name came from the Greek word *aphros,* for the seafoam she rose from when the god Uranus' was castrated. His discarded genitals were thrown into the Cyprus sea.[147]

A craggy rock still heavy in the deep blue water was said to be her birthplace. Any woman who managed to swim around it three times would be granted eternal youth and beauty, as well as fertility and good luck.[148]

This was not withstanding support in battle, as Aphrodite was also occasionally associated with war.

Aphrodite was best known as synonymous with both the ocean and love. Everyone from the pious to the prostitutes considered her a noble, faithful patron of their cause. In Roman times, her name evolved to Venus.

Not only did the legend of Aphrodite in Cyprus sync nicely with Rybolovlev's love of water nymphs real and painted, but the motif of the Venus featured prominent in his collection.

Most famously, Sandro Botticelli's *The Birth of Venus* set the standard for all depictions of love goddesses.[149] Created in 1485 (about 20 years before *Salvator Mundi*), the woman rising from a shell against a seafoam backdrop stood nude, dually vulnerable and

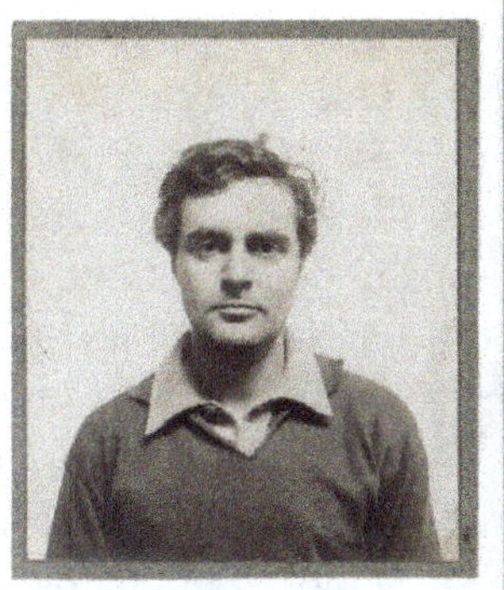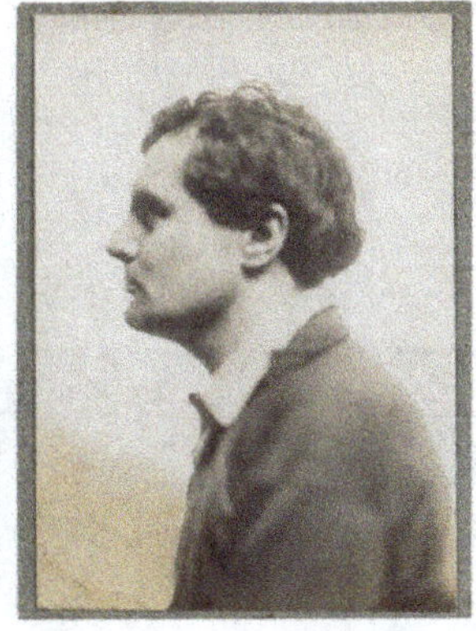

Amedeo Modigliani(1884-1920)
Portraits de Modigliani de face et de profil, c. 1918, mounted, 12.8 x 10.5 cm et 15.2 x 10.6 cm, Lot 175, Books and Manuscripts, Sotheby's Paris, May 2012

strong. Her soft blonde hair fell loose around her shoulders and curved all the way down to her carefully concealed pubic region, while her gaze was cast to the side modestly and mysteriously. The image depicted the exact moment in the legend where Aphrodite was born in Cyprus, emerging from the foam, beset by gods of wind and sea.

Instead of Botticelli's iconic nude, Rybolovlev began acquiring works by Amedeo Modigliani as early as 2006. This was perhaps his favorite artist; of the works Rybolovlev purchased through his Swiss art dealer Yves Bouvier, seven were

Modiglianis: a sculpture called *Tête*, and paintings *Jeune Fille Blonde en Buste, Madame Hebuterne aux épaules nues, Nu dolent, Vénus (Nu debout, Nu médicis), Nu couché aux bras levés*, and *Nu couché aux coussin bleu.*

As the titles indicated, more than half of the works were *nu*, nude women. In particular *Nu debout* (standing nude, also known as *Nu médicis* or, most interestingly, *Vénus)* was explicitly referential to Botticelli's work, especially as it took the pose scandalously further. The work had been sold in November 2006 at Christie's for a high of $15.92 million, but Rybolovlev purchased it through Bouvier at more than double in 2008: $39 million.

Botticelli's Venus stood with hair flowing strategically down and around her body, her hand placed fetchingly around her chest, and her eyes cast downward. While Modigliani's nude's shoulders sloped similarly and the head titled, his version of things was much more direct in its allure. The eyes faced the viewer head on, vividly blue in their electric, unwavering gaze. The model's hair flowed, but in a block, expressionistic style, a ruddy red far richer than the golden light touch of Botticelli's tendrils. The strands brushed across her shoulder only slightly, hiding nothing (including the particularly scandalous touch of pubic hair, something Klimt had experimented with as well). Instead of a hand covering her breast, her fingers pushed her nipple forward, and the flush pink paint of her cheeks indicated immodest, revelatory pleasure.

The Rybolovlev catalogue pointed out the model's resemblance to Jeanne Hebuterne, Modigliani's truest and purest love. Like Rodin's partner Camille Claudel, Jeanne Hebuterne was completely infatuated with the art world. Like Claudel and Picasso's Francoise Gilot, she showed promise herself as an artist, but devoted herself fully to the oeuvre of her lover. She was his close companion in art and sex, and for the most part, the feeling was mutual. The catalogue explained that Hebuterne was given the nickname Noix de Coco (Coconut) among friends, for her chestnut hair and pale skin, evidenced in her portrait, acquired in 2008 for €17 million. In the identified portrait, her arm position is closer to the Botticelli, modestly placed above her chest with just a hint of her nipple exposed above a robe.

The structural facial features of Modigliani's paintings were his signature, undoubtedly highly significant. Like Picasso and his preoccupation with Jacqueline Roque's dark features, Modigliani also sought women who suited his interest in specific shapes and forms—largely, pale, voluptuous women. After all, as he was quoted in the catalogue, "To paint a woman is to possess her."

To be sure, Modigliani was exceptionally handsome in his own right: the Italian Jew had

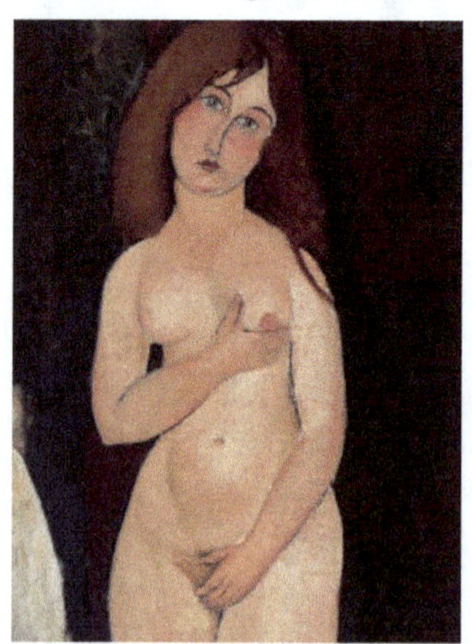

Amedeo Modigliani (1884-1920)
Venus (Nu debout, Nu médicis), 1917, oil on canvas, 99.5 x 64.5 cm

dark, penetrating eyes beneath dark hair that brushed his temples and a roman nose on high cheekbones. Ironically, photos of the artist priced at the lowly €4000-6000 did not sell at a Books & Manuscripts sale at Sotheby's Paris in 2012. It was only the paintings that held their appeal.

The paintings were captivating because they were alive. Above all, Modigliani's voracious appetite for living drove his legacy. As one former lover, art critic Beatrice Hastings, called him, he was, "A complex character. A pig and a pearl."

Just as Rybolovlev had been a sickly child and Toulouse-Lautrec lived despite his handicap, Modigliani had suffered from tuberculosis as a teen. It was only exacerbated by his sheer determination for the best of women, alcohol, and of course, art.

Hebuterne was seduced by the bohemian lifestyle Amedeo Modigliani was surrounded by in Paris. She posed for many of his other works, including the more modest *Madame Hebuterne aux epaules nues*. Even the title suggested a sense of buttoned-up formality uncharacteristic of Modigliani's women. Was it celebratory or distant?

Modigliani died at the age of just 35 from the lethal pairing of partying and chronic illness. His lover followed suit: Hebuterne, pregnant with Modigliani's second child, jumped from a window some months later, following her inspiration even to death. The first, Jeanne Modigliani, went on to write and reflect on the complexities of the couple and the life they lived. Picasso, another artist in Rybolovlev's collection, attended the funeral.

But like so many of the other artists in Rybolovlev's trove, Modigliani was too excited by the female form to stay faithful to a single muse. The nudes he painted were without name or ornamentation, and were mostly woman from the everyday world, such as seamstresses, maids, and waitresses. In his celebration of their bodies, these women of little note became nearly as culturally iconic as the Botticelli Venus.

The Rybolovlev catalogue noted that reclining nudes stemmed from a tradition known as the Odalisque, prominent in Orientalist motifs of harem women. They were enslaved to provide hedonism to their clients, experts in sensuality and providing men with their wildest fantasies. The staging of the Odalisque in French paintings was very similar to the Modigliani compositions, with the woman's head tilted back and her hip rounded along the edge of the canvas. Matisse too was fascinated by the Odalisque concept, drawing inspiration from his time in Morocco.

The striking *Nu couché aux bras levés* (reclining nude with raised arms) was Rybolovlev's first-ever Modigliani, purchased in 2006 for the bargain price of $26.75 million. Legs slightly apart with pubis exposed, the nude deviated slightly from the traditional Odalisque composition. Her long curls fell across her shoulders, and her gaze was stronger than the downcast glance of subdued seduction often featured in older images of the female form.

In *Nu couché au coussin bleu* (reclining nude on a blue cushion, acquired in 2012 for $118 million) the form also lay with her arm raised, sumptuous on a blue pillow.

She was another joyful temptress for Rybolovlev's growing stock. Flirting with the viewer, she spread her legs slightly apart, nipples erect as she pushed her ribcage slightly forward, a shadow cast across her waist. Her eyes were completely black, obscured even as the red lips cracked a slight, close-mouthed smile. Against the blue cushion, brushstrokes were visible, imbuing the backdrop with motion, and the fully fleshed out colorful skin with a pulsating sense of life.

The head was turned to the side, augmenting the trademark long nose and thin brows that featured often in Modigliani's work. The Rybolovlev catalogue drew strong comparisons to African masks in all of his paintings and sculptures, but the recurrent theme came as much from art as from life. He sought to depict women who aligned with his clear vision of beauty in the world.

Rybolovlev acquired *Nu couché aux coussin bleu* through Bouvier in December 2011.

Bouvier had been in contact with Sandy Heller, Steven A. Cohen's art dealer, and negotiated a price of approximately $95 million. Then he emailed Mikhail Sazonov.

"I do not know the price…" He wrote, "If [Rybolovlev] likes this painting, I will look into it."

According to the lawsuit documents, Bouvier had already confirmed the price, and was fabricating the follow-up correspondence.

He emailed Sazonov again the next day, with an informal typo underscoring at once the urgency and casual affectation of the multi-million-dollar deal.

"[T]he owner [referring to Cohen] is…very rich and certainly has other solutions. He is not obligated to sell this painting and not solely to us. For now, we must firstly maintain a trust relationship with him and secondly make him waste time in order to negotiate better."

Bouvier eventually invoiced the trustees for $118 million, and was given the $2.36 million at the standard rate. Unbeknownst to Rybolovlev, Bouvier gave Rappo her $5 million kickback as well—more than he was technically making on the sale. The reality was that Bouvier had turned a profit of $24.5 million.

Later, Rybolovlev's team attacked Sotheby's for covering these email correspondences, believing they had access to the records:

"On October 24, 2014, Sotheby's appraised Modigliani's *Nu couché au coussin bleu* at $110 million at Bouvier's request," the lawsuit noted, "The appraisal approximates the $118 million Bouvier charged to Plaintiffs for this painting, rather than the $93.5 million he paid for it. The transaction history listed in the appraisal omits the 2011 sale to Bouvier at the price the seller was willing to accept."

It was true that Sotheby's played an instrumental role in Rybolovlev's acquisition of Modiglianis. Another example was the summer after the *Nu au coussin bleu* sale, Olivier Valette at Sotheby's contacted Bouvier about *Tête*, a Modigliani sculpture, knowing it may have been of interest to this preeminent Modigliani buyer. By the end of his life, Amedeo Modigliani considered himself more of a sculptor than a painter, and moved his later works into this media. Sculpture was conducive to accentuating the angular facial features Modigliani found attractive in his nudes, and was a worthwhile addition to any major Modigliani collection. The market value was estimated between €80 to €100 million, and Bouvier bargained the price down to €62.5.

However, he still reaped a substantial profit, as was the case with all the Modiglianis in Rybolovlev's collection.

That Rybolovlev purchased such a large number of Modigliani's paintings was noteworthy. Firstly, because he did so for other artists' works acquired through Bouvier, including seven Picassos and two El Grecos. Secondly, this was made especially impressive because there were so few.

Modigliani made just 347 estimated paintings in his lifetime, compared to 26,000 by Picasso, or 34 volumes worth in the Picasso catalogue raisonnée. Because of this, the decision to invest in Modigliani's provided the clearest anchor to the discussion around art as an asset class. In quantifiable terms, there were limited shares of Modigliani stock, and therefore each work was imbued with a higher potential financial value.

This held true in the case of Gustav Klimt, who made 162 paintings, and da Vinci, who of course was known for just 15. But the Modigliani's were exceptional in that they were traded among an active elite network that included some of the most well-connected money managers in the worlds of both art and finance. The best of these were based in New York, and included Stephen A. Cohen of SAC Capital and the Nahmad family, the latter of whom shared many other similarities with Rybolovlev as mentioned in the context of both Geneva and Monaco.

Nahmad Gallery held a Modigliani show in 2006 called *A Bohemian Myth*, which likely drew from the English translation title of his only daughter Jeanne's book: Modigliani -- the Myth. On the website in advance of the exhibition, New York-based Helly quotes from Modigliani's obituary by Francis Carco in 1920:

"A life marked by poverty, worry…by thirst for punishment and a willingness to become a target for the supposedly astute. Life of an artist, life of exultations! I shall not recount the picturesque and bohemianism of it, or the paradoxical and constant defiance of rule, or the absence of all traces of domesticity. But for all that, for all the defects and qualities, the taste for unhappiness and the exceptional, the torrent of graces, the deliriousness and the naughtiness, Modigliani leaves a void behind him that cannot soon be filled." [150]

While the artistic value was irreplaceable, it was perpetuated by this high net-worth network. As of 2014 at the end of the Rybolovlev buying period, Steve Cohen had an estimated net worth of 8.5 billion and 1.5 billion in art. Rybolovlev was estimated to also be worth about 8.5 billion with 1.5 billion in art. *Forbes* listed brothers David and Ezra Nahmad at 1.9 and 1.5 billion net worth respectively, with both residing in Monaco. [151]

The group of blue-chip investors did help to ensure that Modigliani paintings were sound investments as stores of value, because, to a certain extent, their interconnectedness maintained the prices through continued buying and selling.

"If an oligarch buys art it has a temporary effect, but only at that level," Beard said on this subject. "The only way two oligarchs can really affect an artist's market is if they go to battle over the few works that are still extant."

With this strategy, he added, "In the very very short term you can get, just like anything, a pop based on economic forces."

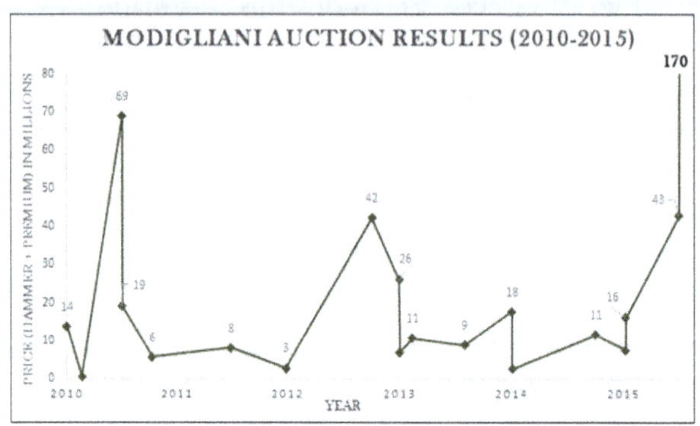

Officially, it was not a surefire strategy, but it was an insurance policy. Going a step further, no one could quite prove that public auction values were predetermined behind closed doors, but it was the subject of art market whispers.

Still, it was worth breaking down into numerical realities. Other art experts specialized specifically in the quantification of art as an asset class.

Professor and Economist David Galenson, author of "Quantifying Artistic Success: Ranking French Painters – And Paintings – From Impressionism to Cubism," spoke about the intrinsic versus the financial value of Modigliani paintings. He did not consider Modigliani one of the most important artists, because Modigliani produced such a small quantity of work before he died…even though this was precisely the rationale for increased exclusivity in private sales. Art historically, there were so comparably few paintings produced just 100 years into the past that their financial tenure was difficult to track.

Galenson affirmed that rising prices could point to macro-economic factors, admitted begrudgingly by some art dealers. "No dealer in anything sells below cost," he said simply, "If it were worth much more you'd sell it for much more." He grew increasingly passionate as he addressed his emerging field of art economics, saying, "Art historians hate what I do, but if they were smarter, they'd know I was right."

He summed up that sales and art history had little in common, with the bold statement, "Believing Larry Gagosian is like believing a used car dealership," Galenson said. "I would say that about any art dealer. Car dealers would be offended by this. They say, 'No, I'm honest.' But they lie to your face."

Larry Gagosian was at the helm of one of the largest art gallery chains in art market history. His headquarters were on 980 Madison Avenue between and 78th Streets in Manhattan — a multi-floor maze full of contemporary art and mysteries. Glossy-haired girls sat at the many desks throughout the space, conduits to sales in the millions. The Nahmads had a contemporary gallery space in the Gagosian building run by the youngest, Joseph Nahmad (born 1988)[152] since he was just 23.

Their primary art space for 20th century artists like Picasso and Modigliani, Helly Nahmad Gallery, faced Gagosian across the street at 975 Madison Avenue. Steve Cohen's art dealer, Sandy Heller, also kept his offices around the corner at 42 E 76th St.

The Modigiliani sales results spoke for themselves. Mei Moses of the Mei Moses Art Index plugged the numbers into his proprietary software, acquired by Sotheby's in 2017.

"What I find quite interesting for Modigliani as an artist is that the average return is about 9%," he said.

Moses defined the rate of return as the difference between the purchase price and the sale price at auction, thus the nine percent spike was suggestive of continued increases in profits. As a benchmark, Moses told *Art Tactic* that the overall rate of return for Impressionism ranged from four to six percent between 1991 and 2013, and five percent for Post-War and Contemporary up to 2000. [153] So Modigliani's rate was close to double the average in his art historical category.

"Modigliani has very positive returns," Moses added, "And has been lower-risk historically than many of his peers."

In death, Modigliani and his paintings surpassed their art historical value. His work was traded as a sort of art currency.

18

MODIGLIANI MONEY

FROM BIRTH, Amedeo Modigliani was something of an accidental posterchild for credit innovation. While his mother laid in labor in Livorngo, Italy, creditors stormed the house to ransack it for valuables. Somehow, the family had finagled that 1884's creditor law through a loophole: nothing on the bed of a pregnant woman could be repossessed. So Modigliani was born into strategic asset manipulation—with as many items as possible placed on the mattress.

Come adulthood as a well-known painter, Modigliani had an exceptional liberal education, but absolutely no business sense. He was reportedly known for crying, "I am Modigliani, a Jew. Five francs!" in his local Parisian café, sketching guests indiscriminately and offering the rapid-fire portraits to anyone interested. In 1918, Modigliani apparently attempted to sell the entire contents of his studio to a Brit for 100 pounds.

When Modigliani died in 1920, young and sick, he had barely been able to complete his select and coveted paintings. But the art market's machinations were immediately in full swing, contributing to the contemporary evolution of his enduring financial value.

Almost immediately following his passing, a network of aggressive collectors sprung up around his art to acquire it.

Two years before his death, Modigliani grew close with French industrialist Roger Dutilleul, who in turn became an important collector after the artist's death, working closely with his Paris art dealer, Leopold Zborowski. Other important dealers in Modigliani's Paris included Paul Guillaume and Leon Rosenberg, both active during the period.

Dutilleul passed away in 1956 and donated the majority of his 34 paintings and 21 drawings[154] to the northern French town of Lille. Doing the math of 34 out of 347 paintings, Dutilleul held nearly 10% of Modigliani's entire artistic output.

The mid-20th century was a time when Impressionists and Expressionists alike were in higher demand than ever before, and American collectors clamored for them as trophies indicative of their sensitive European tastes. Many of the artists in Rybolovlev's collection—not just Modigliani, but Matisse, Picasso and Renoir— became coveted signs of intellectualism and a delight to American audiences.

As Evan Beard described the phenomenon of pops between buyers in the 21st century, American collectors in the early 20th century stirred competition amongst themselves, creating a tense community of buyers while simultaneously stimulating and understanding the artistic interplays.

For example, textile heiresses Etta and Claribel Cone were in the sphere, buying works predominately by Picasso and Matisse. The sisters were made wealthy by denim mills during World War I in North Carolina,[155] subsequently traveling with Gertrude Stein and her brother around Paris, exploring and acquiring the evocative Impressionist paintings.[156] As they got to know the artists by medium and by personality, they grew close with Henri Matisse, who was slightly more toned-down than some of the wilder bohemians. They attempted to store and display all their artwork in an adjoining apartment, and eventually donated their sizeable collection to the local museum in their hometown of Baltimore, known as the Cone Collection at the Baltimore Museum of Art.

Rybolovlev acquired a single Matisse, called *Nu au châle vert* (nude on a green cushion). Like the Modigliani nudes, the form of the brunette was deliberately flattened against a deep red background, to allow the curves and the colors to speak for themselves. As with Modigliani, as well as Maillol and Rodin, Matisse was preoccupied with classical forms, deviating from the increasing abstract expressionism that came to define some of the other Impressionists, and later, the color-blocking and abstractions of Mark Rothko. However, he was fascinated by color theory, and he used the nude to explore its possibilities. The model's supple breasts were central to the composition, with the shawl draped just below her unveiled hip. Eyes closed and lips slightly parted, she was in a light, elegant sleep.

It was not by chance that the Matisse work evoked the Modigliani nudes Rybolovlev had collected. His tastes were increasingly specific. And thanks to the Modigliani network once propagated by Chester Dale, the nudes were highly coveted.

In the era of the Cone sisters and Dutilleul, another American, Albert Barnes, Dale was snapping up Modigliani paintings to eventually build his own museum in Philadelphia. Albert succeeded in creating the Barnes Foundation, which held the impressive 13 works by the artist.

At six paintings and one sculpture, Rybolovlev was fast approaching museum levels of Modigliani acquisition. The Nahmads with their Swiss freeport storage, Steve Cohen with his Greenwich home, the Henry and Rose Pearlman Collection at

Princeton University in New Jersey, the Tate in London, and the Jewish Museum in New York, all had staked their claim in displaying and educating museum and gallery-goers about the Modigliani canon. But Rybolovlev had placed himself in a special category of hardcore Modigliani buyers, surpassing the Guggenheim, the MoMA, and the Art Institute of Chicago with his acquisitions.

There was one other bullish Modigliani investor who drew strong comparisons to Rybolovlev. His name was Chester Dale.

Collector/Museum	Number of Modigliani Paintings (Approximated)
Roger Dutilleul (The Lille Museum)	34 (21 drawings)
Chester Dale (The National Gallery)	25 (26 drawings)
Albert Barnes (The Barnes Foundation)	13
Dmitry Rybolovlev (Cyprus/Singapore Vaults)	6 (1 sculpture)
The Museum of Modern Art – New York	4
The Guggenheim Museum – New York	3
The Art Institute of Chicago	3

Second only to Dutilleul, Dale was the shrewdest, most ruthless Modigliani collector in his lifetime, donating his 25 paintings, 26 drawings and two sculptures by the artist to the National Gallery in Washington, D.C. The National Gallery was founded by American President Franklin Delano Roosevelt in 1937 at the height of the Depression, bringing cultural relief to a nation in the midst of economic crisis, and providing a platform for public art consumption. Dale was instrumental in furnishing the new space with top-quality art. He thought of the paintings as his children, and couldn't bear the thought of them leaving the safety of their viewable place at the museum.

In a documentary about Chester Dale's collection, narrated by long-running National Gallery Director Earl A. Powell III, an actor delivered a quote about Dale from a gallery staffer during his lifetime.

"It was like dealing with the Tsar of all of the Russians or something like that," the staffer had said, "You really didn't dare make a misstep or it might cost you your head [*laughed*]." [157]

Chester Dale was born in 1888. He was an American banker who married an artist named Maude Murray Thompson, walking the glamorous line between the worlds of art and finance. He was infatuated with the enduring demimonde, hobnobbing first with Maude's bohemian circles, and later with Dalí and Picasso. Together they traveled to Paris from the 1920s onward.

When speaking generally about investors, U.S. Trust's Evan Beard addressed the excitement of the art world. He referred to its interesting characters, social aspect and, "elegant and interesting way of living" as the foremost criteria to become an art collector. This held true for Chester Dale, who together with his wife, inspected and analyzed works by some of the most widely appreciated artists of their era.

Maude favored Modigliani portraits over nudes. "In portraits of individuals," the documentary quoted, "We catch again the echo of their times."

Selected Modigliani Portraits in the Chester Dale Collection (By Year Produced)

Title	Year
Monsieur Deleu	1916
Chaim Soutine	1917
Café Singer	1917
Adrienne (Woman with Bangs)	1917
Girl in a Green Blouse	1917
Woman with Red Hair	1917
Gypsy Woman with Baby	1919

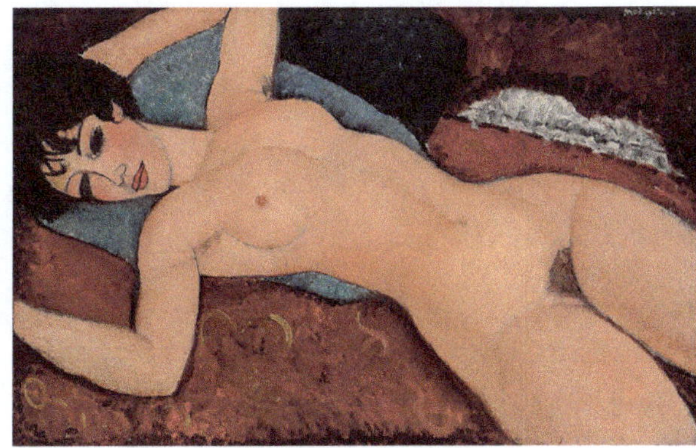

Amedeo Modigliani (1884-1920)
Nu couché aux bras lévés, 1916, oil on canvas, 60 x 92 cm.
Rybolovlev's Collection

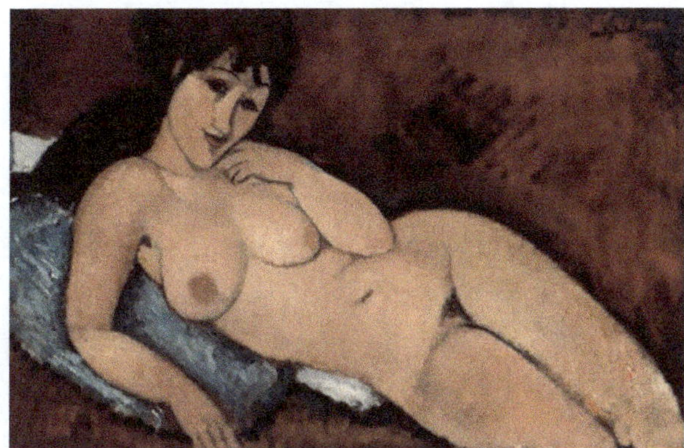

Amedeo Modigliani (1884-1920)
Nude on a Blue Cushion, 1917, oil on linen, 65.4 x 100.9 cm
Chester Dale Collection, National Gallery of Art

They did have at least two nudes in their collection: *Nude on a Blue Cushion* (1917) and *Nude on a Divan* (1918). These works strongly echoed the nudes Rybolovlev had purchased, especially the Nude on a Blue Cushion.

Rybolovlev's nude on a blue cushion was slightly leaner with smaller nipples, and her pose featured raised arms. Dale's nude on a blue cushion was placed somewhat upright in the composition, arm at her neck and legs together. Both women shared the thinly arched brows and dark-eyed smirk that comprised Modigliani's trademark.

Either way, the aesthetic and socioeconomic comparisons between Dale and Rybolovlev's eras were undeniable. From a financial perspective, Chester Dale was uniquely positioned to come of age as an investor during the roaring twenties, and quick-witted enough to survive the crash of 1929 and the ensuing Great Depression. He made a name for himself as an expert in utilities markets, and soon was sizing up works of art as effectively as he did companies. Arguably, Rybolovlev's early years investing in Russian companies drew parallels to Dale's ability to make strategic decisions.

Powell also explained the potential for art as a store of value in Dale's mind's eye. "The prices of paintings might fall," he said, "But their enduring value made them safer than other investments."

That underscored the chronological similarities between Dale and Rybolovlev. Whereas Dale lived through the crash of 1929, Rybolovlev held onto his assets in both 1998 in Russia and 2008 in the U.S. The Russian oligarch was pressured by volatile markets, political instability in Russia, and by 2009, the possible asset seizure during his divorce. The paintings, with their cultural value and their transmutability, were the ideal investment for someone seeking safety in the longer term.

The documentary detailed Dale's ability to make a deal, and his cynicism to that end. He apparently said, "I often thought when I bought some outstanding picture like my Cézanne still life, now in the National Gallery, that instead of buying a picture, I was paying the French national debt!"

Dale's style was the byproduct of his financial background, rather than what Powell referred to as the more refined "courtly decorum of the museum world." He was straightforward, blunt, and unrelenting.

He recollected a barter in documents retrieved by Powell's team, and the nature of the deal had eerily intoned the future of art's financial impact:

"When I asked what he wanted for The *Gypsy Woman*, he told me flatly that it wasn't for sale… Nothing a French dealer has is ever for sale. Except at a price."

"I sat down at his desk chair, pulled out my checkbook, and said, 'What do you want for it?'"

"He mentioned a price that was damn high, so I said, 'I throw in the stone head over there and I'll give you cash."

"He asked, 'dollars'?"

"I said, 'You can take my check to the guaranteed trust company and get any money you want. Even Chinese.'"

In November 2015, Christie's auctioneer Jussi Pylkkänen took his rightful place at the mounted podium. He had been there before, and as art lovers witnessed almost exactly two years later, would be there again to sell Rybolovlev's *Salvator Mundi* on the block.[158]

He was preparing to auction *Nu au coussin bleu,* by Amedeo Modigliani. By then, Rybolovlev had realized the extent of Bouvier's profit through Steve Cohen's art dealer, Sandy Heller, and he wanted to sell for justice.

With his carefully practiced, effortless calm, Pylkkänen began the rhythmic bidding proceedings with near-ritualistic grace, striking his characteristic chord of both signature satire and serious severity.

He took a deep breath and projected confidently in his perfectly polished English accent…

"We move to the beautiful Modigliani. Lot 8, painted in Paris in 1718."

Wrong.

He was off to a slightly sloppy start. Modigliani's *Nu couché (Reclining Nude)* had been painted sometime between 1917 and 1918, explicitly documented throughout the sale process. Maybe it was a typo; maybe it was a slip of the tongue…but it didn't matter. None of the bidders were deterred by this detail.

"75 million dollars, 75 million, 80 million, 80 million dollars, 80 million at 80 million dollars, 85 million now," continued Pylkkänen, not missing a beat to open the bid, shooting the value up by 10 million in a matter of seconds. Artful auctioneering is a sort of posh slam-poetry. If he had corrected his art history, perhaps he would have lost the momentum.

Seven major bidders vied for the masterwork, and soon it was down to just two.

Pylkkänen soldiered on methodically.

"At 85 million now. At 85 million." He ticked up his voice slightly, "At 90."

Then back to the metronome.

"At 90 million. At 95 million."

And with a low tone for impact, "100 million is bid. With Carolina. And selling at 100 million dollars. At 100 million is here.

"105 million is bid.

"105 million I have. And selling, Anna-Maria, with you. 105 million," he said, not stopping for breath.

"Who will give me 110? 110 I have, with Loic."

Swiss-born Loic Gouzer, then the newly-appointed[159] Deputy Chairman of Post-War and Contemporary Art, was the focal point of attention during the sale.

Then the auctioneer added a touch of playful banter with others in the room, probably to keep up the momentum and engage the audience.

"110 million. Not yours, sir. At 110 I have here. 110 million is bid. Loic! Who will give me 150?"

He repeated, "110 I have. At 110 million. 110 is here."

And then shortly, "You coming in?" With an open and rumbling, "110. At 110 million I have. Not yours. 110 million. Be 115. 110. At 110 million far right. Loic has it at the moment…"

He trailed ever-so-slightly.

"At 110." He leaned forward, "110 million is bid and selling. At 110."

It was unusual that he took such a long pause. He was waiting for more bidders longer than a typical auctioneer would. Was he expecting them?

He looked at the screen waiting for incoming bids.

"115 million is bid!" He said, raising back up. "At 115, not yours, Elaine."

It was his first mention of Elaine Kwok, Director of Education in Hong Kong, by name.[160]

"At 115 in a new place is bid. At 115 million. At 115. 120 million is bid. At 120 million, with Loic. 120 I have. Loic, you have it. At 120 million dollars. At 120 here for the Modigliani. At 120. 120 I have. Loic it's yours at the moment!"

He was stalling.

"120 million." He raised his voice "One hundred *twenty* million I have! 120 million. Coming at 125 I have. 1561 in fifth place. 130 with Loic Gouzer. You saw it. There it is on the right. 130."

He was referring to Kwok's paddle number. And then almost as an aside he asked sweetly, "Would you like to come in, sir?"

He resumed. "130 million. Still in two places. At 130 million. At 130 with Loic. At 130 million."

He muttered something about 'the show goes on' that was difficult to hear away from the microphone.

"And five. 135 million."

His eyes darted around. "138 is there! Thank you very much. 140 will be next please." He said it like he was ordering from a menu.

"140 will be next. 138 I have with Loic Gouzer on my right. At 138 million dollars, ladies and gentlemen." He stretched out the word million, tapping the audience. He raised his arm to the painting "Here it is!"

Elaine Kwok raised her arm from the phone bidder section.

"142 million you place. At 142 million dollars for the beautiful Modigliani. Brent, would you like to come in?"

Like it was a swimming pool.

"145 is bid. You heard it, ladies and gentlemen. 145 million with Loic Gouzer."

He gestured towards the screen. "Let's focus over here. 148 million."

After a pause, he leaned forward and said, "149 I have to take!

"Going once!"

But then he continued the sale.

"149 million, 150 will be next," in a tone so assured it could only encourage more bidders. "149, Loic

Gouzer." He puffed up his shoulders. "Modigliani. At 149 is here."

Pylkkänen strategically dodged between Kwok and Gouzer with familiarity. "150 is your bid, at 150 million! Loic what would you like?" asked the auctioneer, calculatedly causal as he turned towards the phones, "I'll take 151 if you'd like it. 150 I have. At 150 million dollars. The Modigliani."

It seemed the sale might have been over.

"Selling here at 150 million. There it is! It's not 170, ladies and gentleman it's 151 million…" Then Pylkkänen held his breath.

It was strange that the auctioneer would say what the value was *not*, unless there was already a predetermined value attached to the painting. In the lot description, Christie's noted, "a direct financial interest in the outcome of the sale," in which a minimal price was being provided to the seller (in this case, Rybolovlev), regardless of the auction's results.

"151 million and two could take it."

Elaine leaned into the phone to discuss with the client.

"Pausing, with you," Pylkkänen said liltingly. "It's getting all the way. Currently with Loic at 151 million dollars. The Modigliani."

Needless to say, there were very high financial expectations for the work. Capitalization was essential.

"152. One more Loic, or are you done? At 152 million, with the ladies here, it's yours Elaine." Pylkkänen dropped his voice with a decrescendo, and the work was sold.

"I'm selling it. Not a chance. All done. At 152 million."

He slammed the hammer.

"Sold here! 1561."

The final price was indeed just over $170 million, after the buyer's premium was added. At the time, it broke the existing public record for the artist by $100 million.[161] Two years later in 2018, it allowed for a Modigliani nude to sell at Sotheby's for $157.2 million, the most any work had ever sold for at their auction house.[162]

Elaine had closed the sale for buyer Liu Yiqian, one of the top art collectors in Asia. The Hong Kong-based businessman and collector was previously known for other watershed sales, such as his hanging scroll collection and his $36 million 'chicken cup' from the Ming Dynasty (1368-1644), which stunned Chinese audiences when Yiqian drank from it casually.

Regarding the stunt, a piece in the *The New Yorker* by Jiayang Fan quoted him as saying, "Emperor Qianlong has used it; now I've used it. I wanted to channel his spirit."

Yiqian was listed as being worth $1.36 billion by Forbes the year prior, making him less wealthy than even the Nahmads, and ranked him quite low on the list of rich Chinese and international billionaires.[163] But like Dale and Rybolovlev before him, he had a strong desire to build a collection, and to add credibility to his country's national art selection.

Like Dale and Rybolovlev, he came of age during a time of socioeconomic upheaval: The Cultural Revolution. Like Modigliani's family, he bore witness to a home invasion as a child, and like the Russians, witnessed the impact of violence on his own family.

He was born in 1963 to factory workers in Shanghai and dropped out of school at 14. *The New Yorker* piece revealed his determination.

"You guys continue reading your books," Fan quoted Yiqian telling his classmates. "I'm going off to make money."[164]

Pylkkänen attempted to explain to Christie's press. "There are a very small number of masterpieces that we dream of handling: this magnificent Modigliani has always been one of them."

There were many so-called masterpieces out there. It was not the sheer art historical context of a beautiful nude that made the sale special, but the network working behind it over the centuries.

Maybe it was the story.

Yiqian called Modigliani "Mudi," in Chinese shorthand, and explained to Fan, "It's not just his art but his life. Every object has its story. Maybe if he hadn't flung himself out of a window at thirty-six, his work wouldn't be anywhere in the millions."

But as Fan dutifully explained, "Liu had his facts tangled: Modigliani died at thirty-five, from tuberculosis; it was his mistress who committed suicide."

The real reason Modigliani was so captivating was its stunning capacity as a store of value.

Just as he had with the chicken cup, Yiqian purchased the Modigliani using his Amex card, in Chinese Yuan due to currency restrictions. With the 170 million miles, his entire family could fly for free.

Chester Dale's words nearly a century prior, had foreseen the flexibility and movability of investing in Modigliani as a tangible asset.

In the world of U.S. Trust, art was backed by credit. In the world of the Chinese buyer, art was access to credit. And the currencies changing hands—French francs to U.S. dollars in Dale's case, Russian rubles to U.S. dollars in Rybolovlev's case, and Hong Kong dollars to Chinese Yuan to U.S. dollars to airline miles in Yiqian's case—all proved that the Modigliani piece was a special form of financial exchange.

To fully understand the evolution, it was necessary to go back to the economic theory behind it.

The question of why art remained a valuable asset class for hundreds of years preoccupied many financial experts. Whole art advisories sprung up around the idea of following valuation trends, and ensuring client portfolios of artwork could show the same return on investment as stock.

Despite centuries of church-related patronage, it was the 19th century when artworks truly blossomed to function as these kinds of cultural trophies, elevating both the art collection itself and the status of the collector. Art was purchased not just for aesthetic pleasure, but social and cultural capital. By the 21st century, the new breed of collector, coming from hedge funds, private equity, and even oligarchy, was viewing art just as much for its asset behavior as an expressive good.

The rationale for why the practice of art buying evolved dated back to a mostly forgotten economist named Thorstein Veblen. Poor Veblen, with his combative behavior in academia, was shunned by economics circles. He was an unpopular socialist who abhorred the auspices of excess in all its forms.

But while his theories were steeped in satire and discontentment, Veblen's insights proved increasingly true when measured against the 21st century luxury market, even if it took the Great Depression of the 1930s to prompt a formal review of his *The Theory of the Leisure Class*, written in 1899.[165] However sarcastic, the book objectively provided a much-needed primer for the social behavior of the wealthiest echelons of society.

The Theory of the Leisure Class chronicled wealth behavior in its entirety, detailing the interplay between leisure and ownership. Veblen began with humanity's most primal needs, and the ultimate ownership—women.

"The ownership of women begins in the lower barbarian stages of culture, apparently with the seizure of female captives," Veblen explained, "The original reason for the seizure and appropriation of women seems to have been their usefulness as trophies. The practice of seizing women from the enemy as trophies, gave rise to a form of ownership-marriage, resulting in a household with a male head."

To this 19th century male gaze, conquest was as intrinsic to masculinity as it was to buying behavior. In the context of Modigliani's nude women during Rybolovlev's divorce, the metaphor of treating women as chattel was explicit.

Veblen was also fascinated by what he called the "Dolicho-blond" as the ultimate standard of beauty. A first-generation Norwegian-American, he even wrote a 28-page paper called "The Blond Race and Aryan Culture" in 1911, long before Hitler and the rise of Nazism. The description evoked the leggy blondes on Dmitry Rybolovlev's yacht, models prized for their light hair and eyes.

Going further, Veblen suggested that the pugnacious style of bartering during deals was also from this same impulse.

"Culture is therefore conceived to come on gradually, through a cumulative growth of predatory aptitudes, habits, and traditions…" he wrote. "Those traditions and norms of conduct that make for a predatory rather than a peaceable life."

Veblen described a "chronic dissatisfaction" now best known idiomatically as 'keeping up with the Joneses,' and the insatiable desire for wealth to postulate for peers.

"If, as is sometimes assumed, the incentive to accumulation were the want of subsistence or of physical comfort, then the aggregate economic wants of a community might conceivably be satisfied at some point in the advance of industrial efficiency;" he offered, "But since the struggle is substantially a race for reputability on the basis of an invidious comparison, no approach to a definitive attainment is possible."

The "conspicuous consumption" term he coined continued into present day, and his legacy in luxury and anthropology had a rightful place in the study of art market behavior.

When speaking about art in his writings, Veblen focused primarily on their value solely as beautiful objects. He was concerned with their inability to provide a productive output to society beyond their cultural capital, and did not address any financial innovations that came out as strategies nearly 100 years later.

"Their exclusive enjoyment gratifies the possessor's sense of pecuniary superiority at the same time that their contemplation gratifies his sense of beauty." He said.

But Veblen's legacy carried into the world of 21st century financial management, even if he was not able to foresee it. A 'Veblen good' became shorthand in economics for an item whose price increased with demand.

In most industries, supply and demand held a relatively stable relationship, with high prices typically deterring the market. But in art, everything was subject to the whims of the leisure class…and the higher the price, the more desirable the item was.

Veblen goods were mostly considered to be things like diamonds, and luxury brands, but art superseded them all as the ultimate Veblen item. Applying Veblen's theory to art, beauty was no longer in the eye of the beholder, but in the eye of the buyer.

In boom times, the record-breaking auction records continued to prove this, as did the statements of many well-versed art historical professionals. For the 2018 film (accompanying the book) *Generation Wealth* by Lauren Greenfield, economists attempted to explain how extreme wealth went so high after 1980.

Greenfield herself echoed Veblen—not to mention Zahia—when it came to beautiful women.

"As women, beauty is currency. It's how you win."

She interviewed her friend from Harvard, Florian Homm, who ended up on the FBI's most wanted list and landed in a German prison.

"Sex is of course an extension of commerce," he said. "What isn't?"

The documentary traced the excesses of the 21st century to the departure from the gold standard in 1976. Because money was no longer backed by blocks of gold in the bank, the bar for what was acceptable was seemingly limitless. This was an interesting theory in the context of blockchain technology, in which cryptocurrencies had no traditional share valuation behind them. In this same vein, art as investment was similarly abstract.

Contemporary art commentary by living makers like Damien Hirst, whose *Beautiful Inside My Head Forever* auction at Sotheby's marked the day of the 2008 crash. His works at that sale, with names like *Midas and the Infinite, New Midas' Lie,* and *End of the Line,* echoed the impact of art's financial investment on the fiscal realities of the era.[166] Steve Cohen was a noted collector of Hirst's work in addition to the Modigliani Heller sold to Rybolovlev on his behalf. A work by the anonymous street artist Banksy exploded at auction a decade later, as the ultimate valuation bubble bursting.

While this financial aspect of art investment was traditionally considered a secondary factor after its beauty and cultural value, it was important to remember that in art, these concepts became one in the same.

Since art functioned like other investments, the line between strategy and corruption began to blur. The investment capacity could also be sinister. Through gambling, wire fraud, and crimes of passion, the art currency took a dark turn.

For Rybolovlev, the art was a store of value during heated divorce proceedings. Increasingly paranoid about asset seizure, he began moving his art collection from Bouvier's warehouse in Singapore to his own stronghold in an underground facility in Cyprus.

19

THE RING

IN HIS HEYDAY, the New York Helly Nahmad was something of a hotshot. Not to be confused with his Francophone cousin of the same name, 30-something Hillel Nahmad was touted in the tabloids as the scion to his illustrious family art collection. He courted models, astounding his peers with his charms. His father David looked on as he dabbled in celebrity, photographed in various stages of inebriation with friends like model Gisele Bündchen.[167] For a time, it seemed that Helly was destined to remain an eligible New York playboy, living the high life and reaping its benefits relatively unscathed. But then Helly got involved in what was later best known by the title of a tell-all book called *Molly's Game,* the illegal gambling ring spanning Los Angeles, New York, Ukraine…and Cyprus.

Those close to him were concerned he may have had a problem, but gambling was a lifestyle for many elites. In Monaco, where the Nahmads had strong ties, the Monte Carlo Casino was built in the 19th century to save the ruling family from bankruptcy. David Nahmad was known to be an excellent game player there, and even won the Backgammon World Championship in 1996.[168]

In Asia's newer havens, Hong Kong art buyers were inclined to gamble on the nearby island of Macau, just an hour away from the art hub by ferry (and presumably, much faster by yacht). Even Singapore controversially opened its first casino in Marina Bay Sands on the main island in 2010.

Plus, Helly invited his fellow Dalton alumni to join the game in New York, including Noah Seigel, called 'The Oracle,' a former chess champion who dropped out of college to focus on bets, successfully utilizing computer algorithm weaknesses to harness his strategies.[169]

Helly eventually bought the entire 51st floor of Trump Tower. In what was deemed by the FBI as the Nahmad-Trincher organization, he teamed up with his fellow Trump Tower residents, Vadim and Ilya Trincher, and ran an illegal ring from his apartment. Bayrock Group, the company of one of the men embroiled in the prostitution scandal, also had offices in the building. Vadim Trincher was a champion as well, earning the title of World Poker Champion in 2009 at the Foxwoods Poker Classic in Connecticut.[170]

Molly's Game author Molly Bloom was managing the logistics. There were multiple games affiliated with Bloom labeled separately by the FBI. Trincher had a second Russian-focused ring with Alimzhan Tokhtakhunov (known as Taiwanchik for his Uzbek Asiatic features), a former footballer turned career criminal who was accused of fixing ice-skating games during the 2002 winter Olympics.[171] This second ring reputedly catered to what the FBI referred to as, "oligarchs living in Ukraine and Russia."[172]

Placing bets on European football teams and more, they laundered money through more shell accounts and companies in Cyprus before being legitimized in American real estate and hedge funds. In New York, JP Morgan branch manager Ronald Uy helped them structure financial transactions and avoid bank reporting requirements.

Bloom was movie-star gorgeous, with the curves and thin brows to rival a Modigliani painting herself. Beyond the Russian game, she was intimately familiar with the key players in the art world, looking to build a, "weekly game for artists, dealers, and gallery owners."

As she alluded to in her tell-all, Nahmad was primarily interested in working with art world connections.

"The game was my entry into any world I wanted to be a part of," she wrote. "The hedge-fund world. The art world. I could do a game with politicians, artists, royalty."

Molly explained that when the game got big, she was "cruising art gallery openings" and reaching out to "gallerinas," a pet term in the industry for junior women at art galleries hired mostly for their looks.

In November 2011, the author of this book was a wayward gallerina herself, seeking opportunities in Manhattan. At the James Hotel bar, The Jimmy, a hedge fund manager from a gallery opening edged closer to her on a sinking black leather couch as he propositioned her to host one of the many games in the wide net of the now-infamous gambling ring. Though he and his friends later denied these interactions occurred, he explicitly said that she could, "provide the girls; provide the drugs," and save enough money to buy a house like, "the last girl—a Russian girl."

She declined all offers.

Bloom also named Leonardo DiCaprio as a regular at her game in Los Angeles. The Hollywood actor was a known art collector, a friend of auction specialist Loic Gouzer, and later, the producer and star of the eponymous Leonardo da Vinci movie, still forthcoming as of 2019. After Molly's game, DiCaprio was involved in a second gambling scandal, when Malaysian billionaire Jho Low paid for him to gamble in Las Vegas, and gifted him a Picasso painting during the course of their friendship.

The worlds of high stakes art investment and gambling were inextricably connected.

Helly Nahmad Gallery, a major hub of Picassos on the Upper East Side, helped to finance the New York gambling ring, as did his father's Swiss bank accounts.[173] In a widely reported wiretap from 2012, Helly said:

"[S]ometimes a bank needs a justification for a wire, right? We can just say, 'Ohh, you are buying a painting' if they need justification. You know what I mean? You just be like, 'Oh yeah, I bought a, you know, Picasso drawing or something.'"[174]

The ring was shut down the following year. Despite his plea to teach art to the homeless and avoid jail time, the New York-based Hillel Nahmad pled guilty to gambling charges on November 12th, 2013. He was also charged with wire fraud, linking the sale of a painting worth approximately $250,000, and was sentenced to a year in prison. After five months, he was released to a Bronx halfway house and eventually was back to work with vigor.

Vadim, Eugene, and Ilya Trincher pled guilty to conspiring to commit racketeering and gambling charges later that week. Molly leaned into her nickname in the media as the Poker Princess and wrote her famous book, which was turned into a movie by Aaron Sorkin that was nominated for a Golden Globe. Taiwanchik was never jailed in the U.S. and was still thought to be at large between Russia and Cyprus.

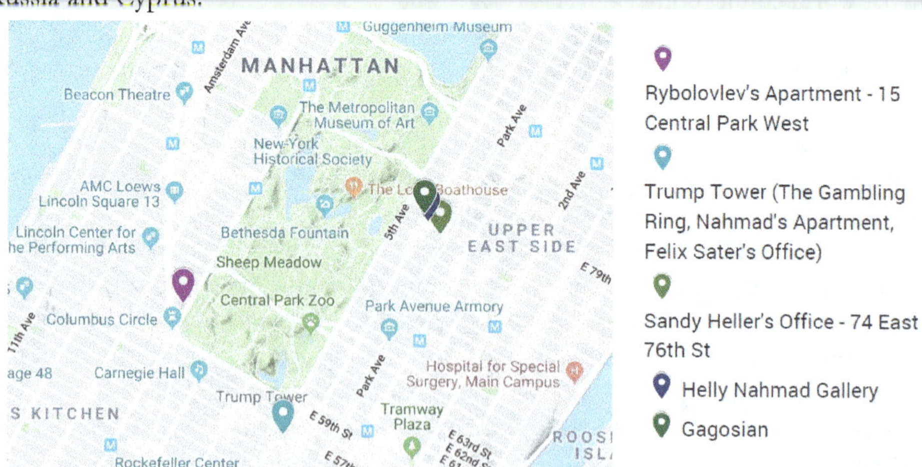

Formally, there was never any connection between Rybolovlev and the Russian rings. The oligarch was not implicated in the Taiwanchik-Trincher oligarch organization, nor was the noted art collector implicated in the high-powered art world games.

It was, however, the same world. Rybolovlev's 15 Central Park West apartment between 61st and 62nd Streets was a four-minute drive to Trump Tower on the corner of 58th Street. Rybolovlev had purchased Trump's Palm Beach home. The Nahmads had ties to Monaco and Geneva. The Russians had ties to Cyprus. Even Leonardo DiCaprio was involved with both the da Vinci and the ring.

Either way, Rybolovlev had his own ring to attend to.

The pristine blue waters and love legends of Cyprus had given way to a much more ominous political climate in the 21st century. Tourists flocked to the region, but it was so rife with corruption that even the signature national dish of the local songbird (ambelopoulia) was a byproduct of controversial illicit activity. [175] Despite the fact it had been illegal to hunt the bird since the region's civil war, an underground poaching business flourished. Hunters caught the birds in the pitch-black of night by trapping the birds with the false chirps of their fellow species.[176] There was a sentiment that the meal was so tasty precisely because it was against the law.[177]

Because Cyprus was quite literally divided, as the country had suffered the post-war split of Turkish and Greek control, it was a vulnerable place in terms of governing bodies well into 2018. Traversing the island meant two sets of jurisdictions, making for ample opportunity to bend the rules.

Apart from Rybolovlev, the Bank of Cyprus was also host to a number of men with ties to the Trump Administration. *The Guardian* chronicled ties between these Americans and Cypriot business dealings: specifically Commerce Secretary, Wilbur Ross, who was previously Vice Chairman of the Bank of Cyprus,[178] and Paul Manafort, who was accused of laundering millions of dollars to hide work for Ukrainian politicos by using Cyprus shell companies…not unlike the companies Rybolovlev used to shield his art activities during his divorce.[179]

Swiss banker Josef Ackermann was invited to become Chairman of the Board at the Bank of Cyprus in 2014.[180] Until 2012, the year Rybolovlev joined the Bank of Cyprus as an investor, he had been the CEO of Deutsche Bank Germany. During the recession, Trump relied heavily on loans from Deutsche Bank to keep building, with an estimated $364 million during the Ackermann years, and a possible $3 billion since the early 90s.[181]

Former US ambassador to Cyprus John Koenig spoke to *The Guardian* in 2017, saying, "There is no reason to look for a sinister narrative. This was a high-risk environment and there were not a lot of external investors interested."

But there were so many ties to President Trump that there was no way to stop the sinister narrative machine. Beyond Ross, Manafort, and Ackerman, the Trump

Tower connections were still clear as day. In one widely reported quote originally leaked by the *New York Times*, Bayrock owner, Mashkevitch partner, and Trump Tower resident, Felix Sater, wrote something especially damning. Referring to Trump, Sater wrote in a November 2015 email to Trump attorney Michael Cohen, "Our boy can become president of the USA and we can engineer it."

RYBOLOVLEV TIES TO DONALD TRUMP

Place	People	Connection
Moscow World Fine Art Fair	Elena was on the honorary committee → Viktor Vekselberg's advisor attended → **Michael Cohen**	Art fair attendee Vekselberg's company paid Michael Cohen through a shell company during the **Stormy Daniels Scandal**
Uralkali	Suleiman Kerimov → Aleksander Mashkevitch & Tevfik Arif →**Felix Sater**	Investors in Trump Soho, **Residents in Trump Tower**
House of Friendship, Palm Beach		Rybolovlev purchased from **DonaldpTrump**
Bank of Cyprus	**Wilbur Ross, Paul Manafort, Josef Ackerman**	Loaned and aided **Trump Companies**
Modigliani	Helly Nahmad → Trincher → Dicaprio	Resided and ran gambling ring in Trump Soho and **Trump Tower**
da Vinci	→ Leonardo DiCaprio	Gambled in **Trump Tower**

What was most interesting about Rybolovlev's overlaps to Trump was that they involved his art investment strategies. The art world investors were linked by social set and taste, as well as financial interests. Following Trump's election, the American FBI worked every possible angle to confirm that Russian involvement interfered in the presidential race.

Spokesmen for Rybolovlev were quick to point out that Rybolovlev's property purchase in Palm Beach had nothing to do with their relationship. After all, they explained, his subsequent Central Park purchase for his daughter to attend a postgraduate program in New York was from Former Citigroup Chairman Sandy Weill, a well-known Democratic supporter.

However, there was one presidential candidate who had an indisputable connection to Rybolovlev: in 2018, Juan Sartori announced his candidacy to run for president of his native Uruguay. Because Sartori was Rybolovlev's son-in-law, those close to the family assumed Rybolovlev was financing him.

The Clinton link may have been more abstract. After all, it was a matter of principle.

If the Russian oligarchs and businessmen accused of throwing the presidential election did so, which of course they all denied, it would have been for two of the values brought up many times in interviews and personal accounts: the power of control, and the need to 'save face'.

Saving face could also be seen as taking revenge.

As the First Lady of the United States during the end of the Cold War in Russia, Hillary Clinton accompanied her husband, President Bill Clinton, while they oversaw diplomatic relations and pushed for Boris Yeltsin to follow Gorbachev as head of state. The Clinton decisions and endorsements were extremely unpopular, but Putin was able to come up after Yeltsin and take advantage of the socioeconomic situation for the better. Hillary, in the meantime, enjoyed the art and culture of the region as part of her diplomatic tour, meeting artists in the early 1990s. Among them, Zurab Tsereteli was instrumental in her exposure. He took many photographs with the Clintons during their travels.

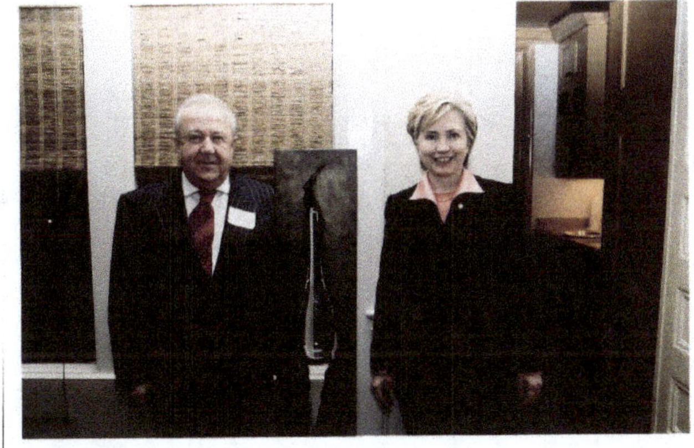

Then-First Lady of the United States Hillary Clinton with Zurab Tseretelli

While Donald Trump was building Trump properties in and with Russia, like the Trump World Tower Moscow, the Clintons were actively interfering in political affairs—in ways that Russian higher-ups perceived were to a detriment.

The previously mentioned American investor, Bill Browder, later had a change of heart in his Russian business dealings. Where he had once been eager to capitalize on the Post-Cold War financial decline, he was subsequently investigated for wrongdoing and enlisted the help of a lawyer named Sergei Magnitsky. When Magnitsky was tortured to death in prison for his connection to the case, Browder vowed to avenge his murder and shed light on the massive corruption in Russian business.

He pushed to pass something called Sergei Magnitksy Rule of Law Accountability Act, which pushed to identify and freeze the assets of Magnitsky's killers. This was drawn up in 2012, the same year Ackerman stepped down at Deutsche Bank, and Rybolovlev joined the Bank of Cyprus. Obama signed it in, but what had often been overlooked in the news was that at the time, Hillary Clinton was Secretary of State. The Magnitsky Act was perceived as an act of war, and it happened under Clinton's policies for international relations. While Trump was actively connected to various businessmen in Cyprus to foster business for decades, Clinton was enacting regulations that hindered it.

Browder said widely in various media that Putin was "obsessed with him" and that he was "enemy number one" of the Russian state. That may have been an exaggeration, but it was true that Putin did comment widely on his disreputability. One particularly interesting accusation was that, according to Bloomberg:[182]

"Putin suggested that Browder illegally siphoned hundreds of millions of dollars out of Russia -- and, for good measure, that he funneled that money into the campaign of Trump's opponent in the 2016 presidential race, Hillary Clinton."

Politifact investigated the claim and found that while Browder did not send the $400 million number Putin had suggested to Hillary Clinton, he had donated $17,700 her campaign, and another $297,000 to the Democratic National Committee on record. His business partners, Ziff Brothers Investments, gave upwards of $1 million to various Democratic organizations.[183] For these reasons, in tandem with the Magnitsky Act, Browder was a wanted man.

When you played for the wrong team, you lost.

It was February 2014 when Elena was lured to Cyprus on business. She was there with the family art dealer, Yves Bouvier, to discuss furniture, paintings, and to see her lawyers in the region. In terms of her tastes, the waterlilies had always been her favorite, before the number of nudes in her husband's collection started multiplying.

Bouvier was happy to oblige. He charted the jet for both of them, and let his other client, Dmitry, know that he would be heading to the island.

"I'd tell Elena when I saw Dmitry," Bouvier said, "And I'd tell Dmitry when I saw Elena."

After all, he had said earlier, "In cases of divorce, I am always neutral." Switzerland.

By this point, the Rybolovlev divorce had become larger than life. It had raged on for five arduous years, with volatility and unpredictability as the only constants. It was hard to know when the next attack was coming from either side.

With the aid of her lawyer Marc Bonnant, who apparently called media outlets himself to offer stories (in violation of Swiss legal code), much of the media around Elena portrayed her as a victim. Bonnant had encouraged her to go after her full half of Rybolovlev's assets. They continued to utilize private detectives to try to track his value through the various shares of the many companies within the Cypriot Trusts.

Elena had the arsenal of Bonnant, private detectives, and years of litigation behind her, not to mention a working knowledge of both French and English (in which her husband paled in comparison). She was empowered—and maybe even excited—about the possibility of retrieving the investments, both in liquidity and in art. She still had no paintings in her own name, but was thinking it might be time to build her own collection.

Her daughter's lawyer, David Wallace Wilson, had won twice against Marc Bonnant in Geneva. Wilson was frustrated with Bonnant's tactics, which he felt were not in the best interest of the client.

Speaking of Elena, he said, "She had such high expectations that her lawyer was feeding her. Marc Bonnant, I will tell you, he was just doing it for his own purse."

Regarding Bonnant, he went on, so frustrated he used an Italian word. "He would have sold only his side and his stardom in doing this… This guy was always 'very *maniere*'. He always had to be the absolute star, the savior of the world."

But the moment Yves and Elena arrived in Cyprus on the jet, the police were waiting to arrest the oligarch's wife. They had set foot on Cypriot soil, and were now under a jurisdiction where she was defined as criminal.

In the days before Elena had planned to arrive, the trustees had prepared all the documents ready for unlawful possession of a colored diamond ring, from Graff jewelers. The police claimed Elena had stolen it, and that its value of anywhere from €25 to 50 million was not rightfully hers.

The ring had been a gift from her husband in 2008, clearly customized to fit her finger. When she first received it, she showed off the beautiful stone to her friends, proud of her husband's affection.

According to Bouvier, the arrest was, "just to terrorize her."

Together, Bouvier and Elena were taken into an interrogation room.

"We'll call the lawyer in Geneva together, Maitre Bonnant," Bouvier told her.

"And call the Russian Ambassador right away."

Just as Rybolovlev had been treated to a stay in Russian prison for what he believed was investment seizure, he was attempting to give his wife the same experience.

It was a negotiation tactic.

Elena went with the police in a car. And Bouvier?

"I was free," he said.

But by selling straight to his wife, Bouvier had betrayed Rybolovlev on a deeply personal level.

She showed legal documents in her name to prove ownership, and was released from police custody shortly afterwards.[184]

Bouvier called Rappo to tell her about the arrest. She made the bold decision to confront her friend about the way he treated his wife, Elena.

Rappo had been there from the beginning. She had been one of the few to successfully maintain relationships with both members of the couple, flying on the family jet, dining with them, and acting as Elena's trusted confidant. But by then,

Rappo and Elena had already stopped speaking. After all, his wife was "totally destroyed" by the divorce battle, fighting without money.

"She went through hell," Rappo said, "And at the end, she started to change. Very unpleasant. Because I think she was exhausted by all that, and because he was winning. So you have the feeling that when you do things like him, this is the way you have to be."

Rappo remembered the highs and lows. She had seen the diamond when Rybolovlev returned with it from London. She had witnessed Elena enjoying her gift.

When she learned about the arrest, she was shocked, and not afraid to confront Rybolovlev about his decision. She recalled the conversation vividly.

"You're crazy! You gave her that present," Rappo cried. "How do you do something like that to the mother of your children?"

Rybolovlev responded without hesitation. "When you start a fight with someone," he said coolly, "You have to cut the oxygen."

Rappo knew what he meant by oxygen. In this case, it was the wealth Elena was fighting so hard for.

"You're crazy…" she said again in disbelief.

"But I'm not ready to give her the money," he answered. "She should have spent a few months in prison. Then she'd have signed anything."

In the end, it was Marc Bonnant who was corrupted during the divorce, bribed with the very money he had promised Elena she would win.

"I don't think she even knows that," said this source, voice tinged with sadness.

How could they be sure?

"Geneva is small," they said simply, echoing Crutchfield. "People talk."

Though Rybolovlev was apparently frustrated that she did stay for months, Elena was released after three days. Regardless, the divorce settlement concluded shortly after his wife's arrest, and Elena's initial ask of $4.5 billion, half Rybolovlev's current net worth, dropped down to a mere $600 million, half his assets at the time of the trusts' creation in 2005—the year he'd invited her to sign the marital agreement in the first place.

It was over…The artwork would be distributed within the proceedings, but mostly remained Rybolovlev's, to stay in Cyprus or wherever he desired.

But before the arrest, in May 2013, the report in *The New York Times* showed Rybolovlev had overpaid his purchase price for his most important work yet—the *Christ as Salvator Mundi*, (*Christ as Savior of the World*, or simply, *Salvator Mundi*) by Leonardo da Vinci.

VI. Saints

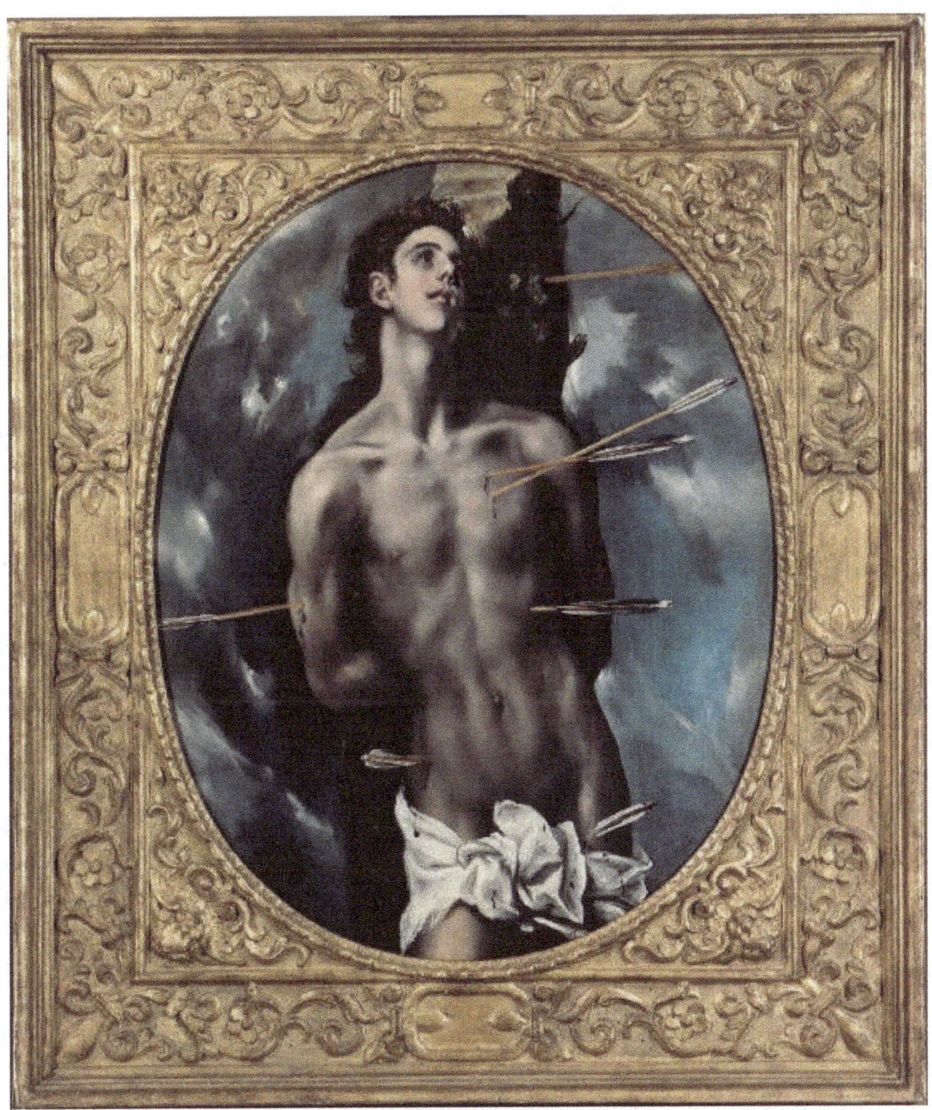

El Greco – Domenikos Theotocopolous (1541-1614)
Saint Sebastian, c. 1600, oil on canvas, oval, 89 x 68 cm

20

THE DA VINCI MACHINE

THE EVOLUTION of a saint in Christian history began with the body. Corporeal preservation of important early Christians manifested in the corpse, and living people came up to the physical remains of the important person's body to worship the dead, and God himself.

In *A Closer Look at Saints* by Erika Langmuir from the Monaco bookshelf of Tania Rappo, this phenomenon was explored at length. The corpse gave way to relics—body parts separated from the original human form—and through a sort of partial-share ownership, they were allowed to travel to various regions for effectual religious practice. Langmuir wrote:

> "Early Christians gathered around the tombs of local martyrs and confessors, venerated these witnesses to the faith through their relics – the saints' physical remains or objects they had touched – not their images. They would have been amazed at the paintings reproduced there…Once saints' relics were 'translated,' that is, removed from tombs to altars, they could be divided, split into fragments – increasingly so as churches and altars proliferated."

As these pieces were highly coveted, a trade around them was born. This proved popular and highly profitable, and it wasn't long before the painted labels below the reliquaries began trading as well. In this sense, the Christian saints created the first European art market.

From there, the question of religious versus aesthetic appreciation arose—not dissimilar to the questions asked by Norwegian economist Thorstein Veblen hundreds of years later. Langmuir described the phenomenon:

> "Where precisely, the modern gallery visitor may wish to ask, did piety end and aesthetic appreciation begin? We tend now to believe that the two are distinct,

yet in past ages the question by never have arisen. The Tuscan peasant wished both to have a bit of beautiful bright color on his wall and to honour his favorite saint…An owner/viewer may sometimes have turned to a saint's image for comfort and edification, and at other times as one would to any picture, for pleasure, but mainly, one suspects, for both reasons simultaneously: spiritual refreshment…The conflation of piety with visual enjoyment was not confined to the rich and sophisticated."

But the rich and sophisticated were among the most active collectors of saintly images. One such collector was Tsarina Alexandra, who became obsessed with icons as the Russian Revolution quickened around her in the early 20th century. Her son, Nicholas, heir apparent to the Russian throne, continued to struggle with hemophilia, and she placed her implicit and increasing trust in her friend Rasputin. More than just a fixture at Russian court, he appeared to be a spiritual force (see pg. 29). Part saint and part scoundrel, he was dubbed 'The Mad Monk.' Eventually adversaries organized a coup against him, spurred on by tabloid reports of his misconduct, and after a staggering number of ill-fated attempts at drowning, shooting, and poison, Rasputin was finally killed in 1916.[185]

In her imperial bedroom, it was the saints who the Tsarina imbued with the most confidence. With her private chapel, she displayed more than 300 Russian Orthodox icons by her bedside at Alexander Palace, glittering gold images each providing uniquely significant sources of solace. Kneeling, she prayed that they would ward off enemies—but her prayers fell on deaf ears, and she was assassinated along with her family in 1918.[186]

Towards the tail end of Rybolovlev's accumulation of pictures of women, he too began to collect religious iconography by some of the most critically important artists in the category, dating to the 16th century. Soon he owned two works by El Greco (Domenikos Theotokopoulos), purchased in 2011 and 2012 before he acquired the da Vinci in 2013.

It was the season for opulence, quite literally: Dolce & Gabbana's couture show the year of the da Vinci sale, Fall 2012 for Spring 2013, featured a Byzantine theme inspired by the old cathedrals of Sicily. Among the models who walked were Rybolovlev's yacht friends from 2018—Ginta Lapina and Daria Strokous. Lapina's bejeweled tunic featured the faces of dazzling saints below her royal crown, awash in golds, reds, and blues.[187] Strokous wore a low-cut corset, practically bulleted with heavy details.

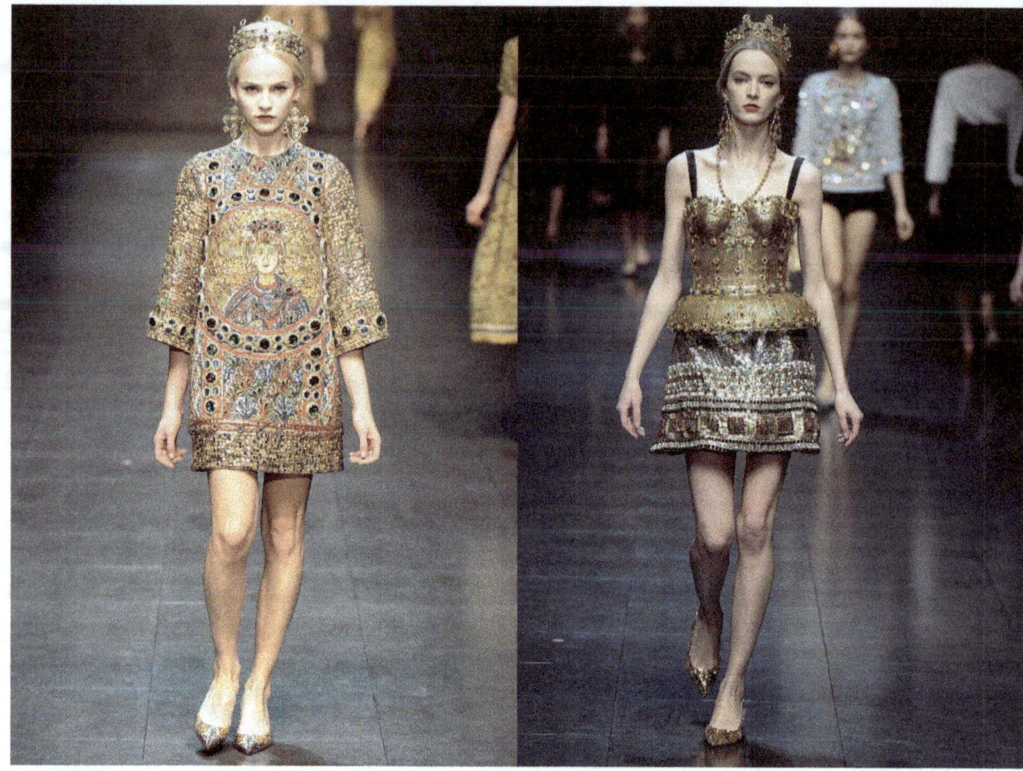

Dolce & Gabbana - Runway RTW - Fall 2013 - Milan Fashion Week (Left to Right: Ginta Lapina, Daria Strokous), Getty Images ®

The El Greco paintings in Rybolovlev's collection bore significant reference to the icons of Russian Orthodox saints. El Greco was a Cretan, whose study of Byzantine saints served him well in the more commercial context of Spanish enterprise. Beyond the medieval world of 'translated' relics, El Greco leveraged his knowledge of Latin for formal documents and religious ideology, Greek from his home country, Italian vernacular from his studies, and Spanish in his new home to navigate the ornate and elaborate world of spiritual iconography…as well as the art market itself.

El Greco featured prominently in Russia. Not only was a duplicate of the altarpiece for the Santo Domingo el Antiguo held in Saint Petersburg,[188] but the Saint Petersburg Hermitage also had *Saints Peter and Paul* painted ca. 1587-1592, a rich oil on canvas, as well as other saintly depictions that bore reference.[189] The latter work entered the collection in 1911 from the private holdings of Peter Pavlovich Durnovo, a successful lawyer from a wealthy family.[190]

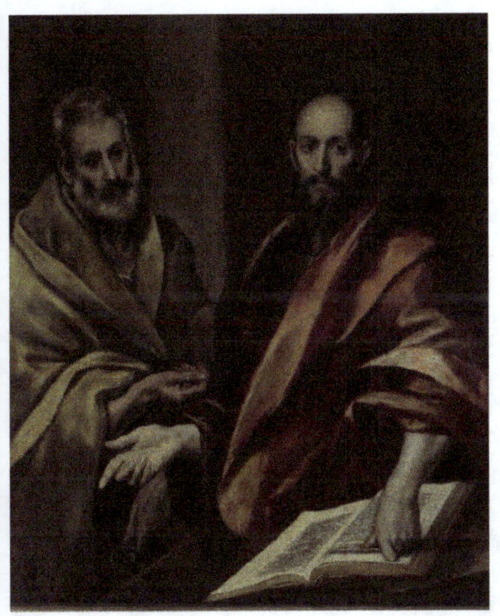

El Greco
Saints Peter and Paul, ca. 1587-1592, oil on canvas,
121.5 x 105 cm

In the Hermitage painting, the two saints stood side by side in contemplation. Both had dark eyes that turned away from the viewer, with hands outstretched from the heavy folds of their robes. The color scheme was sepias and burgundies, far deeper, darker hues than the voyager expressionists, the flashes of gold in Klimt's work, or the dappling pastels of the coveted waterlilies. These were serious, religious works, rounding out the collection of Rybolovlev not just as a lover of lust and joy, but as an introspective art world impresario. More than any other works in his collection, they evoked his original home, and the art historical foundation of his upbringing. They were a departure, but they were also a return.

It was interesting that Rybolovlev began more work with religious subject matters after he moved to Cyprus, a bastion of cultural diversity. Cyprus was the site of brutal conflict in the 1970s between Turkish invaders and the local Greek Cypriot community, with the former eventually overtaking a portion of the island. North and South Cyprus were extremely different politically, and ultimately, the entire area teetered on shaky ground. Geneva, Monaco, and Cyprus all had Russian Orthodox churches as well, which drew from a similar Byzantine aesthetic tradition. Yet with the Turkish Muslim and Greek Orthodox populations coexisting, the religious imagery of Cyprus was to be treasured.

In the era of Spanish inquisition, El Greco's own religious background was often debated. Greek Orthodox, Catholic, or even Jewish, his background was as mysterious as the stylization with which he imbued his saintly depictions. But his Cretan heritage touched the world of Cypriot conflict. El Greco specialist Fernando Marias wrote he was known to have served in the Turkish army during the Veneto-Turkish war.

Undoubtedly, his heritage was important to him: El Greco translated in Spanish to 'The Greek,' which he proudly signed on his paintings. He was the son of a tax collector from Crete, a territory which, like Cyprus, was overseen by foreign invaders. In his lifetime, Crete was part of Italy, so like Rybolovlev, El Greco was able to move without restraint to a more commercial center (in his case, Venice, then Toledo) as he looked for better opportunities.

"Eccentric, madman, mystic, philosopher; all four terms have been applied to El Greco," Marias wrote in *El Greco: Life and Work.* He was a genius, but combative, and difficult to understand.

Rybolovlev owned *Saint Sebastian* and *Jesus et Madonna (Christ Taking Leave of his Mother)*, purchased in 2011 and 2012 for an undisclosed sum and for €48 million respectively. Both were also unusual for him in that they featured male subjects rather than female—and fully clothed. Apart from the Picasso paintings, these were his first male portraits. Certainly, they were his only realistic ones.

El Greco, however, was not fixated on women. In his personal life, his mother and the mother of his son were both shadows, and the portraits he concentrated on were predominately male. Marias explained that El Greco abandoned his wife in Crete to pursue his career. Speaking of his partner, Marias wrote, "Her existence is purely conjectural, anonymous and instantly forgotten."

Conversely, El Greco was very close with his son, Jorge Manuel. They worked together on artistic and logistical matters throughout his life, and on his deathbed, El Greco bequeathed everything to his only child, without any mention of the afterlife he so carefully depicted.

In the case of El Greco's *Christ Taking Leave of his Mother*, the subject matter was a motif prevalent in religious iconography across Europe, particularly during the Northern Renaissance running concurrent to El Greco's life in Spain. It told the story of Jesus Christ departing from his mother, the Virgin Mary, knowing that his martyrdom awaited. In the best-known

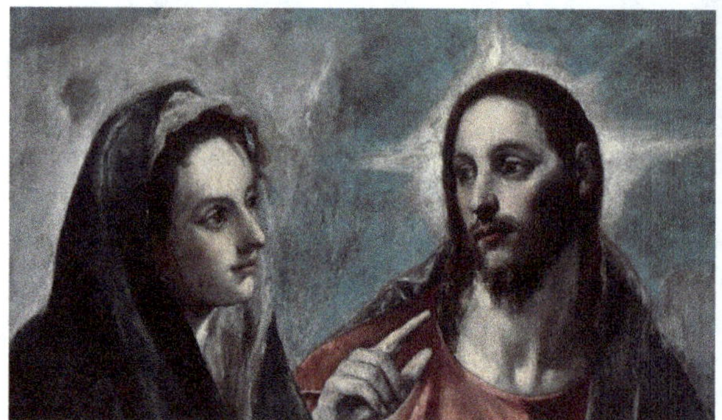

El Greco – Domenikos Theotocopolous (1541-1614)
Christ Taking Leave of his Mother, c. 1578-1580, oil on canvas, 64 cm x 92.5 cm

example of this work by Albrecht Durer, the Virgin was depicted beside herself with grief, prostrating and attended by women providing emotional support, whereas Christ was often set with Saints Peter and John.[191] It was a historically macabre motif, at the apex of doom and sadness.

But in his rendering, El Greco eschewed the weight of darkness. His scene beset Christ in a heavenly light, with his cheekbones catching above the shadow and his gaze at his mother filled with soft melancholy and longing rather than impending doom. His finger pointed outwards and upwards, though his gaze did not waver, and the backdrop and robes took on an ethereal blue. In the foreground of a misting cloud, the Virgin Mary appeared youthful, even peaceful, as she was swathed in the light of her son's spiritual glow.

El Greco was not like other religious painters of his era. Instead of the more rigid, contextual iconography designed to engage believers, El Greco was concerned with the inner life of his works, and his own personal expression. He was rather whimsical and flighty, prone to elongated forms. In the world of Byzantine art, personal artistic sensibility was secondary to the regimented aesthetic as it served to praise religious deities, and the politicized world of Biblical representation was strict.

The work in the Hermitage was just a taste of his tendency towards deeper expressive work and experimentation with form.

In the case of Rybolovlev's *Saint Sebastian,* the short-haired man's pallid form was completely nude save for a cloth around his waist. Agonizing as the arrows cut from his chest down to his legs, he cast his eyes upward towards the heavens, mouth only slightly open, similarly at peace. It was an oval painting, encompassed in an elaborate gold frame that highlighted the bright tones of the arrows that pierced him everywhere, and set back the strong movements of the dark clouds behind the body.

The scene was taken from a legend of Christian persecution in the 3rd century, in which the saints were hunted down. A Gaulois soldier (from French territory), he enrolled in the Roman army and spent his life between France and Italy. When given the choice to renounce Christ or die, Saint Sebastian chose the latter—and suffered the consequences.[192]

Despite the all-encompassing nature of the religion's artistic merit, there remained important markers in both words to denote each saint's individual significance. The long torso and expressive face turned upwards were clear markers of a work by the artist, and arrow wounds on a shirtless Sebastian delineated this particular saint over years of study. According to *Saints and Their Symbols* by Rasa Giorgi, also in Rappo's collection, Sebastian was the patron invoked against the plague, as well as "protector" of athletes and policemen.

Langmuir spoke of saints as trustworthy, an important value in Rybolovlev's world. When it came to depictions of saints, she wrote, "Suffering, death, and the fear of death, and the grief, guilt, and gratitude of survival are here sublimated into an image of serene trust and hope."

Her book explained that saints were vehicles of religion, of art, and of storytelling. In their interplays and overlaps, their impact was truly revealed:

> "Real or legendary, the saints and martyrs assumed to be in Heaven remain among us on earth…Like the ancient myths, the stories of their lives and deaths make exciting reading, yet it is mainly through images that they teach us what it means to believe; to sin and to repent; to suffer and to rejoice; to endure or do battle; to live in solitude or in fellowship with others—or simply to enjoy images. They remind us of who we are, and what we can become, of the limits and potentials of our own nature."

El Greco deviated significantly from Medieval traditions in his urge to tell a passionate story. With his unique sense of elongated and distorted forms so unusual, some art historians speculated whether perhaps he had astigmatism.[193] Vision theories were generally dismissed, but they spoke to the sense of mystery around this curious, atypical style.

In modern history, he was later deemed egocentric, combative and prone to conflict. Imbued with an artistic fervor that translated into hyper-confidence, El

Greco's lack of doubt in his own abilities was so certain that it became a detriment. He reportedly said, "I was created by the all-powerful to fill the universe with my masterpieces."

While El Greco was most likely not as religious as his paintings portrayed him to be, it was this sense of flourish in his work that revealed his truest spirit. The egotism and the elongation were two sides of the same coin.

"What he embraced was the world of a self-consciously, erudite style, or *maniera*," wrote Keith Christiansen for the Metropolitan Museum of Art. "The paradox is that, at a time when the blatant display of artifice inherent in Mannerism was being criticized as an indulgence, and artists in Rome were striving to rid their paintings of anything that might seem like mere display, El Greco took the opposite route. He made elongated, twisting forms, radical foreshortening, and unreal colors the very basis of his art."[194]

Despite El Greco's unwavering faith in his own ability and strategic relocation to Spain, he was not well-received anywhere in his lifetime, or in the centuries that followed. As art historian and Baltimore-based professor Richard Kagan told *The Guardian* in 2014, "He neither had followers nor supporters in the 17th and 18th centuries when critics regarded him as an oddball, a man apart," said Kagan, an authority on the painter's Spanish period. "His work was viewed as capricious, extravagant even."[195]

Furthermore, his abrasive confidence consequently failed to foster strong ties with important artists and patrons of the era, among them Michelangelo, for whom he offered to repaint the Sistine Chapel, and important Roman art patron Cardinal Alexander Farnese. It was suspected that he left Italy for the wealthier Spain because he was unable to make a name for himself in Italy.[196] This drew parallels to da Vinci, who left the Florence of Michelangelo and Machiavelli for Milan, and Rybolovlev himself, who was always looking for the right home to provide him with his most imminent personal and professional needs. But from 1577 onwards, El Greco was based in Spain, and went onto become one of the nation's greatest painters.

Once success started to come, his combative nature revealed itself. During his lifetime, El Greco was embroiled in a surprising nine lawsuits, instigated either by him or his client, and they continued throughout his career. They were even on the question of valuation. A religious altar, a *Martyrdom of Saint Maurice,* and *The Disrobing of Christ* were all implicated in the various valuation disputes. [197]

The motif *Expulsion of the Money Changers* featured numerous times in El Greco's work. The description for another artist's rendering was featured in the Hermitage, and the accompanying explanation sampled from the Bible: "Jesus went into the temple of God, and cast out all them that sold and bought in the temple, and overthrew the tables of the moneychangers, and seats of them that sold doves. And said unto them, It is written, My house shall be called the house of prayer; but ye have made it a den of thieves." (Matthew xxi: 12-13)[198]

In his day-to-day life, El Greco was far more preoccupied with money than with God. The religious scenes paid well, but El Greco was constantly in conflict over their values and his own salary.

"He bombarded his own clients with lawsuits," said El Greco expert Fernando Marias in the Spanish newspaper *El Pais*, "And was impertinent to Philip II himself!...He was extremely interested in money, always seeking new commercial strategies, always in the red."

The list of lawsuits was seemingly endless. El Greco's first legal conflicts were in his home region of Candia in 1563, when the Duke issued a sort of restraining order against another family for "harassing" El Greco and his constantly-in-trouble brother, Manusos.

Perhaps the financial backlash was a result of the surprisingly modern tactics around investing in El Greco's paintings. Appraisals for "sale by lottery," or auction, was recorded in 1577. Instead of taking the higher bid, however, he took the lower one. That same year, for his contract with the church of Santo Domingo, he brought down his price from 1500 to 1000 ducats, "since the five hundred additional ducats that the contract mentions, were only offered to me out of kindness." His contract clearly noted he was to be paid in installments.

He also constantly had the value of his artwork "assessed" to ensure it was worth what he was paid. 10 years after his low prices, *The Burial of the Count of Orgasz* was finished in 1587 for a parish celebration. When the valuation proved too high for the parish, at 1200 ducats, they requested to have it appraised again—but the new appraisers said it was worth 1600 ducats. In short, Marias explained, "the parish's plan had backfired." A civil lawsuit ensued throughout the following year, and went back to the original estimate.

Later in life, El Greco was supposed to have filed suit against the tax collector, because he did not want to pay tax on his own paintings. Then charges were mounted against the artist, but eventually both suits appeared to be dropped.

However, the most astounding case concerned *The Disrobing of Christ*. El Greco went head-to-head with the governing bodies at the cathedral council in Toledo.[199] The valuation of his work was 227 ducats, but El Greco was certain it was 900. El Greco was defiant throughout months of proceedings, and only relented when he was imprisoned—apparently, for no other reason than to close out the proceedings.

Just to terrorize him. After all, it was a negotiation tactic.

Rybolovlev's El Greco failed to sell at Christie's in 2017, even with a low estimate of just £4 million in London, less than 1/10th what he had paid Bouvier for the work six years prior. This confirmed in his eyes that he was cheated by Bouvier. If he could not find a public forum buyer at the value he paid, perhaps it was incorrect.

To others, however, his plan had backfired: in his conviction that Bouvier had cheated him, Rybolovlev was initially devaluing the works. It was a lose-lose: if they sold below Bouvier's value, he lost money. If they sold at or above Bouvier's market value, he lost face.

Either way, at first it appeared that the market for Old Masters lacked the tenacity of the Modigliani trade, or the highly competitive collecting of early 20th century Impressionist lovers. It was a subdued, somber environment—but still something was not right.

Scandals were starting to add up: the da Vinci article and the ultimate betrayal of buying with Elena were signs of mounting distrust between Bouvier and Rybolovlev. After having his wife arrested and settling divorce issues, it would have made sense to tackle the issue of the art dealer as well, through similar tactics of litigation around the globe.

But first, Rybolovlev fell deathly ill.

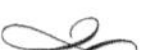

Regarding Russian relations, Bill Browder wrote, "Inquiring after a person's health could feel like asking someone to reveal a state secret." This proved true. Rybolovlev's media team was aghast when questioned about his difficulties with prostate cancer in 2014. They merely mentioned a tumor. However, it was reported and known among friends that the tumor was of the prostate.

Then there was Dr. Samadi.

The Iranian-born Dr. Samadi was a celebrated, even celebrity, urologist working at Lenox Hill Hospital on Manhattan's Upper East Side. The hospital was less than five blocks away from Gagosian and Nahmad Gallery, and he reportedly earned more than $6 million annually from his dealings as a practicing doctor.

Men who came in contact with him were in awe. "God," and "wizard" were used to describe him, and he regularly gave university lectures and went on camera to talk about the latest innovations. More than just urological issues around the prostrate, he purported himself to be something of a libido expert as well, speaking about how men in their fifties could maintain sexual function—through Viagra, and through his new and important surgery. The "uncontrollable libido" Rybolovlev described to his daughter, detailed in the divorce files back in 2008, would have substantially benefited.

His crowning achievement, however, was his operation equipment. The standard procedures for prostate surgery had always been manual and invasive, but Samadi's new state of the art equipment was managed by controlling a robotic device instead. It was first publicized in 2012, the year before Rybolovlev purchased the *Salvator Mundi*.

Samadi called it, "the da Vinci machine."

No doubt, the title of the machine was a reference to Leonardo da Vinci's Vitruvian man, in which the sketch of an anatomically strong and proportionate male spreads across the page. The nude man had all his operations about him— presumably, a healthy libido and a healthy prostate.

Rybolovlev selected Dr. Samadi as his surgeon, rejecting doctors in Geneva that had often dealt with prostate issues without incident. But he was not able to have the surgery in Monaco and then the United States refused his visa. He was forced to be operated on in the Dominican Republic.[200]

For all his charisma, Samadi and his da Vinci machine were not 100 percent fail-safe. One patient, a retired restauranteur named Philip Nadler, received a surgery in New York from one of his students unbeknownst to him initially, and suffered from a complete loss of libido. Accusations of performing too many operations per day and overseeing rather than operating continued to arise.

Oddly, some of the controversy around Samadi's preferential treatment of one operation over another echoed comments by Old Master conservator Julian Baumgartner, who had no connection to the medical world of Manhattan. When discussing the *Salvator Mundi*, he spoke about the importance of objectivity in painting restoration, and compared the process to a medical emergency room.

"I try very hard not to consider whether it's a $20 painting or a $20 million painting," Baumgartner had said, "You certainly wouldn't want to be a hospital where Brad Pitt and you didn't receive the same treatment."

He continued, "As a conservator, you want to ignore the value other people put into it. It allows you to work freely. How would you ever think to work on a painting worth that much?"

Celebrity or not, Rybolovlev suffered post-surgery complications after working with Samadi. "I was at a near-unconscious state," he told Knight.

He eventually recovered enough to come back to his senses, and close out his time collecting with Yves Bouvier.

When Rybolovlev decided to purchase the da Vinci the year after Samadi's machine hit the market, it was the only work that Bouvier had not presented himself. Rappo never even saw it. After refusing sculptures of men by Bernini and Rodin, Rybolovlev had independently determined his taste for male anatomy in art with Old Masters.

The days of appeasing his wife's sense of style with Chagalls and waterlilies were slowly fading away. The number of nudes was dwindling. Through his newfound interest in Old Masters, he had embraced the old and the new, life and death. And on speculation, it might be said that an operation with 'the da Vinci machine' was instrumental in saving his life.

He had truly become an art collector.

As of 2015, Dr. Samadi had performed 5,600 operations. That year, he brought his team to Cyprus to teach them everything he knew and open an institute there, when Rybolovlev's health was still floundering. In August 2016, he also came under scrutiny for commenting on Hillary Clinton's possible ill health on Fox News, and in 2017, the da Vinci machine was extolled in a long article for the *Monaco Gazette*.

But by then, the scandal now known as the Bouvier Affair was in full swing.

21

WALK THE BLADE

"HE SAID that I was his friend," Yves Bouvier began, speaking of his important client, "[But] we don't speak any common languages…he never came to my home. He never came to my birthday party."

But while Bouvier may not have trusted Rybolovlev with his more intimate moments, the Russian trusted him with just about everything. From purchases to invitations, art fairs to art storage, their relationship was enmeshed and instrumental in many ways. When Rybolovlev had first moved to Geneva, the family leaned on Rappo and Bouvier alike to ensure they fit in. When he was in the heat of divorce proceedings, he had entrusted Bouvier with his most valuable assets, not to mention the exchange of more than $2 billion to ensure those assets were collected and transported appropriately around the world for more than a decade. From Geneva to Singapore, Monaco to Cyprus, nearly every aspect of the process had input, or even management, from Bouvier himself.

This was his form of trust.

After all, as Bouvier later said of Rybolovlev, "He is someone who confides in no one."

Elena had been arrested on February 25th, 2014 and the divorce proceedings were soon to close out. But the previous year, Bouvier had been in Cyprus one more time to review the new storage facilities Rybolovlev was building, underground in a warehouse owned by a company called Neocleous. He was there to ensure they were up to his standards to protect a museum-quality collection. From there, Rybolovlev would be OK to store the artwork on his own if and when he wanted to keep it in the home of his golden visa.

"Cyprus has close cultural ties with Eastern Europe," a Neocleous report dated to April 2012 explained, "Based on a common Orthodox religion, and following the break-up of the Soviet Union, it rapidly developed into the offshore center of choice for investment into Russia and the CIS, performing the same role as Singapore does for South East Asia and Hong Kong for China."

The report continued with time-sensitive updates, "Indeed, contrary to predictions that the Cyprus banking crisis would bring about the demise of Cyprus as an international financial sector, investment into Russia via Cyprus increased significantly in 2013, reaching the highest level ever since 2008." 2008 was the year Rybolovlev purchased Trump's House of Friendship in Palm Beach.

Neocleous was the foremost law firm in Cyprus, located at 195 Arch. Makarios III Avenue in the district of Limassol. They oversaw the management of Rybolovlev's trusts, on par, apparently, with Mossack Fonseca of the Panama Papers in terms of control. Neocleous made plans for an even more imposing tower to be constructed, at 10,000 m², with panoramic sea views of the Mediterranean. And beneath the Neocleous offices was a trove of Rybolovlev's most private and protected works. Thanks to this underground storage, Rybolovlev was no longer beholden to Bouvier, able to physically and artistically distance himself. The paintings were following suit.

As requested, Bouvier affirmed that the Cyprus warehouse was in top shape.

It seemed that the artwork would be seamlessly transitioned, and their relationship did not need to remain as intertwined. But Rybolovlev had one last favor to ask.

Bouvier was invited to Rybolovlev's home alone in Saint Tropez. He took a private jet at a moment's notice, ever at the beck and call of his trusted multi-billionaire client.
Together, they sat poolside and had a rare, intimate conversation, mediated by a translator. Because after almost 20 years of travel between Moscow, Geneva, and Monaco, Rybolovlev still did not speak a word of French. The two didn't talk much one-on-one.

To Geneva's international set this was mortifying. Not only was it bad form to speak just a single, impractical language, but how could anyone really get to know you? Every word was pre-screened.

On that spring night in Saint Tropez, the translator was none other than Tetiana Bersheda.

Bersheda had been an instrumental figure in Rybolovlev's life since 2009. She was a young lawyer then, no more than 25 years old, but a talented linguist at the top of her game. She spoke Ukrainian, Russian, French, and English at a working legal level, and her resume also boasted basic knowledge of German, Spanish and Italian. The only child of an economics professor father, she was fluent in Russian, French and English, communicating with media and divorce courts around the world on Rybolovev's behalf.

As she told *Paris Match* in 2016, "I told him that I wasn't familiar with divorces. He responded that his case needed an advantage in commercial litigation, in trust and corporate law."[201]

That quickly changed.[202] In 2011, Bersheda was divorced herself, from the husband she had met when she was 19, also a lawyer.

She had been the one to survive all the intense proceedings, according to Bouvier and Rappo, because there was no risk she wouldn't take for her boss.

The same story cited one of her friends, Paul Boury, who said she would, "cut off her own hand" for him, and that in seven years, she'd never detached from her cell phone or taken a vacation.

Bouvier echoed that sentiment. Her boss was everything. Father figure, suspected one-time lover, boss…he was an amalgamation of all role models and authorities. She never told him no.

In another instance, when she was not invited on a group ski trip to Rybolovlev's Hotel Alpina chalet in Gstaad, Switzerland, she apparently got so angry that she smashed all the glass around her.

Yet another source close to the conflict said that Bersheda was "academically gifted, but morally bankrupt." The term used in French was *sans foi ni loi*—without faith or law.

But when Bouvier sat beside her in Saint Tropez, it was still a huge shock what he claimed was asked of him.

In 2013, Rybolovlev had apparently propositioned Bouvier to buy the house to hide it from Elena during the final divorce proceedings, and he would buy it back once the assets were fully protected. Not only was this an unusual request, but a reference to the allegedly innocuous Trump purchase of the House of Friendship.

Bouvier had declined.

This time, Bersheda translated a much bolder request. In Russian, Rybolovlev said, "I made your fortune. Now you must save mine."

He asked Bouvier to pay off the judges in his divorce from Elena, to close out the case in his favor.

According to Sixtine Crutchfield, it was something he could theoretically make happen. He was on "tutoyer," or informal, terms with many of the judges due to a lifetime in the privileged circles of Switzerland. And certainly, he had done the Rybolovlevs so many favors before.

This one was too much for him. It had gone too far. While he was a daredevil, Bouvier wasn't really a rule-breaker when it came to the Swiss legal system. There was too much at stake with his many businesses.

"He is kind and appropriate. Always, always, always," said Geneva Freeport manager Alain Decrausaz, "I see him with customs, and he's always excellent. With declarations he knows to always get it right. He has done his work. And today as well, if the companies continue to function, it's because everything was done correctly."

To be "correct" in Switzerland was an important cultural value. Legality may have been malleable in variant regions around the world in the eyes of law-abiding Swiss citizens, when judging Cypriot trust law or freeport regulations in more relaxed ports, but Bouvier would never have jeopardized his reputation at home. Bouvier laughed off the request and thought it was forgotten. Speaking of Rybolovlev, he simply said, "I didn't think he was serious," and went back about his business around the world.

But soon, Bersheda had dutifully prepared and mailed a list of judges to the office, and a package was received at Bouvier's Geneva office that fall. Bouvier refused again.

He texted his friend, art dealer Jean-Marc Peretti, "I'm in the shit," he wrote, "He's totally crazy."

Sixtine Crutchfield reflected on the escalation of events, "It should never have happened," She said firmly.

"…It was none of Yves' business, that divorce, so he shouldn't have tried to involve him. If that's what the truth is, if it's about the divorce, then the whole professional side of this is ridiculous. And I told Yves that."

Decrausaz compared the conflict to a schoolyard fight.

When Bouvier formally refused in October, he recalled, Rybolovlev presented him with an ultimatum: to sell all the work in the collection by Christmas.

There was no way he could do it.

Frank Michel, who later represented both Rappo and Bouvier during Monaco proceedings, described the challenge of Rybolovlev's pressure to sell.

"The problem is that an artwork so rare was very difficult to resell in a few weeks," Michel said, "As Bouvier explained, it's that, he could not be the seller. He had to take his time, and he had to come across a person who was passionate and who had sufficient funds to acquire works so incredible. It's not like selling your car."

Michel further explained Rybolovlev's financial benefit. "Thanks to his complaint, he had avoided the 50 million payment he was supposed to provide. So that was the first motive."

But from Rybolovlev's investor's perspective, the sale request was the ultimate test. It had been so easy for him to buy the works; couldn't a seller be found just as easily? As the challenges revealed themselves, he grew more and more frustrated— and most dangerously, more suspicious.

Never one to shy away from a challenge, Bouvier continued to work with Rybolovlev. He did his best to sell the works, and did not spend too much time worrying about the consequences. After all, he had other freeport ventures coming up in Luxembourg, not to mention a bit of a taste for life on the edge.

"He was always one to walk the blade," Crutchfield said later, "I think he just didn't realize it would be this bad."

On November 22nd, 2014, Rybolovlev's 48th birthday, the two men had a conversation at *La Belle Epoque* penthouse in Monaco. Rybolovlev asked Bouvier about whether the price of the da Vinci had been too high. The dealer insisted they had purchased the work for far below market value,   and in turn, Rybolovlev said he would pay up on outstanding debts.

Festivities commenced that evening with a birthday party at the Monaco Yacht Club. The five-floor waterfront space was known even in Monaco to be incredibly exclusive. Massive ships could dock at its doors, and people who had lived their whole lives in the country had never been invited inside.

It was a lavish affair, topped off by an alleged strip tease. Rybolovlev was reportedly known to enjoy them, and had even invited guests to join him for more intimate performances in the past.

Tania Rappo and Yves Bouvier were both present as usual. When they went out onto the yacht club terrace with Rybolovlev, he noted that they seemed uneasy.

Bouvier did not tell Rappo what happened, but Rybolovlev again asked him to sway the judges, and again, Bouvier had refused.

The tension was palpable, but Rybolovlev attempted to put his art dealer and his close friend at ease. He asked Rappo to translate to Bouvier, saying, "Tell him not to worry. We're still friends."

But Rappo knew her friend well. the 22nd was the ultimate turning point. She knew better what he was capable of, having witnessed his treatment of Elena. And she knew the power of Russian "loyalty," which Rybolovlev had always valued, and how quickly its emphasis could become a losing situation.

Echoing Rybolovlev's comments about friendship later in the case, she said, "He understood that he could not manipulate him. Either you become slaves, or you become dangerous. It's a very Russian thing." (See page 29.)

Meanwhile, Bouvier was still unable to find buyers for the other works on such short notice. Apart from the divorce ultimatum, one of the incentives was to receive payment for the most recently acquired piece, Mark Rothko *No. 6 (purple, green and red) (1951),* bought at $222 million.

22

TRAGEDY, ECSTASY, DOOM

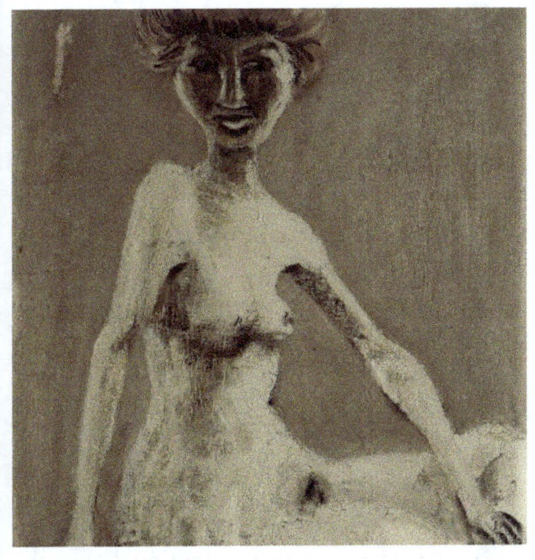

Mark Rothko (1903-1970)
"Untitled (nude)," 1939, oil on canvas, 60.6 x 46 cm
© 1998 Kate Rothko Prizel & Christopher Rothko/
Artists Rights Society (ARS), New York

MARCUS ROTHKOWITZ (or Rothkovitch) was the fourth child born to a pharmacist[203] in Dvinsk, Russia. It was 1903, on the cusp of the revolution that would go on to shake up Moyshe Seghal (Marc Chagall)'s artistic practice in the subsequent decades. As was the case for Chagall, Rothko's family were religious Russian Jews. He remained immersed in Judaica throughout his childhood, speaking Russian and Yiddish, and studying at a Hebrew day school.[204]

But by 1913, the Rothkowitz family had moved to Oregon, and the artist eventually known as Mark Rothko became quintessentially aligned with Americana.[205] In many ways, the artistic lineage of Rothko had more to do with the old masterworks than with the Picasso pictures and sumptuous nudes created in his own century.

Like El Greco's elongations, the deliberate departure from the confines of subject matter allowed him to explore emotive and spiritual ideology unencumbered. The absence of representation was not erasure; it was a means of further depth. As Rothko once said, "There is no such thing as good painting about nothing."

That being said, Rothko experimented with a variety of subject matters before he found his trademark, distinctive style. He dropped out of Yale after two years in 1923, abandoning a scholarship to move to New York. One nude painted in 1939, had an expressionist quality more typical of the French and German Pre-War periods. The gestural dark features and sinewy forms were more comparable to Modigliani's *Nu dolent*, acquired by Rybolovlev in 2008 for €18 million, than the works Rothko later became known for. It almost looked like the Giacometti *Femme de Venise IX*, sinewy and eagerly pushing towards the abstract.

Like Rothko's human experimentation, *Nu dolent (Nude Sketch)* was an earlier work, dating to 1908, far more visceral and somber than the later temptresses sprawled on cushions. In fact, the verso of the canvas even had an inscription — 'sketched head of a man.' Perhaps the intensity of the emotion expressed in the gesture had initially necessitated a man's face and body, until Modigliani's love of the female form got in the way. As the Rybolovlev catalogue quoted from his 1907 writings, Modigliani's brooding mirrored Rothko's as well.

"What I am searching for is neither the real nor the unreal," he had scribbled in his sketchbook, "But the subconscious, the mystery of what is instinctive in the human race."

Like Rothko, Modigliani was Jewish, though his religious experimentation opened his mind to seances and the occult. To this end, the somber tones and blocks were closer to Rothko's paintings and the suffering of saints than the playful eroticism more prevalent elsewhere in the collection.

It was surprising to see Rothko had also experimented with the female form, because his sense of reverence for the higher thinking had yet to materialize.[206] Because for all the indoctrination of his religious upbringing, abstraction as a vehicle for the spiritual freed him from the restrictions of any pre-judgments of Anti-Semitism, allowing him to think universally. Rothko used a technique his contemporary, noted art historian Clement Greenberg, called color blocking: sectioning his canvas into bold hues, at once overwhelmingly vibrant and diffusing gently into a floating unknown world. Quite literally, they were dematerializing on a higher plane.

Rothko's vision of reflection later morphed into a non-denominational chapel in Houston. 14 Rothko works surrounded the space, designed as a refuge and place of reflection for people from all faiths and positions. Their website reported 100,000 people of all faiths visited each year.[207] Tibetans and Taoists, Torahs and Qurans—nothing was out of place in Rothko's chapel. It was the ultimate in contemporary spirituality.

In terms of artistic practice, Rothko's spiritual conscious was widely celebrated. He differentiated himself from the other Abstract Expressionists working alongside him in New York during the mid-20th century, and his vivid colors were given context in their ethereal depth.

One strong example of Rothko's categorical transcendence was its similarity to tantric Indian paintings, which emerged in the 1970s. Om Prakash, Sohan Qadri, and Natvar Bhavsar all experimented with color and composition as a means of gaining intellectual insight into the unknown. Their legacy carried through into South Asian art collections, and rippled through cross-cultural realms of understanding.

But as ethereal as Rothko's painting remained, internally he was consumed with anxiety and misery to rival El Greco's prostration. In his eye towards the darkness, he took on an intensely personal burden.

"Only tragic and timeless subject matter is worthy of painting," he once said.

It was his version of humanism.

"I'm interested only in expressing basic human emotions—tragedy, ecstasy, doom," he said separately,

"…If you…are moved only by their color relationships, then you miss the point."

On the flip side of the heavenly spirit was a dark, dragging sense of doom. To Rothko as an artist, in this sense, they were one in the same.

As a man, Rothko had all-consuming, incurable anxiety. He lived in fear of being replaced by Pop Art movements, and was reluctant to show his work to anyone who may have been able to criticize it.

Two months after his separation from his second wife of 25 years, Biestle, at the age of 66, depression overwhelmed him. He plied himself with anti-depressants and slit his right wrist in his New York City kitchen, where he was found dead in a pool of blood.[208]

At Art Basel Miami Beach 2018, Nahmad Galley presented an exceptional Rothko.

Bouvier spent years procuring the second work by the artist on Rybolovlev's behalf. He had confirmed his interest at a hotel in Gstaad initially, and proceeded discreetly from there. The final transaction was conducted over the phone with Sazonov, and Rybolovlev bedridden in a Russian hospital. Though formally unconfirmed, it appeared he was still recovering from his prostate surgery complications. Bouvier facilitated the purchase without Rybolovlev ever even seeing the painting in person.

Rybolovlev recovered in Skorpios, where Rappo and Bouvier flew to see him. But the appointment only lasted 30 minutes, as he was really very unwell. It was 2014, the year prior to Dr. Samadi's presence in nearby Cyprus.

Once Rybolovlev was feeling better, Bouvier was called to an appointment in Saint Tropez for the divorce proceeding request. Of course, Bouvier rejected it, and according to him, set the subsequent events in motion.

No. 6 was the last work Rybolovlev ever bought with Bouvier. When it came time to pay Bouvier in full, he invited him to Monaco to settle the accounts.

23

FALLEN ANGELS

EDEN ROCK – St Barths was a five-star hotel on the island of St. Barthélemy. The sweeping vistas had nothing but blue skies and sandy beaches, a playground for the ultra-rich of the art world elite. Roman Abramovich notably purchased a home there in 2009 for nearly $90 million.[209]

The resort oasis drew its name Eden from the Old Testament tale of Adam and Eve. The first man and woman were created in bliss in a garden of the same name, awed by one another and by the magical garden in which they lived. Surrounded by beauty, nutrition, and the power of innocent self-discovery, the Old Testament story became the ultimate connotation for perfection. In fact, the word paradise came from the Persian word *pairidaeza* for enclosure or park, proving that the Garden of Eden was as enthralling as any place of peace.[210]

Another depiction of mythical paradise was *Domaine of Arnheim* by Rene Magritte, a painting purchased in 2012 for $43.5 million. At first glance, the serene scene of mountains was nondescript, but Magritte's trademark surrealism revealed the shape of a bird in the scraggy landscape, and two eggs neatly positioned in the foreground that came to him in a dream. As Christie's Head of Impressionism Olivier Camu explained, he went onto make three paintings of Arnheim, deriving from the proto-Germanic term for Eagle, each with a different motif related to the bird in the pale blue and white.[211]

The title was drawn from a short story by Edgar Allen Poe of the same name, describing a place that did not exist beyond the imagination. Poe wrote:

"Meantime the whole Paradise of Arnheim bursts upon the view. There is a gush of entrancing melody; there is an oppressive sense of strange sweet odor, -- there is a dream -- like intermingling to the eye of tall slender Eastern trees --

bosky shrubberies -- flocks of golden and crimson birds -- lily-fringed lakes -- meadows of violets, tulips, poppies, hyacinths, and tuberoses -- long intertangled lines of silver streamlets -- and, upspringing confusedly from amid all, a mass of semi-Gothic, semi-Saracenic architecture sustaining itself by miracle in mid-air, glittering in the red sunlight with a hundred oriels, minarets, and pinnacles; and seeming the phantom handiwork, conjointly, of the Sylphs, of the Fairies, of the Genii and of the Gnomes."[212]

Rybolovlev sold *Domaine of Arnheim* at Christie's London in 2017 for £10 million—at a significant loss.[213]

However, Eden was also a place for realization. Coaxed by a serpent who tempted her with greatness, Eve, created by a piece of Adam, took a bite of an apple (or pomegranate) of knowledge, and with one taste, she was awakened to the realities of her own shame. Forever after, Adam and Eve could never recreate the magic of their beautiful garden. Humanity was doomed to live out their legacy of understanding, even in its most painful iterations.

Rybolovlev had purchased the early bronze of Eve by Rodin in 2012 for more than €26 million, first conceived in 1881. It was set for the Gates of Hell like *Eternal Spring*, with the voluptuous woman casting her face down and her arms swirling around her, aware of her own condemnation, expelled from paradise. Because the model was pregnant, the work was left unfinished, a powerful testament to gesture and the evolution of knowledge. It was cast at the turn of the century.

On New Year's Day 2015, Rybolovlev attended a luncheon at Eden Rock St. Barths alongside some of the other top art world players.

Sandy Heller, the New York dealer who worked with Steve Cohen and kept his offices near Gagosian, decided to discuss the recent sale of the *Nu couché au coussin bleu*. He turned to the Russian oligarch and said casually, if indiscreetly, "It looks like you bought the Modigliani."

Rybolovlev still did not speak any English or French—just Russian. He replied through a girlfriend, "Which Modigliani? What price did you sell it for?"

"$93.5 million," Heller explained.

But Dmitry had paid $118 million.

According to Rybolovlev's team, this was the moment when he realized he had been cheated far beyond the 2 percent commission. Instead of approximately $2 million, Bouvier had made $24.5. His team began tracing the records, and realized Bouvier's profits were estimated to total between $75 and $80 million overall—close to $1 billion.

The bite of the apple had been taken. Eden's bliss, the Bouvier-Rybolovlev partnership, was officially over. Heller and Rybolovlev followed up with a meeting to sort through the variant prices, matching up documents and rapidly setting the case against Bouvier into motion.

Bersheda and the team immediately went to work, answering round-the-clock calls. The values of all the artworks were traced, the emails pulled, and the mounting case against Yves Bouvier was made around the world. By January 12th, 2015, less than two weeks later, Tetiana Bersheda quietly filed a criminal complaint with Monaco's Palais de Justice.

Everywhere the pair had done business was culpable territory. Just as the divorce battle had spanned the globe, cases against Bouvier were eventually filed in Geneva, Paris, Singapore, Hong Kong, and, by 2018, New York.

They also had steadily moved the art from Singapore to Neocleous in Cyprus prior to taking legal action, throughout the coming month of February in the lead-up to Bouvier's arrest. Bouvier, coordinating the transport, had no idea what was to come.

In charging forward with Bouvier, the Rybolovlev team decried the need for transparency in the art market. But they leveraged secrecy to their own benefit. Valuations and roles shifted in and out of public view for the purposes of safety. Protector, seller, advisor, storer…all of it was washed away by the look in Bouvier's eye, assured enough to skim a billion?

Secondly, what Bouvier had done was deemed fraudulent. But in the art market, with Veblen's conspicuous consumption and the inconsistent valuation process, was it even illegal?

Once the emails were revealed, Bouvier made no attempt to deny that he had taken more money from Rybolovlev than the agreed-upon two percent from his client. Ever the adrenaline junkie, he pressed for the toughest questions.

"Ask me anything," he said, "Even those questions that will make me angry."

It turned out that Bouvier's business practices had history ruffling feathers in court—particularly for his sales practice.

Lorette Jolles was born in 1917. She was educated in Paris, impressively graduating from law school in 1939. Her sister had a PhD in Psychology, and her brother-in-law attended art school, rubbing shoulders with the Parisian artistic elite.

But despite the family life of European privilege, they could not ignore the realities of mounting tension in the lead-up to World War II. As a Jewish family, they faced deportation and imminent death, not to mention the confiscation of all their professional credentials and valuables. They were smuggled out of France to Palestine in a successful effort to escape the Nazis. Lorette was prepared to never be well-off again.

She spent the majority of her life in Montreal, Canada, married to the business-savvy Daniel Shefner. Together the couple made frequent trips to Europe to

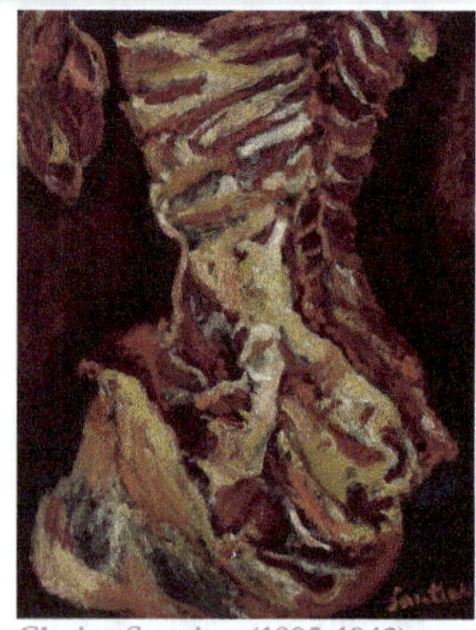

Chaim Soutine (1893-1943)
"Le Boeuf" c. 1923, oil on canvas, 81 x 60 cm © 2019 Artists Rights Society (ARS), New York

appreciate its cultural capital… by then long after the war, in the 1960s, 70s, and 80s. Though Daniel never professed himself to be an aesthete, he had a strong business acumen, and when Lorette's brother-in-law explained the significance of artist Chaim Soutine (1893-1943), he listened. The Shefners purchased the important work *Le Boeuf* in 1981, for what was then an impressive sum of $68,000. It was signed on the lower right, and the family had documents to prove it was legitimate.

It hung in the living room—not in a freeport or a secret vault, but among the family to be enjoyed.

They were close-knit after all, with an undeniable sense of humility. As Lorette's children married and she became a grandmother, then a great-grandmother, she was adored for her kind and gentle nature.

"She didn't have an enemy in the world," said her son, Barry Shefner.

His wife, Susan, echoed this sentiment. After everything she'd been through, Lorette was a thoroughly kind and gentle woman. "She wasn't angry. She never saw bad. Only good. You always wish you have a teacher with your child that only sees good in your child. The child is the most rotten person, but they only see good. That was my mother-in-law."

To be sure, however, the painting was not quite as beloved. "You know, it's wonderful in the gallery," Barry said, "But in a private home, it's a little gory."

Whereas the artists in Rybolovlev's collection preoccupied themselves with the characters they saw in the cafes and the comely women of the whorehouses, *Bon Appetit* reported Soutine was drawn to the world of food. He loved the rawness of life—quite literally, purchasing raw beef from the butcher to study. As it decomposed, Soutine would pour blood over the carcass so it would maintain its color, and injected it with formaldehyde to preserve it. Soutine's studio emitted a stench so foul that his neighbors called the police. When he finished painting the beef, he buried it.[214]

It was noteworthy that the techniques around meat carcasses later denoted a work by Damien Hirst (b. 1965), collected by Steve Cohen, owner of Rybolovlev's portentous Modigliani and client of Sandy Heller, for an astronomical sum. Cohen was the high-profile owner of Hirst's *The Physical Impossibility of Death in the Mind of Someone Living* from 1991, in which a shark was submerged in a formaldehyde-filled tank. Cohen acquired the work in 2004 for £6.5 million, but the shark still decomposed and had to be replaced in 2006.[215]

In 1986, five years after the Shefners purchased the painting, Lorette's husband notified Soutine specialists Maurice Tuchman and Esti Dunow of its existence, so it would be included in the catalogue raisonné of the artist. This comprehensive list of all artists' works proved it was authentic, increased its value, and ensured it was included in discussions around the artist. Daniel Shefner died in 1986, months after he wrote the letter, but Lorette maintained a relationship with the specialists.

The specialists celebrated the *Le Boeuf*, and as a result, the owner. They sent the Jewish Museum to Lorette's home in Montreal, and in 2002, they featured the painting on the cover of a museum exhibition catalogue as marketing for an upcoming auction, implying it might be for sale (it was not). But Lorette didn't mind. She was happy to attend the events, and to acknowledge that she had such a historically important painting. In an unrelated exhibition, Tuchman and Dunow worked with Nahmad Gallery to showcase works by Soutine and Francis Bacon years later, in 2011, prior to the gambling ring scandal.

In March 2004, Tuchman and Dunow spoke of an exceptional opportunity to sell the painting for $800,000 to an anonymous buyer with whom they were allegedly corresponding. In a letter, they told Lorette that "the market for Soutine works was in decline," and presented her with comparables that showed lots unsold at auction (bought-in) or severely undervalued.

They weren't exactly selling the painting as they claimed. Instead, they were working in tandem with two galleries: Galerie Cazeau-Béraudière in Geneva, and an investment company called Longtel Trading.

It was confusing. Galerie Cazeau and Gallery Béraudière were occasionally represented as separate companies, with Jean-Francois Cazeau and Jacques de la Beraudiere considered separate. Longtel was for all intents and purposes a private corporation of "Swiss investors," veiled, as was often the case, in secrecy.

Barry facilitated the sale for his mother, and was happy to oblige Tuchman and Dunow's request. After all, he thought, "They were doing this as an accommodation."

But in the retelling, his wife Susan shouted, "Accommodating? They were getting a huge commission!"

"We didn't know," Barry answered. "I took for granted what they were saying was correct."

Not only had the specialists deliberately obfuscated the identity of the buyer, but they also falsely portrayed the market as declining, when in reality, the painting was worth far more than the paltry $800,000 they offered.

By then, the widowed Lorette was 87. She was thinking of her daughter, Ariela Braun, 57, for whom the family had created a trust in 2002. Besides, she trusted the specialists, with whom she had worked by then for many years.

Lorette decided to move ahead with the sale, at the final price of $1 million. She mentioned to her son, Barry, that she had done so, and while he was unsure she made the right decision, he did not realize the extent of it until he got a call from another relative, down in Washington, D.C. on vacation.

"You'll never guess what I'm standing in front of," his father-in-law said, "That painting that used to hang over the sofa in the living room."

Le Boeuf was hanging in the entrance of the National Gallery of Art in DC— arguably one of the most important museums in America. It appeared that Tuchman had promptly resold the *Le Boeuf* to the museum for double—$2 million— within the year, in November 2004. Though the museum claimed they had purchased the piece from "a French gallery," the provenance on the website clearly stated Tuchman as the owner, as did a sticker he had made for the back of the painting. After a lifetime of studying the artist, it was the only Soutine for which he had ever been able to claim ownership.

Furthermore, the director of the gallery, Earl A. Powell III, had been Maurice Tuchman's boss at the Los Angeles County Museum of Art many years before. Tuchman served as Senior Curator for 27 years at LACMA, but filed a lawsuit against them in 1993 when he was demoted upon Powell's departure for DC. He was rehired and awarded a cash settlement.[216]

When Barry realized the Soutine painting had been sold too low, he bought it back for $1,975,000, in the form of $1,325,000 cash and $650,000 to come over seven years. The extension was due to reaching an understanding that the painting could be displayed at the museum during the transition. Tuchman and Dunow agreed to contribute $210,000 to the repurchase. Barry understood that the museum was "embarrassed" at the terms of the sale, and were OK with making such a small profit. The National Gallery not only raised the value of the painting, which quickly shot from $800,000 to $2 million, but also insured *Le Boeuf* for $10 million—much more on par with the true value of the piece.

In terms of the scandal with Rybolovlev and his later lawsuit against Sotheby's, the power of insurance to prove out a higher value, irrespective of the prices more visible during the transaction, was seen as deeply problematic, as it conflicted with the sale price. In other words, insurance valuation had one motive, and sale price had another.

Furthermore, the Soutines were selling for even more than $10 million at auction. In February 2006, *Le Boeuf écorché*, from the same series, sold for $13.8 million. In February 2007, a portrait of *The Man in the Red Scarf*, sold for $17.2 million.

Lorette Shefner died that year, at 90. Reviewing her estate, Barry discovered the deceptive documents from the art advisors acting as financial experts, and realized the extent that the family had been cheated. The family insisted the work was worth between at least 4 and $6 million. Lorette had been defrauded.

Speaking of the realization, Barry said, "It was up close and personal, because this was my mother…I didn't know the extent of it initially, but money wasn't the motivating factor…it was a matter of getting justice."

The Shefners contacted an attorney immediately, filing the complaint in New York on May 12th, 2008: *The Estate of Lorette Jolles Shefner by and through its executors Mr. Barry Shefner, Ms. Ariela Braun, and Mr. Leon Miller, Barry Shefner and the Ariela Braun 2002 Family Trust against Maurice Tuchman, Esti Dunow, the Galerie Cazeau-Béraudière, the National Gallery of Art, Lontrel Trading, and John Does 1-10.*

Susan fiercely defended the family, shrewd where they were gentle. "I gotta tell you," she said, "I was just told by this jeweler that I'm very tough. So, I'm very tough. But you have to be tough to win this! Are you kidding me?"

And their claim was successful. The Shefners were able to recover their losses around *Le Boeuf* in court.

"The proof is in the pudding," Susan said. "They gave it back."

The courts returned the painting to the Shefner family at the full value of the original sale, buy-back, plus legal fees and other expenses. It was resold at auction in 2015—not for $1 million, $6 million, $10 million, or even $17.2 million: It was $28 million: 28 times the price Tuchman and Dunow had paid Lorette in 2004.[217]

The Shefners had set a precedent in cases of defrauding in the art world, with the only retribution case of its scale for anything other than the Holocaust (most notably in the case of *Portrait of Adele Bloch-Bauer,* pg. 69).
But in the process, they learned quite a bit about art market fraud.

"I was the happiest person in the world to pay tax on the Soutine when it was auctioned," Barry said, "It was the happiest day of my life to write the check to the Canadian government. Why is that such a problem?"

By the time of the auction, many years after the first realization, they were well-versed in the complexities of deception and corruption.

And that was due, at least in part, to Yves Bouvier.

As a factor in the settlement for the case regarding the Soutine, the Shefners were awarded a painting by Willem de Kooning, *Woman in the Garden II,* 1967. The family viewed the de Kooning at the New York Armory Show, and decided they would like to acquire it from the gallerists who cheated them.

That was where Bouvier stepped in. Through a company called Diva Fine Arts, S. A., he explained that he was the true owner of the painting, and that it was not able to be given to the Shefners.

Bouvier commented on his implication in the case, which surfaced during the mounting conflict with Rybolovlev.

"Ok Shefner, that's easy," Bouvier said. "It's a conflict between the seller and the Parisian gallery."

The issue did not concern him. He was just a witness.

But when Susan spoke of Bouvier, her voice was thick with conviction and intensity. Her tone had changed, and she was at once furtively angry and coolly clear in her certainty of his misconduct.

"I want to explain this to you," she said, "You listen."

She barely paused for breath.

"He fought us, spent a couple million dollars, fighting us on a million-dollar judgement. Why would he do that? For what? You know why? Because the people whose money he's hiding are the scum of the earth. And he is terrified that he's going to walk off the curb and get hit by a taxi if he doesn't *hide their money!* So he can't let one go. Because if he shows weakness with one, he can show weakness with all!"
She continued later, "We're the only people that won with Bouvier. You know that, right? Because he couldn't play with me."

Through his lawyer, Bouvier confirmed that the legal fees paid as third-party intervenor in the Shefner proceeding in New York State court were a fraction of what Susan Shefner suggests and were commensurate with the value of the painting that was the subject of the litigation.

Lawyer Daniel Levy noted that a review of the court docket shows that the appellate court in New York dismissed all of the claims that the Shefners made against Bouvier as having no legal basis.

During the proceedings, it was revealed that Bouvier controlled a company Diva Fine Arts S.A. and a company Diva Fine Arts Inc. One was in Panama and the other was in the Virgin Islands. To the plaintiffs, they were methods of moving and concealing massive sums of money, untraceable to the Swiss government. To Bouvier, having various companies in various jurisdictions is not an indication of illegal conduct and such assertions are baseless. The use of companies in Panama, the Virgin Islands, and elsewhere is rather typical in the art market.

According to Rybolovlev's case, not only had Bouvier skimmed what the oligarch deemed to be the approved commissions, but apparently, he had not reported the values to Switzerland. As a Singaporean resident, the practice was viable, but the sales Bouvier made to Rybolovlev as a Swiss citizen prior to 2009 may be another matter.

The massive Panama Papers scandal revealed that the firm Mossack Fonseca was embroiled in a huge scandal that involved 11 million internal documents with everyone from the King of Saudi Arabia to Nahmad Gallery, to Dmitry Rybolovlev himself with Xitrans Finance LTD.[218] Rybolovlev's connection to offshore companies was brought up during his divorce proceedings, as his wife Elena was convinced he was using the companies to hide his valuables from her.

A statement from the Rybolovlev family office during the 2016 scandal formally denied these rumors. "The use of Xitrans Finance as a holding entity to constitute a remarkable art collection has been publicly disclosed in numerous publications worldwide and is perfectly legitimate," they wrote.[219]

Apart from the companies uncovered during the proceedings, in 2012, the Shefners followed a trail and contacted the Landeskriminalamt, or LKA, the equivalent of the German FBI. German art forger Wolfgang Beltracchi (born Wolfgang Fischer, 1951) was creating counterfeit paintings from the time he first faked a Picasso at age 14.

Together with his wife Helene Beltracchi (the love of his life, whose name he took), Wolfgang schemed auction houses, dealers, and collectors for decades. The couple did everything right: not only was Wolfgang a talented art forger, mimicking the Degenerate art of Max Ernst and Fernand Leger, but his wife crafted elaborate provenance alleging her family's safe stow of Jewish paintings during World War II in Germany, even going so far as to fake a photo of her 'grandmother' at home with the paintings. It was Helene herself, in costume, in a doctored photograph.

They fooled Christie's, the Centre Pompidou in Paris, and even the actor Steve Martin.

But some of the Beltracchi masterpieces were sold through DivaFine Arts.

"With Beltracchi, I was one of the losers." Bouvier added later, "I bought works from very reputable dealers with certificates of authenticity from recognized experts. I never had any contact with Beltracchi or his wife. I just purchased paintings in view of reselling them, but they proved to be fakes!"

Despite his talent with forgery, Beltracchi was also a gifted artist when he was not imitating better-known masters. One painting, photographed by *Vanity Fair* writer Joshua Hammer, was called *The Fall of the Angels*. In the piece, a purple, demonic figure fell crashing in a horrific scream, head upside-down and mouth agape in violent hues of red and violet. Beneath him, a crowd in pale blues, tans and greens looked on, faded and dispassionate as they blurred into the background.[220]

The motif came from Catholicism: the devil himself was a fallen angel, who rejected God and was damned to hell.[221] Fallen angels were those who fell from grace, and Beltracchi's depiction was as literal as it was figurative. Not only was the demon falling through the canvas, but the world of mischievous and criminal art players had fallen apart around him.

However, Beltracchi was bold and confident in interviews. He boasted that he had faked 50 some-odd artists,[222] and that when he was obligated to notify the buyers of the forgeries, none of his works were returned.[223]

As Bouvier's reputation plummeted thanks to the media efforts of Rybolovlev's lawyer, Tetiana Bersheda, who went full force into her media onslaught against Bouvier, and echoed what she contended was largescale criminality. Speaking of his fraud with Rybolovlev, she told *Monaco Matin*, "This case is the art market what Madoff was to finance in 2008."[224] Bouvier says that, apart from Rybolovlev, no other client has ever made a complaint against him. In addition, Bersheda has been charged and is being sent to trial in Monaco in December 2019 for defaming Bouvier.

The Shefners were also convinced that Rybolovlev got "ripped off," Barry said, "But unfortunately, used Russian tactics to try and get back" at Bouvier.

Bouvier spoke of computer hacking and private detectives Rybolovlev hired to follow him around for millions of dollars, and questioned their legality. He snapped photos of them as they followed him and carried on with his life.

Tania Rappo was skeptical of Bouvier's criminality, not least because of animosity towards Bersheda, but especially after the divorce request came to light.

"Now, I believe in coincidences," Rappo said, "But you know, there are some coincidences that one has to study very carefully—very carefully. How come two months after they had that [divorce] scandal, he became the worst criminal in the world?"

The ultimate question was: how could Rybolovlev not have known? Where were the trustees? With his hands-on approach, was it possible that he had blindly trusted, or was it, as Bouvier claimed, all tied to his refusal to move ahead with blackmail during the divorce?

"It's absurd to say that they had not even verified the prices were correct," Rappo's lawyer Frank Michel said. "He determined the price…He chose the paintings himself."

Particularly in Singaporean and Swiss courts, they spun around trying to trace the relationships. Why were sales contracts no longer being used after the first four sales? Was Bouvier an art advisor or art seller?

Bouvier later explained that Russian culture was beholden to contracts, while the Russian team spoke of the importance of countenance and tacit trust.

There were no clear answers.

Both he and Rappo were certain of their innocence, in that they had done nothing illegal. "I received commissions like *everybody* in that business," Rappo said, drawing out the words 'every body' with perfect diction, "My commission on the totality of the stuff is around five percent."

Rappo cited the sale of *Nu au coussin bleu*, the very same sale discussed by Heller and Rybolovlev at Eden Rock. During the legal proceedings, she saw in the filings that Joachim Pissarro, Camille Pissarro's grandson and the author of the Rybolovlev catalogue essays, had received a $4 million commission for facilitating the sale between Heller and Bouvier.

"No one bothers him!" She said emphatically.

"It seems to be very normal that he receives that commission, but for me, it's abnormal. So you see, that is a very important point."

Speaking of Rappo, Bouvier later said, "The commission continues for the decorator even if they're not in the room."

But in February 2015, neither party had any idea of the scandals mounting against them. And Bouvier had still not yet been paid the last $50 million for the $222 million Rothko acquisition. He never would be.

Rybolovlev innocently invited the dealer to settle the payment at La Belle Epoque, his home in Monaco. Bouvier dutifully chartered the jet and flew to Nice, France. There were no airports in the principality, so there was no way to stop him immediately upon arrival off the plane in France when it came to jurisdiction.

Then he arrived in Monaco and headed into danger.

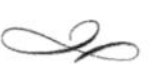

Even from the exterior, the Belle Epoque apartment was resplendent. By the standards of private islands and secret entrances, it was indiscreet: the building was easily accessible from Avenue d'Ostende, and upon entry, two sweeping staircases led up and up to the cavernous rooms of the formidable building.

There were two bank headquarters inside as well: BNP Paribas and HSBC. Rybolovev had such a strong relationship with HSBC that there was a trading room in the back of the bank devoted almost entirely to his accounts.

Bouvier arrived by chauffeur for their appointment at 9am, one hour earlier than planned. He walked along the water to kill time, taking in the fresh air and admiring the large boats. Monaco was almost always sunny with mild weather, even in the winter, and the nearby water's edge was as pleasant as it was beautiful.

It was February 25th, 2015, exactly a year to the day of Elena's arrest in Cyprus. Yet when Bouvier arrived in the lobby, he was still alarmed to see 10 policemen.

"I thought they were bodyguards," he said, "So I walked towards them!"

Then they all flashed their police IDs, and explained they were there to arrest him. Still, though, he was in disbelief. Perhaps he was caught up in an investigation into Rybolovlev's activities, he thought. He never imagined they were after his own.

It was also, he felt, an excessive amount of police. "There was no need for 10 people to stop me, especially in Monaco." Bouvier said, "When you have an appointment at a place with one entrance, you might say that's a little excessive."

The police placed him in handcuffs, though the cuffs were carefully concealed as he was escorted out of the building.

"That's polite," the author said.

"That's Monaco," Bouvier answered.

They brought him to be read his rights (under the Monaco legal system) then left him to wait in a locked, windowless room with a stiff bed. Not only was he completely caught off guard, but the subsequent proceedings were a form of extended bewilderment. He had no watch to track the time, no pen or paper to track his thoughts. Just as Rybolovlev had been during his time in Perm, he was literally and figuratively in the dark.

His mind raced. Maybe Rybolovlev had been arrested, too. Maybe they thought Bouvier was involved in something his client was doing. They were at his home, after all, not Bouvier's.

"It was like you see in the movies," he said.

Then they asked him "silly" questions: name, profession, education, residence. When asked his profession, he said businessman. Not art seller, not shipper.

"Because I do many things," he said matter-of-factly. "I am a *homme d'affairs*."

They asked him if he wanted a lawyer. It took him a full five minutes to say yes, because he was so sure that this would blow over. But eventually, Charles Lecuyer arrived. He was provided by the principality on Bouvier's behalf.

But he insisted he was not afraid.

"I wasn't proud," he said, "Maybe I wasn't reassured. But I did not have a sentiment of fear."

He was released on a bail of €10 million, and flew commercial home to his girlfriend and a small group of close friends, who waited somberly in Geneva

From a legal standpoint, it was strange that Bouvier would be stopped in Monaco. He claimed he had no major business there apart from his dealings with the principality's beloved Rybo.

The link was Tania Rappo.

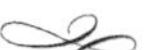

Tania Rappo lived in an apartment building called La Radieuse with her husband, Olivier, by then her partner of more than 25 years. In French, 'La Radieuse' was the feminine of "The Radiant One," and Rappo certainly lived up to her building's name. In her late sixties, she was still as strong and joyful as ever, passionate about beauty and truth, determined to uphold her reputation despite what was to come.

The night before Rappo was placed under investigation in February 2015, she had dinner with the Rybolovlevs for the last time. Rybolovlev pushed her to drink more and more, rather forcefully urging her to have fun.

"Have another vodka!" He kept saying.

But Bersheda was illegally recording her, as she confirmed that perhaps the art dealer had indeed overcharged her friend.

"When I replay the film in my head," Rappo told *Monaco Matin*, "It is so clear he knew I would be arrested."

Just as with Bouvier at La Belle Epoque, a pack of guards awaited her in the lobby of La Radieuse. They escorted her to her interrogation as well, where they questioned her at length about the so-called kickbacks she had received from Bouvier.

She held her head up high. She knew that she was dealing with a dangerous man, standing firm in her conviction of her own innocence.

Unlike the two "pathologically private" men doing business, Rappo claimed she had made no attempt to hide her financials. She had received her money primarily to a single HSBC account in Monaco, with corresponding paperwork clearly citing each painting and the amount due to her.

Furthermore, not everything presented to her during the interrogation was accurate. The investments she and her husband had made in properties were switched into Bouvier's name. Was it inefficiency or corruption? Either way, it didn't make sense. A policewoman called HSBC bank to verify, puzzled.

Rappo continued to explain that the papers were false. She was convinced she was being framed, but she was equally convicted in her sense of security.

She cited the French saying used around destroying reputations. "When you want to get rid of a dog," she said, "Say it has rabies."

It was her favorite way to describe Rybolovlev. She had used almost the exact same quotations exactly three years earlier, for a feature in *Town & Country*.[225]

Regardless, her resilience was unprecedented. She was the only person in the story—not Elena, not Dmitry Rybolovlev, not Bouvier, not even Crutchfield, or any of the men who worked in the freeport—who revealed a deeper passion for art as a saving grace. For Bouvier, it had been a source of passion, and a driving force in his business dealings into the billions. For Rybolovlev, it had been an investment strategy during a difficult divorce, and for his wife, it had been a way to gain entry into elite society and learn about the world around her. For Crutchfield, it had been a mechanism for joyful discovery and exchange. But for Rappo, art was religion.

She had been raised by a single father in Eastern Bloc-Bulgaria and faced many hardships. Her great escape had been translation, learning French, and being a voracious reader. She had worked in publishing in Bulgaria, translating previously banned books from the French at the fall of Communism

Sixtine Crutchfield compared her strengtl

Wind.

When presented with this, Rappo only alluded to her personal struggles. But she did not shy away from describing her unfaltering courage.

"God never gives you, as Madame Kennedy says, a cross harder than you can carry. I don't have such an extraordinary life," she said, gazing out the window to the Monaco sea from her parlor at La Radieuse. "What I can tell you is that what saved my life in moments of difficulty was art and nature. Those are the two things which always give me energy. That's what kept me alive."

She paused, then switched into French, turning back from the window with a fierce and unwavering gaze. Her eyes, like Bouvier's, were light, but they glowed with a turquoise blue-green that was striking against her other, darker features.

"It's difficult to destroy me."

She suddenly revealed a gold cross beneath her back blouse. She was religious, she explained, but not practicing. Her nuclear family was a bit like the Rothko Chapel in Houston: she was Bulgarian Orthodox, her husband was a practicing Catholic, her daughter had converted to Judaism, and her son had married a Buddhist. But like Mark Rothko, she understood the implicit power of spirituality, and its power to transcend any one community.

"There is art, nature, and faith. It's these three things that are the sources of life, of the force of resistance, if you will." She thought back to the Rybolovlev's power. "There had been no hope over three years…all the systems worked for him and his lies. Yet I knew, and somewhere, I had a hope that could not be defined with words. It was just a profound tranquility. And it's so absurd…it couldn't be defined, but I did not despair.

And you see? There was a miracle."

24

ALONE

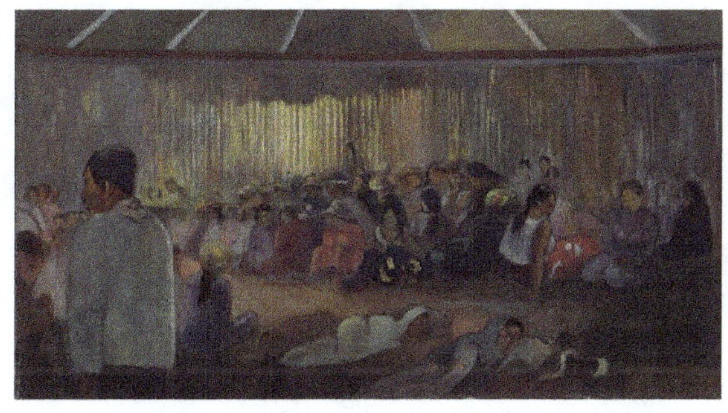

Paul Gaugin (1848-1903)
Te fare hymenée, 1892, oil on canvas, 73 x 92 cm

RYBOLOVLEV PURCHASED two works by Paul Gauguin at the very beginning and the very end of his business relationship with Bouvier. They were bookends on the Modigliani nudes and water serpents of Monet and Gustav Klimt, indicative of a descent—and possibly, a disengagement—into the depth of hedonistic beauty.

Paul Gauguin (1848-1903) was a painter who celebrated the joys of life in all its forms. Vibrant colors, travel, and women were all insatiable interests of his, and he spent a substantial portion of his life immersed in them, much to the dismay of his bourgeois French family.

Gauguin had never set out to be an artist, instead developing his skills as a sailor in his teens making wood carvings on the sea.[226] He failed at many things, including art investment,[227] before embracing his soulful destiny as a lifelong traveler, explorer, and well-known painter. He had gone from banker to art collector, to finally picking up the brush himself after Impressionism was a solidified category of French painting. With his own unique set of experiences, he was differentiated not just in his personality, but with his work. Camille Pissarro fostered his love of art collecting, and encouraged him to explore his own creativity. From there, Gauguin became part of the broader Impressionist collective.

In his constant pursuit of the beautiful and the unknown, the artist explored many Biblical motifs: of a brightly colored Jesus in *The Yellow Christ*, and of the garden of Eden in *Where Do We Come From? What Are We? Where are We Going?* But he became an icon to other artists in the Rybolovlev collection—among them, Pablo Picasso—for his colorful depictions of Polynesian women.

Rybolovlev purchased *Te fare hymenée (La maison des chants)* in 2008 for €54 million. The work was painted in 1892 during Gaugin's first stint in Tahiti, where he went onto travel many times. The 'house of song' featured in this painting was a testament to compositional prowess rarely seen in Gauguin's portraits, allowing the strokes of the architecture to frame a blur of expressive women. On the far right, a woman with long hair in red sat with her back to the crowd, while a woman in purple at her side cast her gaze down, lost in contemplation.

It was a scene as festive as it was calm, alluding to a time for both joy and introspection. Gauguin was blurring his own line between dream and reality, exploring the euphoria brought on by his travels through the colors and compositions of his paintings. They danced with his brushstrokes and his heartfelt love of the land.

Prior depictions of his Danish wife, Mette, from his early artistic practice in the 1870s were rigid and appropriate. The Rybolovlev catalogue showed a slick white marble bust of her icy expression now held in the Courtauld Institute of Art in London, so far from the vivacity later beloved in his paintings. The catalogue also cited Gauguin's disparaging attitude towards European life when he saw it adapted globally:

> "It was Europe—the Europe which I had thought to shake off—and that under the aggravating circumstances of colonial snobbism, and the imitation, grotesque even to the point of caricature, of our customs, fashions, vices, and absurdities of civilization."

By the 1890s, the artist had abandoned a wife and five children in France for extended travel in the isles of French Polynesia, pushing away from capital cities and into coastal villages. But his lust was for more than just new places. In stark contrast to his life in Europe, Gauguin's exoticized, full-figured forms of the native women were his primary focus. As he adjusted, he even incorporated their language into the title of many of his works. Another excerpt from Gauguin explained:

> "I am feeling better every day; I can already understand the language quite well; my neighbors—three live close by, the other much further away—almost view me as one of them; walking daily barefoot on the stones means that my feet are used to the ground; my body, which is naked more often than not, is no longer afraid of the sun; little by little, step by step, civilization is peeling away from me...All the joys—animal and human—of a free life are mine. I have escaped everything that is artificial, conventional, customary. I am entering into the truth, into nature."

Yet as Gauguin grew more comfortable in his lifestyle, so too did his lens on the local women. He took native brides in each place between the ages of 13 and 14, and was thusly accused of pedophilia in future reviews.

Many art historians, proclaimed as feminists or otherwise, addressed Gaugin's problematic attitudes towards women, and the complexities of a colonial era where this man without borders or boundaries was able to thrive. As his artistic practice heightened in parallel to his lifestyle, the woman in red became a motif recurrent throughout his work.

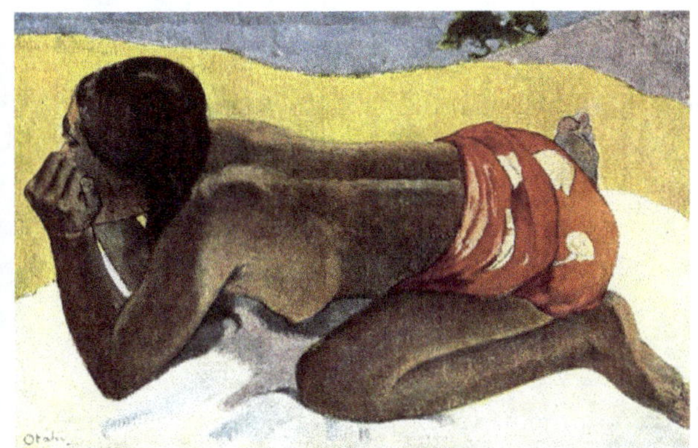

Paul Gaugin (1848-1903
Otahi, 1893, oil on canvas 50 x 73 cm (20 in. x 29 in.)

A strong example of this was *Otahi*, which translated simply to "Alone." Rybolovlev purchased it for $120 million in 2013.

Otahi featured the increasingly common trope in his work of a woman turned away, exposing her breasts and back on her knees. The Rybolovlev catalogue pointed to a more menacing overtone to this kind of work, addressing the vulnerability of the women in his compositions turning away, perhaps in fear. Another scene of his girlfriend Tehura, called *Spirit of the Dead Watching*, recalled a moment where she was immobilized and terrorized, lying inexplicably stretched across the bed. He later abandoned her when she was pregnant.

But there was another side of the story. His British descendent, Mette Gaugin, gave an interview to *The Independent* following brutal criticism of his Tate retrospective. She cited stock market problems and a troubled marriage in a country where he did not speak the language (Denmark), and a sense of wanderlust and affinity with native peoples that propelled him to seek a different lifestyle. Citing Spanish heritage, he felt at peace among the Polynesians.[228]

Others argued that the very controversy that disquiets art lovers was what imbued the paintings with their captivating historical impact. It was the not knowing, the uncertainty, and the delicate frequency of fear that were enduringly interesting.[229]

In any case, the loneliness of *Otahi* was undeniable. The woman's face was obscured by a dark palm, with only her breast and leg catching the light. Surrounding her were bright colors to contrast her rich skin and hair, but they almost served to overpower her, intoxicated by her own sense of knowing and unknowing, forever masked to the viewer.

Gauguin himself was aware of his own failures. He wrote:

"I was sometimes good and do not congratulate myself for that. I was often bad and do not regret that. I look at all these saints, I do not see sign of life, and I am filled with doubt. They make sense in cathedral alcoves, but only there…All my doubts have vanished. I am and always will be a savage."

The title of "Alone," referred both to the subject of the painting and to a life of solitude. Gaugin's excesses and voyages started to unravel when he was diagnosed with a condition later thought to be syphilis. His golden period from 1892-1893 was plagued by suffering: coughing fits brought on by the poorly treated illness, financial problems, and being forced to return home to sleepy and unpromising France. By 1897, he had huge sores on his legs, with many on the islands taking him for a leper.[230]

Upon his death in 1903, his belongings were auctioned in France. *The Independent* reported that one of his paintings sold for just two francs…compared to his sewing machine, at 80.

Rybolovlev sold *Otahi* for under $50 million in 2015. It was less than half what he had originally paid Bouvier.

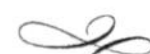

The Bouvier Affair quickly became a media frenzy. Yves Bouvier was painted as a sly thief, emblematic of deep-seated corruption in the world of freeports. In a public relations initiative spearheaded by Tetiana Bersheda, Rybolovlev was a powerful man blinded by trust, eager for transparency in the art market. Rappo was a destructive intermediary, with one tabloid implicating her criminal activity as far as the Corsican mafia.

It bordered on the ridiculous.

"I had a dentist who was a Corsican," Rappo said, "That's about all I know."

The Rybolovlev media team was large and cautious, relying heavily on source material and accounts of friends and colleagues to avoid presenting the oligarch with something he did not want to be a part of. Bouvier, however, emailed freely, quietly facilitating introductions with his most outspoken allies. Rappo invited journalists to her home, with prominently displayed photos of her grandchildren and family vacations. Both Bouvier and Rappo acted in ways that frustrated their lawyers, who begged them not to give any more interviews. But they relentlessly professed their innocence.

As the affair took shape, what had begun as an example of distrust and disingenuity in the art market took on a more nefarious element as a quest for power and control. Even during his time with Bouvier, Rybolovlev turned a shade of grey at the thought of marketing and exhibiting his works. But during the case, the Rybolovlev team stopped publishing the resale values of the artwork involved in the Bouvier case, because it served to refute their argument that the trust had been cheated.

Sandy Heller, Cohen's art dealer, who had spoken to Rybolovlev at Eden Rock, was hired to manage new and old artwork in the Russian's collection. He defended his client to a detriment, offering values of artworks far below what Bouvier and the Sotheby's insurance records provided.

The attempts to trace the values of the work were increasingly complex.

"It used to be that the only place where you could get an honest read on what was going on with the auction results, but of course, that's no longer the case…" art dealer Robert Simon said, "With this world of guarantees and third-parties, irrevocable bids and loans and all that, it's not as if the auction prices are necessarily the true barometer of what something sells for."

In one example, in the beginning of the litigation, Heller had estimated the value of the da Vinci at a mere $80 million.

Les Noces de Pierrette, one of Rybolovlev's earliest acquisitions through Bouvier, was sold in 2018 to Bernard Arnault. He was the richest man in France (and the fourth richest man in the world), known in the art world for his Fondation LVMH in Paris, designed by Jean Nouvel. Though it was only said in whispers, the purchase was apparently millions more than the original price.

Such was the complexity of an art collection. At first, in Rybolovlev's fury at Bouvier's betrayal, he was eager to sell all the work as swiftly as possible. But working with the elites in the art world, he was still a businessman. There was no reason not to respect and augment the value of some of the world's most famous paintings.

It was impossible to finitely quantify the value of a painting, since it was so dependent on the perspective of the buyer and the network around it. Instead, the ultimate problem was the question of transparency.

The case between Bouvier and Rybolovlev was initially intended, according to Rybolovlev's associate as "a kind of trigger" for the unregulated and fairly experimental strategic art investment market.

"It doesn't matter who the winner is," Rybolovlev's associate explained in January 2016, "The market will be diminished specifically and some control over the freeports will be installed."

A series of exposés that year in Mediapart.fr drew parallels to suggest that Bouvier's projects around the world were deliberately copied at the Russian freeport, Vladivostock. Rybolovlev had ties to the area, all the while as Bouvier was rapidly losing ground as 'The Freeport King.' The case against Bouvier was fostered in Monaco in February, and the announcement of Vladivostock's inception was publicized in Russia by July, piloted by Rybolovlev's longtime colleague from the Uralkali sinkhole crisis, Yury Trutnev.

Trutnev was elected Mayor of Perm in the pivotal year of 1996, around when Rybolovlev spent time in prison for murder. He was Governor of the Perm Region and Natural Resources Minister in 2008 during a mining scandal faced by Rybolovlev's company, Uralkali. By 2016, Trutnev was Deputy Prime Minister and Presidential Plenipotentiary Envoy to the Far Eastern District. The defense believed Rybolovlev was discrediting his art dealer to gain control of the Eastern freeport region, moving Chinese and Korean business through Russia instead.

In addition to alcohol distribution that had been the bread and butter of freeports in Europe for many years, diamonds were a major market, especially in Russia and Asia. The secret world of extensive luxury led as far as Zambia, where Rybolovlev was often traveling in the months leading up to the sale of the da Vinci. He offended local airport staff by refusing to shake their hands.

The local newspaper, *The Zambian Eye*, quoted one staffer. "They could not come out of the plane, and when they did, they were just spraying themselves with anti-mosquito spray," He said laughing, "Very afraid of dying. I don't envy that kind of life."

Though there was no confirmed connection, Israeli-Russian diamond magnate Lev Leviev purchased Grizzly emerald mine in Zambia in 2017,[231] but by 2018, was caught in a smuggling scandal. Leviev returned to Moscow for questioning that December.[232]

The photo from *The Zambian Eye* featured a tall blonde that could easily have been Daria Strokous, who was confirmed to be Dmitry Rybolovlev's girlfriend in late 2018. She had published photos of herself and friends languishing on *My Anna* that summer. Her Wikipedia page said she had even spent part of her early childhood in Benin, Africa.[233]

With her pale skin and wide-set blue eyes, she was almost hauntingly beautiful. But Strokous had a sense of darkness beneath her fair exterior. An aspiring actress beyond her modeling career, she explained in a 2011 interview on a fashion channel that her supporting role in *Contagion* was just the beginning of her exploration of character.

"All my favorite movie characters, are usually, you know, the villains," she said, "I don't know what it is. I think it's more…it's kind of more complicated inside, you know, how it feels inside. Because when you're good you're always, you know, kind of, same. You're like really sweet, or you're saving the world. The villain is a bit different because you have to have some kind of, why you're doing. The reason for that."[234]

Whereas Rybolovlev had been kicked out of his wife's home on Christmas Eve 2008, ten years later, he spent the holiday with Strokous, cozily watching movies.

Just as had been the case with the divorce, the proceedings would drag on for years. Rybolovlev had "cut the oxygen" for Bouvier: his anonymity. Without the discretion and secrecy he had prized, the ability to do business suffered greatly. He was forced to sell the family business of Natural Le Coultre to André Chenue,[235] abandon his project for a freeport in Lichtenstein, and halt plans for a Paris "Art City" called R4, planned to be designed by Jean Nouvel. At first, it seemed, he was ruined.[236]

"The idea was to destroy me in all domains," Bouvier said. "The idea was to hurt me."

He was not entirely devoid of business, however. He maintained a facility within the state-owned Geneva Freeport, and his Singapore operation was still open for business. Because of the way freeports were structured, other vendors were still able to use the spaces. One source suspected that Rybolovlev was still using the Singapore Freeport Bouvier owned, just with a different vendor.

Whatever Rybolovlev's motivations—disloyalty, freeport control, legitimacy in art—it wasn't long before his own methodology of imprisonment was called into question.

This was the miracle to which Rappo had referred.

In subsequent proceedings, proof that the team at HSBC was involved in preparation for Bouvier and Rappo's arrests provoked a criminal investigation into Monaco's Minister of Justice Philippe Narmino, Narmino's son, and a rapidly expanding suite of Monaco's police, banking professionals, and beyond. Bersheda had apparently built relationships with the professionals in order to prepare the case against Bouvier, and to maintain control in the region. When it was discovered she had illegally recorded her conversations with Rappo, the investigating magistrate was able to uncover previously deleted texts on Bersheda's phone regarding these cultivated ties, thus demonstrating enough to move forward with allegations on corruption, influence trafficking, and bribery.

Rybolovlev himself was implicated, although he had a habit of refusing to answer questions.

10 men were charged in the trials that followed for what was known in the press as Monaco-gate. It was not the first instance of backlash against the Russian's team for misconduct. As early as 2015, Bersheda's recording from dinner with Tania Rappo was considered illegal, and seen as a way to tackle the dangerous oligarch's suspect approach to justice.

Michel had eagerly told *Town & Country* writer Vicky Ward at the time, "Rybolovlev will be charged, and then there will be a trial involving one of the most powerful men here. Monaco has never seen the like."

But Monaco-gate was on a much larger scale. Philippe Narmino, had exchanged extensive text messages with Rybolovlev's team, and even spent time at his home in Gstaad immediately prior to Bouvier's arrest. HSBC Associate Director Gerard Cohen, a longtime associate of the late Edmund Safra, was also reportedly present at Eden Rock when Rybolovlev claimed he first realized he had been betrayed.

Meanwhile, Bersheda had worked to maintain her relationships with many people in Monaco. Like Narmino, she was also a fixture at Gstaad.

She sent hundreds of texts to Narmino Jr., the minister's working for the HSBC bank that adjoined Rybolovlev's home, as well as the Minister of the Interior Paul Masseron and Jean-Pierre Dreno, among others. Some of them were personal and intimate, wishing people well and sending gifts, and others were preparatory in the lead-up to Bouvier's arrest. Tickets to AS Monaco games, weekends at the chalet…the generosity was extensive. While Narmino retired in the midst of the ensuing scandal, Masseron had left the force during the ongoing case against Bouvier and Rappo—and joined up at Rybolovlev's private bank 11 days later.

"They have been working," Rappo said. "They're a team."

The case kept expanding. Christophe Haget, Frédéric Fusari, Regis Asso—all were men who worked for the police force, and all were held accountable for Rybolovlev's tactics, either in its investigation or its incrimination.

Rappo's lawyer alleged that she was incriminated solely to ensure that the case was conducted in Monaco.

Rappo's lawyer Frank Michel was decrying this injustice as early as December 2016. "What is very, very strange is that when you take the dossier, Tania Rappo is not mentioned in the complaint," he said. "Nor in the following declarations made by Rybolovev, by his employees. No one said, 'Tania Rappo took commissions,' et. cetera, et. cetera, et. cetera. Moreover, the previous Attorney General who we suspected had favored Rybolovlev ordered investigations into Tania Rappo's account. He didn't have any reason. And his investigations showed that she had commissions, which she never hid."

Far from it: she requested invoices from Bouvier to legitimize the funds at the bank. After all, they were into the millions, and she wanted to keep accurate records.

Michel explained that the defense alleged Rybolovlev knew perfectly well that Rappo had been receiving remunerations throughout, and had mobilized the Monegasque authorities to look into her accounts knowing what they would find. Of course, they saw the records of what she had received.

"Why bring Rappo into the dossier?" Michel explained, "For reasons of territorial jurisdiction…there was no rapport with Monaco."

Fraud and money laundering investigations were started against Rappo. By accepting Bouvier's allegedly fraudulently obtained funds, they suggested, she had essentially cleaned his dirty money.

"In this manner, they artificially created a link so that the penal procedure could be done in Monaco, because Mr. Rybolovlev was persuaded that in Monaco, with the justice system, he could do whatever he liked."

Speaking of Rybolovlev's culpability, Bouvier said, "I think people are coming to discover the true face of this man."

Ultimately, Rappo was placed under investigation for just money laundering, while Bouvier being investigated for both money laundering and fraud.

"But that could change," Michel said.

Things changed constantly. Michel stopped working with Rappo following his statements due to an undisclosed dispute, but joined Bouvier's team thereafter.

The case in Singapore was thrown out, claiming the proceedings should have been handled in Geneva. Rappo said the judge told her, "It's not criminal to be lucky."

Despite attempted cases against Bouvier in Monaco, France, Geneva, Singapore, Hong Kong, and even Gstaad, many were either thrown out, or no charges had been brought against him.

Detainments and inquiries began in summer 2018.[237] As a result, Rybolovlev's team could not comment on the ongoing investigation. Rybolovlev also refused to answer more than 600 questions during the proceedings. Then he sought refuge in Moscow.

After the Uralkali sinkholes resulted in tension with Putin, Rybolovlev had portrayed himself as someone who had few ties to Russia, with some even considering him something of an outlier from the world of oligarchs—a dissident.

But Rappo, whose command of the Russian language had allowed her to become close friends with the family initially, was also well versed in the complex world of Russian political subterfuge. She referred to Mikhail Khodorkovsky, a Russian billionaire who fell out of favor with Putin, and ended up imprisoned at a camp in Siberia. Conditions for Khodorkovsky were atrocious: one morning in 2006, he woke up to a slash across his face, covered in his own blood.[238]

Despite the scandal in Monaco, Rybolovlev had managed to stay safe, and was able to return to Russia without incident.

"If you are dissident, you don't leave Russian with seven billion," Rappo said, "You go like Khodorkovsky, in a camp. They take *all* your business, and you don't have a penny. That's what a dissident is. Someone who pretends to be a dissident who leaves Russia and an enormous catastrophe to buy Monaco Football Club, that's not a dissident."

25

GATHERING ALL POWER

ON OCTOBER 2ND, 2018, Saudi Arabian journalist Jamal Khashoggi walked into the Saudi consulate in Turkey. He had fallen out of favor with the Saudi ruling family, despite years on good terms, namely because he disapproved of the King's son, 32-year-old Crown Prince Mohammed bin Salman. As the tension mounted, he fled to the United States, where he wrote for *The Washington Post*, increasingly outspoken in his condemnation of the state. Under 'MBS,' Khashoggi decried throughout the media, Saudi Arabia would never be a democracy. He was "acting like Putin," and becoming a "Supreme Leader."[239]

"I still see him as a reformer," Khashoggi said of MBS in an Al-Jazeera interview with British media personality Mehdi Hassan that March, "But he is gathering all power within his hand. And it would be much better for him to allow a breathing space for critique, for Saudi intellectuals, Saudi writers, Saudi media, to debate. The most important, needed transformation in the country."

Though he was wary of returning to a homeland subsequently steeped in danger, Khashoggi was eager to obtain divorce papers in order to remarry his new fiancé, Hatice Cengiz, and felt assured that the treatment he received in Turkey was protecting him. As Cengiz waited outside the consulate for her soon-to-be husband, she could not imagine that he would never walk back out.

In the reports that followed, it was revealed that Khashoggi was murdered inside the Turkish consulate by a team of envoys sent from Saudi Arabia. After a struggle, they gave him a lethal injection and smuggled the body out of the building—all while Cengiz stayed waiting. She decried the injustice in the months that followed in reports around the globe, defaming the Crown Prince and the blind eye in diplomatic relations.

"This is a Saudi journalist..." Hassan said on MSNBC after Khashoggi's death. "This is not some Democratic opposition member, dissident."

On November 4th, 2017, MBS had launched an anticorruption campaign, set to recover $100 billion in 'ill-gotten' funds.[240] This ended with 200 businessmen in confinement in Riyadh's Ritz-Carlton that month, and a remaining 56 by March. The Crown Prince claimed this was part of a greater attempt to turn Saudi Arabia into a more ethical and religiously tolerant place.

"What he is doing, I called for, and I got fired for...," Khashoggi had continued to Hassan before his death, citing numerous examples, "To limit the power of the religious establishment. I demanded that...and no one should be jailed for that."

Hassan in turn decried this corruption "crackdown" as more of a "shakedown," less about catching criminal activity than extorting wealth. The initiative resulted in a gain for at least $106.7 billion, as confirmed by the Saudi Arabian attorney general for BBC. Properties, cash, and other investments were handed over to the prince in attempts to save their lives.[241]

It echoed the tactics of Post-Cold-War Russia, and the scramble for wealth among oligarchs and mafia hitmen that Rybolovlev had survived.

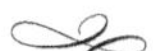

On November 15th, 2017, just under a year before Khashoggi's death and weeks after the corruption campaign was launched, the *Christ as Savior of the World* by Leonardo da Vinci was sold. The purchase was by Bader bin Abdullah bin Mohammed bin Farhan al-Saud, known as Prince Bader. The total price was the unprecedented $450 million.

At the time of the sale, Saudi Prince Bader was otherwise unknown to Christie's, even with the company's robust database, legal and research teams. He answered important due diligence questions with vague, curt answers, and initially intended to pay for the work in its astronomical lump sum—a very different strategy to some of the credit-backed tactics of the Chinese and Russian buyers. Bader eventually facilitated the transaction in $58 million payments.

Furthermore, the ground-breaking depiction of Jesus Christ seemed an unlikely acquisition for a Muslim billionaire, especially from a country steeped in turmoil.

Then it was revealed that Prince Bader was merely a representative of the Crown Prince—MBS himself.

Not only was the billionaire a famously wealthy ruler of a Muslim country, but his decision to purchase the most expensive painting of all time sent a powerful message. Despite thwarting a political platform against excess and disrespect with such an ostentatious acquisition, it was this image of Christ that was to solidify the religious tolerance he purported to achieve.

Savior of the World.

Then, the prince did something additionally extraordinary. He bequeathed it to the Louvre Abu Dhabi for permanent display.

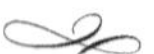

The Louvre in Paris was one of the first public museums in history. After the French Revolution necessitated the security of the rulers in a stronghold rather than outside the city in the 18th century, it was the revolutionaries who insisted on the necessity for art in a public space.[242] It was not until 1993 that the entire building was open to the public as a museum.[243]

The crown jewel of the museum was *La Jaconde*, or the *Mona Lisa*, by Leonardo da Vinci. Her enigmatic, smoky depiction had captivated centuries of museum-goers, and as time went by, the Louvre and da Vinci became synonymous.

But like all precious commodities, the evolution of the Louvre necessitated export. At the time of the Moscow World Fine Art Fair, there was a Russian distributor of luxury brands that took its name from the famous museum. The Louvre at the Moscow Art Fair had a catwalk, where models strutted behind the company's block letters.

For the Louvre Abu Dhabi museum, skeptics in the Arab art world compared the phenomenon. The power of the museum name was as valuable as a designer handbag. It was all about the branding. As was the case in Paris, no Louvre would be complete without a da Vinci.

As previously indicated (see pg. 20), the traffic of tourists to see masterpieces at the Louvre in Paris had maintained into the millions. It would be safe to assume that the Abu Dhabi Tourism Board was hoping for similar results, especially given their push for press tours into 2019.

The official contract to build was signed in 2007, and construction began in 2013. Upon completion five years later, founding Director Manuel Rabaté came from France to see the project to fruition, alongside a team of Emirates-based women, Hissa Al-Dhaheri and Noor Suwaidi.[244]

Curators at the Louvre Abu Dhabi adamantly lauded its differences.

"The name Louvre evokes this spirit of the universal," Rabaté said fervently in a French interview, "This rapport with the encyclopedic. With the Enlightenment. This idea of embracing the world...this idea of connection has always been valid in the United Arab Emirates. So with that, you enter into the collection."[245]

Although the Abu Dhabi museum was a collaboration with the French Louvre, architect Jean Nouvel customized his design of 23 galleries to the landscape of the Emirates. The dome of the museum was chiseled to catch the light the way the palm trees did in the desert, and the building was surrounded by shimmering blue waters. On Saadiyat Island, a hub for NYU Abu Dhabi and other cultural centers, it was truly a desert oasis, not just for the treasures inside, but as an architectural marvel.

Most explicitly, the Abu Dhabi museum was intended as a crossroads of culture. In cohesion with the Emirates' storied history as a trading center, the museum would be a return to this ideology. In a region fraught with conflict and misconceptions, Western art from an Eastern perspective was a way to study and appreciate differences, fostering an important dialogue the world over.

The ability to bridge between peoples was priceless.

The museum opened in November 2017, almost simultaneously with the da Vinci sale, and the push to get this message out was aggressive.[246]

"What I was most interested in was understanding how societies are formed," Noor Suwaidi told *Vogue Arabia*, "And what makes cultures what they are."[247]

She was an artist herself, first realizing her passion for paintings when she discovered them in her twenties. It was Suwaidi who had pushed to acquire Giovanni Bellini's *Madonna and Child* (1480-1485), and she who most sincerely addressed the impact of the museum on her people and those around the world. In a publicity film spearheaded by the Abu Dhabi Tourism Commission published online with the *The Art Newspaper*, she spoke from the heart about the power of Old Master paintings to empower viewers, specifically the Middle East:[248]

"I always say that these museums that will be located on Saadiyat Island are gifts. Gifts from the UAE to its people, the Arabian Gulf, the Arab World, and to the world. These are cultural gifts and their effects won't be seen in a day or two; their effects will remain for the ages. The story of the Louvre and its collection is the story of humanity; human civilizations and their development. But for the first time, we tell those stories from an Eastern point of view to the West...the Louvre Abu Dhabi views human civilization from all directions."

Work by Paul Gaugin also featured in their collection.

What made the *Salvator Mundi* by Leonardo da Vinci such a worthwhile addition to the museum collection was its overwhelming power to stimulate the viewer—to tears, to dialogue, to marvel. It was the crowning work not just for a Louvre museum, but for a place seeking to challenge its own artistic cannon.

The staggering price point of $450 million was secondary to the magic of the painting itself.

Art dealer Robert Simon confirmed the effect on audiences while experiencing the viewing process firsthand when Christie's displayed the piece in London. He was impressed by the impact it had on everyone in its wake.

"It's very hard to say what any work of art does to an individual," Simon said, "Except that a painting has the ability to communicate over 500 years in a very basic, very powerful way. That's what Leonardo can do."

He went on.

"People, particularly the press, are so focused on the dollar amount. That's what's given it so much attention in the last year, as opposed to the painting itself, which is extraordinary, as phenomenal, rare things are...It's a tremendously powerful and spiritual work with an amazing presence that undercuts all aspects of religion and subject matter. I find it to be hugely moving and spiritually uplifting."

The lives of those who came into contact with the work were forever changed. "This thing was the most extraordinary professional accomplishment in my life, so I'm very proud of it," Simon concluded. "If there's anything, I would love for the attention to go back to the painting and people could start to look at it and appreciate it."

However, the speculation around the authenticity of the work continued, especially as it was delayed from its expected showcase in Fall 2019.

The cycle had started again. Political intrigue, billions at stake, and a shroud of mystery that extended as far as the artwork itself. Such was the nature of the art market from the time of da Vinci's great patron Il Moro, of El Greco's fervent lawsuits and swift imprisonment, of Gauguin's sexually-fueled creative exploration and of Modigliani's untimely demise. Through the great collections and inspirations of Rodin, Giacometti and Maillol, of Van Gogh, Renoir, and Monet, and the religious power of mastery in color and light, the realities of art extended far beyond their subject matters. They provided insight into the humans who coveted and scorned them, the people they had loved and lost, and the worlds they created and destroyed through their own desires for fortitude and inevitable vulnerabilities.

The art revealed these truths. It was just a matter of closer inspection.

Together, Yves Bouvier, Tania Rappo, Elena Rybolovleva and Dmitry Rybolovlev had put together one of the most extraordinary art collections of all time. And through its acquisition, the collection broke them apart.

Rybolovlev continued to work with art dealer Sandy Heller in New York, and pursue his businesses around the world, protected by his large and loyal team. He was suspected to still hold goods in the Singapore Freeport through one of the private dealers under Bouvier's purview, even though Bouvier was no longer privy to his assets.

His ex-wife Elena eschewed media attention and remained, for all intents and purposes, in Geneva, removed from the Swiss contacts who had helped her when she first moved to the city. Unlike her husband, she had learned to speak near-perfect French.

His lawyer, Tetiana Bersheda, became the founding CEO of LexSnap, a new technology software around divorce law.[249] Her website promoted her as a member of the law faculty at four Swiss universities, as well as a lecturer at the University of Geneva.[250] She was based in London.[251]

Rappo defended herself emphatically and sought refuge in beautiful things. She traveled frequently between London, Paris, and Monaco, enjoying the best of everything as well as she could despite the pressure of the ongoing lawsuits. She insisted she lost no friends during the litigation.

Bouvier maintained optimism that his name would be cleared. He hoped, when everything was over, that he could continue his art ambitions in California, focusing on contemporary artists rather than Old Masters, Impressionists, or Expressionists.

As of 2019, however, he was no longer acting as an art salesmen, and had no clients. His enterprises were within the world of freeports and shipping, not of art consultation.

The Geneva Freeport spokesman, Andre Decrausaz, insisted they had lost no clients despite the negative coverage of the business model.

The Bouvier Affair continued, of course, but the acquisitions were no longer the primary focus of their story.

ACKNOWLEDGEMENTS

Thank you to my professor, Jim Stewart, for believing I was the student to take on this incredible story, and to Kelly Crow, his former mentee, who ensured I would revive it without doubting myself again.

To the boyfriends and bosses who let me down, you paved a way forward that was entirely self-motivated and without further regret. Every closed door was a window on this path. Thank you to Niall McKinney for hiring me into a flexible consultancy that gave me the perfect amount of space to remotely pursue this unlikely dream.

Thank you to Marilyn White for the introduction to Sixtene Crutchfield. I am endlessly grateful to the named and unnamed sources throughout the writing project, but if I could only thank one person, Sixtene would be it.

Thank you to the friends and gracious AirBnB hosts who gave me a place to stay while I was figuring this out: the Ekstrand family (especially the wonderful Anna Mikaela), Jessie Twersky, Dan Clarke, and many more from Singapore, Bali, Hong Kong, Geneva, Monaco and Paris. Shoko Aono, Zainab Chaudhary, Lucy Cross, Hamdi Fariz, Cole Harrell, Amal Hassan, Alexandre Khadivi, Sameen Khan, Caleb Leon, Daanish Masood, Brian Mayer, Rob McQuilkin, Billy Norwich, Sean Pi, Rebekah Shufelt, Gregory Soros, Louis Webre, and Lynn Xiting gave me words and gifts of encouragement sometimes without even realizing, pushing me to get this far to the finish line.

Thank you to my family for raising the kind of headstrong woman who could disappear into her own mind halfway across the world for the better part of a year, and to the incredible friends who helped put the finishing touches on the editorial process together.

Emily Corwin and Melissa Sommerweiss made for patient guinea pigs with my earliest manuscripts. Anam Khan, a news entrepreneur, was a fantastically thorough and scrupulous editor. Alex Geana, a lifestyle photographer, took professional headshots with kindness. Alison, a graphic designer, spent hours perfecting the cover and manuscript and building my spirits.

I am lucky to know all of you. For this first book, acknowledgements feel more like destiny than courtesy. Not only could I not have done it without you, but I would not be the person I have since become. Tears, fears, flights, dim sums and fondues later, I am truly indebted.

Thank you for everything.

REFERENCES

[1] Saltz, J. (2017, November 14). Jerry Saltz: Christie's Says This Painting Is by Leonardo. I Really Doubt It. Retrieved October 24, 2018, from http://www.vulture.com/2017/11/christies-says-this-painting-is-by-leonardo-i-doubt-it.html

[2] (2017, November 12). The Last da Vinci | Christie's. Retrieved October 25, 2018, from https://www.christies.com/features/The-last-da-Vinci-Salvator-Mundi-8598-3.aspx

[3] Haring, B. (2019). Leonardo DiCaprio Testifies To Federal Grand Jury In Malaysian Fund Probe: Report. *Deadline Hollywood*. Retrieved from https://deadline.com/2019/01/leonardo-dicaprio-testifies-to-federal-grand-jury-in-malaysian-fund-probe-report-1202529345/

[4] Mead, R. (2016). *The Daredevil of the Auction World.* [online] The New Yorker. Available at: https://www.newyorker.com/magazine/2016/07/04/loic-gouzer-the-daredevil-at-christies [Accessed 1 Oct. 2018].

[5] https://www.vogue.com/article/prince-albert-leonardo-dicaprio-ocean-environment-gala

[6] The National Gallery, L. (2019). *Pentimento | Glossary | National Gallery, London.* [online] Nationalgallery.org.uk. Available at: https://www.nationalgallery.org.uk/paintings/glossary/pentimento [Accessed 11 Oct. 2018].

[7] Lewis, B. (2019). Would the 'royal' Salvator Mundi please stand up?. Retrieved from https://www.theartnewspaper.com/news/would-the-royal-salvator-mundi-please-stand-up

[8] Curbed NY. (2011). *World's 93rd Richest Person Buys $88M 15 CPW Penthouse.* [online] Available at: https://ny.curbed.com/2011/12/19/10414666/worlds-93rd-richest-person-buys-88m-15-cpw-penthouse [Accessed 20 Oct. 2018].

[9] DeGrasse-Isaacson: Anybody Can Become a Genius. (2017). Retrieved from https://www.youtube.com/watch?v=7NcNpHcrfv4

[10] Lodovico Maria Sforza, called il Moro, 1451-1508, 7th Duke of Milan 1494-1500 [obverse]. (2019). Retrieved from https://www.nga.gov/collection/art-object-page.45469.html

[11] Burckhardt, J., & Middlemore, S. (1878). The Civilization of the Renaissance in Italy. Retrieved from http://rubens.anu.edu.au/htdocs/bycountry/italy/rome/popolo/burckhardt/1-5.html

[12] Sampaolo, M. (1998). Palazzosforzacesarini - The Historical Roots of the Sforza Family. Retrieved from https://www.britannica.com/topic/Sforza-family

[13] Bloks, M. (2016). The almost Queen of England - Bona of Savoy - History of Royal Women. Retrieved from https://www.historyofroyalwomen.com/bona-of-savoy/almost-queen-england-bona-savoy/

[14] Delaware State Bankruptcy Laws - bankruptcyhq.com. (2019). Retrieved from https://bankruptcyhq.com/delaware-state-bankruptcy-laws/

15 Hall, K. (2016). What might Trump be hiding in those tax returns he won't disclose?. Retrieved from https://www.mcclatchydc.com/news/politics-government/election/article105029036.html

16 Bloomberg. (2017). Here's How You Get Someone to Bid $450 Million for a Painting. Retrieved from https://www.bloomberg.com/news/articles/2017-11-17/the-da-vinci-homerun-how-a-wild-idea-turned-into-450-million

17 8 Major Pieces of Art in Beyoncé and Jay-Z's "Apesh*t" Video. (2018). *Architectural Digest*, (June 2018). Retrieved from https://www.architecturaldigest.com/story/8-major-pieces-of-art-in-beyonce-and-jay-zs-apesht-video

18 Cascone, S. (2014). Louvre Expects 12 Million Visitors Per Year by 2025. *Artnet*. Retrieved from https://news.artnet.com/exhibitions/louvre-expects-12-million-visitors-per-year-by-2025-69408

19 Polukhina, J. (n.d.). Rybolovlev, who dropped the scales. Novaya Gazeta [Moscow]. Retrieved from https://www.novayagazeta.ru/articles/2016/10/05/70066-rybolovlev-sbrosivshiy-cheshuyu

20 Power of habit. Dmitry Rybolovlev tried to bribe Monaco law enforcement authorities. (2018, November 9). *Crime Russia*. Retrieved from https://en.crimerussia.com/oligarchs/power-of-habit-dmitry-rybolovlev-tried-to-bribe-monaco-law-enforcement-authorities/

21 Mikhail Gorbachev: The man who lost an empire. (2016, December 13). *BBC*. Retrieved from https://www.bbc.com/news/world-europe-38289333

22 Corless, D. (2014, September 28). Just plane rude: the day Boris Yeltsin 'overslept'. *The Independent* [Ireland]. Retrieved from https://www.independent.ie/life/just-plane-rude-the-day-boris-yeltsin-overslept-30615643.html

23 Wood, T. (2018, August 30). The crisis that created Putin. *Jacobin Mag* [Brooklyn]. Retrieved from https://www.jacobinmag.com/2018/08/rouble-crash-yeltsin-putin-free-market

24 Pohl, O. (2004, July). The assassination of a dream. *New York Magazine*. Retrieved from http://nymag.com/nymetro/news/people/features/10193/index1.html

25 Boycko, M., Shleifer, A., & Vishny, R. (1997). Cambridge, MA: MIT Press.

26 Theft of the century: privatization and the looting of Russia. (2002, January 2). *The Multinational Monitor* [Washington, DC].

27

28 Isakov, V. (2018, March 11). *Russia Berezniki 11 March 2018: men's and women's 10 km sprint at the winter Olympics* [Photograph]. Retrieved from https://www.alamy.com/russia-berezniki-11-march-2018-mens-and-womens-10-km-sprint-at-the-winter-olympics-image178386288.html

29 History Channel Editors. (2018). Boris Yeltsin. In *History Channel*. Retrieved November 11, 2018, from https://www.history.com/topics/russia/boris-yeltsin

30 Kovensky, J. (2014, August 18). From Nazi resistance to Ferguson's unrest: The weird history of the Molotov Cocktail. *New Republic*. Retrieved from https://newrepublic.com/article/119127/history-molotov-cocktail-nazi-germany-ferguson

31 Fedorin, V., & Sazonov, A. (2008, May 3). Dmitry Rybolovlev, the owner of "BRIC". What's the salt? *Forbes* [Russia]. Retrieved from http://www.forbes.ru/forbes/issue/2008-05/11470-v-chem-sol

32 Rachkova, O. (1998, January 17). The case of contract killing. *Kommersant* [Russia]. Retrieved from https://www.kommersant.ru/doc/190514

33 Ganney, M. (2018, January 29). Trump publishes list of Putin cronies worth $1bn each who now face sanctions over US election meddling as Russian president blasts the 'hostile step'. *Daily Mail* [United Kingdom]. Retrieved from https://www.dailymail.co.uk/news/article-5327919/Trump-administration-declines-apply-new-Russia-sanctions-now.html
34 Perm gangster-businessman Prokop on wanted list for murder. (2017, March 3) *Crime Russia*. Retrieved from https://en.crimerussia.com/gromkie-dela/perm-gangster-businessman-prokop-on-wanted-list-for-murder-/
35 *Geneve Golf Club*. (2018). Retrieved from https://golfgeneve.ch/en/home
36 Sotheby's. (2006, May 3). Marc Chagall, Le Grande Cirque. Retrieved from http://www.sothebys.com/en/auctions/ecatalogue/2006/impressionist-modern-art-evening-sale-n08195/lot.52.html - sold at a loss?

38 http//www.wsj.com/articles/when-chagall-and-malevich-battled-in-russia-1533828420?mod=searchresults&page=1&pos=1 (by the author)
39 Marc Chagall (1887-1985), Le grand cirque. (2015, November 12). Retrieved from https://www.christies.com/lotfinder/Lot/marc-chagall-1887-1985-le-grand-cirque-5944967-details.aspx
40 Natural Le Coultre. (2014). *Welcome to Natural Le Coultre*. Retrieved from https://www.nlc.ch/wp-content/uploads/pdf/presentation-booklet_nlc.pdf
41 Kinsella, E. (2015, March 9). Is Swiss Freeport King Yves Bouvier free on €10M bail, or not? *Artnet*. Retrieved from https://news.artnet.com/market/is-yves-bouvier-free-275272
42 Ananth, V. (n.d.). The secret history of Swiss bank accounts. *LiveMint* [India]. Retrieved from https://www.livemint.com/Politics/novevubtiXoiKubIr0U6SM/The-secret-history-of-Swiss-bank-accounts.html
43 Waldman, K. (2012, January 27). How hard is it to open a Swiss Bank account? *Slate*. Retrieved from https://slate.com/business/2012/01/mitt-romneys-swiss-bank-account-how-do-you-open-a-bank-account-in-switzerland.html
44 Publiart. (2009, October). Natural Le Coultre, le transport au sommet de son art depuis 150 ans. Retrieved from http://fr.worldtempus.com/article/publiart-natural-le-coultre-le-transport-au-sommet-de-son-art-depuis-150-ans-6495.html
45 Roch, C. A. (1919). *La famille Le Coultre*. Retrieved from Imprimerie Albert Kundig website: http://www.aubertcombier.ch/textes/Lecoultre.pdf
46 Geneva Freeports. (n.d.). Ports Francs & Entrepôts de Genève SA | Rte du Grand Lancy 6a - Genève. Retrieved from http://geneva-freeports.ch/en/
47 Griogoryeva, Y. (2018, April 25). Manege central exhibition hall in Moscow - Sights of Russia 2018. Retrieved from https://www.moscovery.com/manege-architecture/
48 Ahouse, J., & Dolenko, E. (2005, August 18). The Hector Berlioz Website - Berlioz in Russia Moscow - Concert January 1868. Retrieved from http://www.hberlioz.com/Russia/1868Concert.htm
49 Russian gas blast kills 21. (2004, March 16). *Telegraph* [United Kingdom]. Retrieved from https://www.telegraph.co.uk/news/1456978/Russian-gas-blast-kills-21.html
50 Real time net worth - Roman Abramovich #140. (2019, January 9). *Forbes*. Retrieved from https://www.forbes.com/profile/roman-abramovich/#191117d6134a
51 Vice Media buys Dasha Zhukova's Garage art magazine. (2016, July 5). *Financial Times*. Retrieved from https://www.ft.com/content/6d85f52a-42a4-11e6-9b66-0712b3873ae1

[52] Billionaires build a museum for Russia's contemporary art market. (2018, June 30). *The National* [Arab Emirates]. Retrieved from https://www.thenational.ae/business/money/billionaires-builds-a-museum-for-russia-s-contemporary-art-market-1.745577

[53] Popyk, L. (1989, October 12). Picasso's 'Noces de Pierrette' up for auction. *United Press International*. Retrieved from https://www.upi.com/Archives/1989/10/12/Picassos-Noces-de-Pierrette-up-for-auction/6082624168000/

[54] Kazanjian, D. (2012, April 27). Life After Picasso: Françoise Gilot. *Vogue*. Retrieved from https://www.vogue.com/article/life-after-picasso-franoise-gilot

[55] Decroes Jacobs, C. (2018, February 8). The last love of Jonas Salk. *Nautilus, 57*. Retrieved from http://nautil.us/issue/57/communities/-the-last-love-of-jonas-salk

[56] Murphy, E. (2008, May 17). Picasso's heirs and the mystery of the evil stepmother. *The Independent* [United Kingdom]. Retrieved from https://www.independent.co.uk/news/world/europe/picassos-heirs-and-the-mystery-of-the-evil-stepmother-829927.html

[57] Dorment, R. (2004, January 14). Picasso's saddest love. *Telegraph* [United Kingdom]. Retrieved from https://www.telegraph.co.uk/culture/art/3610082/Picassos-saddest-love.html

[58] Pablo Picasso - Jacqueline Roque. (n.d.). Retrieved from https://www.pablo-ruiz-picasso.net/theme-jacquelineroque.php

[59] Brazilian restorer engages in mystery of paintings by Pablo Picasso. (2017, August 10). *Fantastico* [Brazil]. Retrieved from http://g1.globo.com/fantastico/noticia/2017/10/restaurador-brasileiro-se-envolve-em-misterio-de-quadros-de-pablo-picasso.html

[60] Kinsella, E. (2015, May 14). Dealer Olivier Thomas detained in France after theft accusations by Picasso heir. *Artnet*. Retrieved from https://news.artnet.com/art-world/picasso-stepdaughter-accuses-dealer-298137

[61] Rea, N. (2018, February 7). Picasso's stepdaughter is opening a museum that will house the largest-ever collection of the artist's works. *Artnet*. Retrieved from https://news.artnet.com/art-world/picasso-jacqueline-museum-aix-1218407

[62] Hallinan, B. (2018, February 13). New museum in southern France will host world's largest Picasso collection. *Conde Nast Traveler*. Retrieved from https://www.cntraveler.com/story/new-museum-in-southern-france-will-host-worlds-largest-picasso-collection

[63] Ament, P. (2006, November 3). Pot ash history - invention of a potash process. Retrieved from http://www.ideafinder.com/history/inventions/potash.htm

[64] Grant, B. (2014, June 16). What is potash: using potash in the garden. Retrieved from https://www.gardeningknowhow.com/garden-how-to/soil-fertilizers/using-potash-in-garden.htm

[65] Encanto Potash Corp. - about potash. (n.d.). Retrieved from http://www.encantopotash.com/english/aboutpotash/default.aspx (5% used in commercial and industrial products such as soap)

[66] What is potash? | Canpotex. (n.d.). Retrieved from https://www.canpotex.com/our-potash/what-potash (The remaining 5% is also part of emerging opportunities in glass making, pharmaceuticals, food processing, textile manufacturing, and as a de-icer.)

[67] Langley, A., & Cowley, E. (2006, October 12). Russia's Uralkali discontinues plan for London IPO. *Wall Street Journal*. Retrieved from https://www.wsj.com/articles/SB116060539932589854

68 Crystal of sylvinite for BKK. (2007). *Filtration Industry Analyst, 2007*(7), 3. https://www.sefar.com/data/docs/es/10583/AS-PDF-Sefar-Vision-Headquarters-BKK-EN.pdf?v=1.2

69 Sheva, N. (2006, October 11). ICL stock lost 1.6% as Uralkali pulls back from London IPO. *Haaretz* [Israel]. Retrieved from https://www.haaretz.com/israel-news/business/1.4873308

70 History | PJSC Uralkali. (2016). Retrieved from https://www.uralkali.com/about/history/

71 Romm, J. (2018, March 23). Why are sinkholes seemingly stalking Trump's residences? Retrieved from https://thinkprogress.org/is-the-white-house-sinkhole-climate-change-or-just-karma-8dea4dbdfea2/

72 Vincent, J. (2014, February 18). What are sinkholes, how do they form and why are we seeing so many? *The Independent* [United Kingdom]. Retrieved from https://www.independent.co.uk/news/science/sinkholes-what-are-they-how-do-they-form-and-why-are-we-seeing-so-many-9136235.html#r3z-addoor

73 *Uralkali: one year after the accident. Rybolovlev's case* [Video file]. (2012, March 31). Retrieved from https://www.youtube.com/watch?v=yoxexl8caXA&t=1s

74 Occupational Safety and Health Administration. (2017, June 5). Safety and health topics: hydrogen sulfide. Retrieved from https://www.osha.gov/SLTC/hydrogensulfide/hazards.html

75 Uralkali calls Russia govt to table over mine probe. (2008, November 21). *Reuters* [United Kingdom]. Retrieved from https://uk.reuters.com/article/sppage023-ll720283-oisbi/uralkali-calls-russia-govt-to-table-over-mine-probe-idUKLL72028320081121

76 Helmer, J. (2007, September 24). Russian potash IPO makes London debut. Retrieved from http://johnhelmer.net/russian-potash-ipo-makes-london-debut/

77 (Estimates by Ramsay)

78 Press releases | PJSC Uralkali: Uralkali CEO receives special prize at Ernst&Young Entrepreneur Of The Year Awards. (2012, December 3). Retrieved from https://www.uralkali.com/press_center/press_releases/item4123/

79 Belarus to sue Baumgertner over Uralkali affair. (2014, February 10). Retrieved from http://www.rapsinews.com/judicial_news/20141002/272264823.html

80 Sechin weighs in on Uralkali purchase. (2013, September 18). *The Moscow Times* [Moscow]. Retrieved from https://themoscowtimes.com/articles/sechin-weighs-in-on-uralkali-purchase-27746

81 Russia's Uralkali approves delisting from LSE, launches market buyback. (2015, November 23). *Reuters* [United Kingdom]. Retrieved from https://uk.reuters.com/article/russia-uralkali-delisting/russias-uralkali-approves-delisting-from-lse-launches-market-buyback-idUKFWN13I00L20151123

82 Momente, F. (2017, July 7). MATHIEU FOSCHIA APPOINTED HEAD OF FINE ART LOGISTICS NATURAL LE COULTRE, SINGAPORE | Fine Art Logistics Singapore. Retrieved from https://www.falnlc.sg/mathieu-foschia/

83 Le Freeport. (2011). The ultimate infrastructure. Retrieved from http://www.singaporefreeport.com/facility

84 (BNP Paribas is a French bank.)

85 Gouvernement Princier de Monaco. (n.d.). Occupation of the Rocher by François Grimaldi / The beginnings of independence (Middle Ages) / Periods / History and Heritage / Government & Institutions / Portail du Gouvernement - Monaco. Retrieved from https://en.gouv.mc/Government-Institutions/History-and-Heritage/Periods/The-beginnings-of-independence-Middle-Ages/Occupation-of-the-Rocher-by-Francois-Grimaldi

86 Kissane, K. (2011, July 9). Is this a kiss to build a dream, or a curse to end one? *The Sydney Morning Herald* [Sydney]. Retrieved from https://www.smh.com.au/world/is-this-a-kiss-to-build-a-dream-on-or-a-curse-to-end-one-20110708-1h6qm.html

87 Russian oligarch suspected of massive money-laundering spree out on bail. (2017, December 6). *Monaco Life* [Monaco]. Retrieved from http://www.monacolife.net/russian-oligarch-suspected-of-massive-money-laundering-spree-out-on-bail/

88 Samuel, H. (2018, October 9). Roman Abramovich undervalued his €100m Riviera chateau to pay less tax, French court rules. *The Telegraph* [United Kingdom]. Retrieved from https://www.telegraph.co.uk/news/2018/10/09/chelsea-owner-roman-abramovich-undervalued-100m-riviera-chateau/

89 Gold Creative. (2012). *La Belle Époque Monaco* [Video file]. Retrieved from https://vimeo.com/37401187

90 Joseph Safra real time net worth. (n.d.). *Forbes*. Retrieved from https://www.forbes.com/profile/joseph-safra

91 Dunne, D. (2000, December). Death in Monaco. *Vanity Fair*. Retrieved from https://www.vanityfair.com/culture/2000/12/dunne200012

92 *The murder of Edmond Safra and Vivian Torrente (crime documentary)* [Video file]. (2018, February 17). Retrieved from https://www.youtube.com/watch?v=VScz1b91MDE

93 Nice: Musée National Marc Chagall. (2017, May 18). Retrieved from http://ee.france.fr/en/discover/nice-musee-national-marc-chagall-0

94 MUSÉE NATIONAL MARC CHAGALL Museums Reception venues in Nice Famille Plus Nice Côte d'Azur. (n.d.). Retrieved from http://en.nicetourisme.com/nice/183-musee-national-marc-chagall

95 Artnet. (n.d.). *The Mediterranean (Cap d'Antibes)* [Painting]. Retrieved from http://www.artnet.com/magazine_pre2000/features/klein/klein11-19-4.asp

96 History of the Water Lilies cycle | Musée de l'Orangerie. (n.d.). Retrieved from http://www.musee-orangerie.fr/en/article/history-water-lilies-cycle

97 Flowers in Mythology - Myth Encyclopedia - Greek, god, story, legend, names, ancient, symbolism, Hindu, Japanese, world. (n.d.). Retrieved from http://www.mythencyclopedia.com/Fi-Go/Flowers-in-Mythology.html#ixzz5VTKBXVov

98 Bouguereau, W. A. (1873). *Nymphs and Satyr* [Painting]. Retrieved from https://www.clarkart.edu/Collection/6158

99 http://cultbytes.com/opinion/the-woman-question-deification-as-objectification-at-the-neue-galerie/ written by the author

100 *Altmann v. Republic of Austria, 317 F. 3d 954 - Court of Appeals, 9th Circuit 2002 - Google Scholar.* (2002). Retrieved from https://scholar.google.com.sg/scholar_case?case=8884093045915597586&hl=en&as_sdt=6&as_vis=1&oi=scholarr

101 Vogel, C. (2006, November 9). $491 million sale shatters art auction record. *New York Times.* Retrieved from https://www.nytimes.com/2006/11/09/arts/design/09christies.html

102 https://www.telegraph.co.uk/news/2017/03/01/gustav-klimt-painting-sells-record-47971250-sothebys/

103 Super Yachts. (2018). Drettman Yachts sell My Anna. Retrieved from http://www.superyachts.com/news/drettmann-yachts-sell-my-anna-t-2395.htm

104 Boat International. (n.d.). ANNA 1 yacht for sale. Retrieved from https://www.boatinternational.com/yachts-for-sale/anna--93291

105 *Yacht overview M/Y ANNA.* (n.d.). Retrieved from https://www.yacht-zoo.com/yachts/my-anna-i/

[106] Yacht Charter Fleet. (n.d.). ANNA 1 Yacht Charter Price - Feadship Luxury Yacht Charter. Retrieved from https://www.yachtcharterfleet.com/luxury-charter-yacht-22890/anna-1.htm

[107] Abramovich's wife warns his new squeeze - he'll dump you too. (2007, March 23). *Daily Mail* [United Kingdom]. Retrieved from https://www.dailymail.co.uk/femail/article-444314/Abramovichs-wife-warns-new-squeeze--Hell-dump-too.html

[108] David Diesling LinkedIn. (n.d.). Retrieved from https://www.linkedin.com/in/david-diesing-848516159/

[109] Paumgarten, N. (2006, October 23). The $40-million elbow. *The New Yorker*. Retrieved from https://www.newyorker.com/magazine/2006/10/23/the-40-million-elbow

[110] Gaylord, M. (2006, September 16). He ran his hands over them and caressed them. *The Telegraph* [United Kingdom]. Retrieved from https://www.telegraph.co.uk/culture/art/3655307/He-ran-his-hands-over-them-and-caressed-them.html

[111] 5 minutes with... Auguste Rodin's Eternal Spring | Christie's. (2018, March 19). Retrieved from https://www.christies.com/features/5-minutes-with-Auguste-Rodins-Eternal-Spring-8950-1.aspx

[112] Eve | Rodin Museum. (n.d.). Retrieved from http://www.musee-rodin.fr/en/collections/sculptures/eve

[113] Sherwin, S. (2018, May 4). Auguste Rodin's The Kiss: an adulterous couple transformed into everyday icons. *The Guardian*. Retrieved from https://www.theguardian.com/artanddesign/2018/may/04/auguste-rodin-the-kiss

[114] Eternal Springtime. (2018, October 20). Retrieved from https://www.mfa.org/collections/object/eternal-springtime-59515

[115] Thompson, J. (2017, February 1). *Brief history of 'The Kiss' by Auguste Rodin* [Video file]. Retrieved from https://www.youtube.com/watch?v=hCkxNNtvCfA

[116] Sooke, A. (2015, November 19). The shocking story of the kiss. *BBC*. Retrieved from http://www.bbc.com/culture/story/20151119-the-shocking-story-of-the-kiss

[117] Biography of Auguste Rodin - Victoria and Albert Museum. (2014, November 17). Retrieved from http://www.vam.ac.uk/content/articles/b/rodins-life-and-work/

[118] Bird, M., Shaw, C., & Sentek, Z. (2016, December 16). Kazakh moguls, the pal of Donald Trump, teen models, and the yacht of the father of the Turks. *The Black Sea* [Bucharest, Romania]. Retrieved from https://theblacksea.eu/stories/football-leaks/football-leaks-kazakh-moguls-the-pal-of-donald-trump-teen-models-and-the-yacht-of-the-father-of-the-turks/

[119] Yacht Charter Fleet. (n.d.). SAVARONA Yacht Photos - Blohm + Voss | Yacht Charter Fleet. Retrieved from https://www.yachtcharterfleet.com/luxury-charter-yacht-23048/savarona-photos.htm#yacht-tabs

[120] Kazakh miner ENRC plans London IPO. (2007, November 13). *Reuters* [United Kingdom]. Retrieved from https://uk.reuters.com/article/eurasian-ipo-idUKWLA283720071113

[121] Suleiman Kerimov's motives eyed in ENRC deal. (2013, May 17). *Financial Times*. Retrieved from https://www.ft.com/content/516b44ba-c48c-11e2-bc94-00144feab7de

[122] Committee to Investigate Russia. (n.d.). Tevfik Arif. Retrieved November 2018, from https://investigaterussia.org/players/tevfik-arif

[123] Bird, M. (2016, December 16). Donald Trump's disastrous relationship with the dodgy Kazakh business world. The Black Sea [Bucharest, Romania]. Retrieved from https://theblacksea.eu/stories/donald-trumps-disastrous-relationship-with-the-dodgy-kazakh-business-world/

124 *Donald Trump on David Letterman* 17 October, 2013 Full Interview [Video file]. (2013, October 22). Retrieved from
https://www.youtube.com/watch?v=PR_SoJpWzOA&feature=youtu.be&t=14m44s
125 Clough, A., & Pacenti, J. (2017, March 9). Why did a Russian pay $95M to buy Trump's Palm Beach mansion? *The Seattle Times*. Retrieved from
https://www.seattletimes.com/nation-world/why-did-a-russian-pay-95m-to-buy-trumps-palm-beach-mansion/
126 Ronin Gallery. (n.d.). Toulouse-Lautrec, Henri de. Retrieved from
https://www.roningallery.com/artists/henri-de-toulouse-lautrec?dir=asc&order=price
127 D'Angelo, M. (2015, August 19). 5 things you didn't know about Toulouse-Lautrec. *Huffington Post*. Retrieved from https://www.huffingtonpost.com/madelaine-dangelo/5-things-you-didnt-know-a_b_8004704.html
128 Wolf, P. (2005). *The Effects of Diseases, Drugs, and Chemicals on the Creativity and Productivity of Famous Sculptors, Classic Painters, Classic Music Composers, and Authors* (Vol. 129, No. 11). Retrieved from Department of Pathology and Laboratory Medicine, University of California, San Diego; Archives of Pathology & Laboratory Medicine website:
http://www.archivesofpathology.org/doi/full/10.1043/1543-2165%282005%29129%5B1457%3ATEODDA%5D2.0.CO%3B2
129 Musée d'Orsay: Edgar Degas In a Café. (2007, July 31). Retrieved from
https://www.musee-orsay.fr/en/collections/works-in-focus/search/commentaire_id/in-a-cafe-2234.html
130 Eggler, M. (2014, October 9). MoMA | Absinthe Makes the Heart Grow Fonder: An Evening of Cocktails with Toulouse-Lautrec's Muses. Retrieved from
https://www.moma.org/explore/inside_out/2014/10/09/absinthe-makes-the-heart-grow-fonder-an-evening-of-cocktails-with-toulouse-lautrecs-muses/
131 Ronin Gallery. (n.d.). Utamaro. Retrieved from
https://www.roningallery.com/artists/utamaro
132 Ronin Gallery. (n.d.) Demimode: the floating world and Toulouse-Lautrec. Retrieved from https://www.roningallery.com/education/demimonde-the-floating-world-and-toulouse-lautrec/
133 Reverie d'Opium by Henri de Toulouse-Lautrec. (n.d.). Retrieved from
https://www.auctionclub.com/public/historic/henri-de-toulouse-lautrec-151864/reverie-dopium-2883384
134 South China Morning Post. (2018, September 22). The Opium war (or how Hong Kong began). Retrieved from https://www.scmp.com/article/974360/opium-war-or-how-hong-kong-began
135 Ting Sun-Pao, J. (n.d.). 1860 - 1898, The establishment of entrepot trade: Opium trade and the blockade of Hong Kong (History of the Port of Hong Kong and Marine Department). Retrieved from
https://www.mardep.gov.hk/theme/port_hk/en/p1ch3_4.html
136 The French Chamber of Commerce and Industry in Hong Kong. (2016, March 31). HKE80: Panorama of the French Community in Hong Kong. Retrieved from
http://fccihk.com/blog/2016/03/hke80-panorama-french-community-hong-kong
137 Hugo Lopez. (2013, January 30). *Zahia de Z à A* [Video file]. Retrieved from
https://www.youtube.com/watch?v=w26isWJM5rY&t=1539s
138 AP. (2014, January 30). Franck Ribery and Karim Benzema are cleared of having sex with underage prostitute Zahia Dehar in France. *Adelaide Now* [Australia]. Retrieved from

https://www.adelaidenow.com.au/sport/football/franck-ribery-and-karim-benzema-are-cleared-of-having-sex-with-underage-prostitute-zahia-dehar-in-france/news-story/908a98fde087bc6ad46073b471ab9b49

[139] Michael, C., & The Metropolitan Museum of Art. (2010, May). Henri de Toulouse-Lautrec (1864-1901) - Heilbrunn Timeline of Art History. Retrieved from https://www.metmuseum.org/toah/hd/laut/hd_laut.htm

[140] LaChapelle, D. (n.d.). *Zahia Dehar* [portrait]. Retrieved from http://www.lachapellestudio.com/portraits/zahia-dehar/

[141] Farolfi, S., Pegg, D., & Orphanides, S. (2017, September 17). Cyprus 'selling' EU citizenship to super rich of Russia and Ukraine. *The Guardian*. Retrieved from https://www.theguardian.com/world/2017/sep/17/cyprus-selling-eu-citizenship-to-super-rich-of-russia-and-ukraine

[142] Orphanides, S. (2012, January 16). Russia may grand loan for Bank of Cyprus stakes, Alithia says. *Bloomberg*. Retrieved from https://www.bloomberg.com/news/articles/2012-07-16/russia-may-grant-loan-for-bank-of-cyprus-stakes-alithia-reports

[143] (65% the city of Moscow, 13% in the Moscow region and 7% in Saint Petersburg.)

[144] Ledyaeva, S., Karhunen, P., & Whalley, J. (2016). *Offshore jurisdictions (including Cyprus), corruption money laundering and Russian round-trip investment* (19019). Retrieved from National Bureau of Economic Research, Cambridge, MA website: https://www.nber.org/papers/w19019.pdf

[145] Chrysopoulous, P. (2017, December 8). Greek gov't gives Russian billionaire Dmitry Rybolovlev permit to revamp Skorpios Island. *Greek Reporter* [Greece]. Retrieved from https://greece.greekreporter.com/2017/12/08/greek-govt-gives-russian-billionaire-dmitry-rybolovlev-permit-to-revamp-skorpios-island/

[146] Dangremond, S. (2015, October 20). The daughter of a Russian Billionaire is getting married on the same Greek Island where Jackie Onassis was wed. *Town & Country*. Retrieved from https://www.townandcountrymag.com/society/news/a4018/ekaterina-rybolovleva-juan-sartori-skorpios-wedding/

[147] Aphros = foam. (n.d.). Retrieved from http://faculty.washington.edu/alain/Clas430/Aphrodite.htm

[148] Birthplace of Aphrodite = Petra tou Rominou. (n.d.). Retrieved from http://www.visitcyprus.com/index.php/en/discovercyprus/rural/sites-monuments/item/732-birthplace-of-aphrodite-petra-tou-romiou

[149] Botticelli, S. (1485). *Birth of Venus* [Painting]. Retrieved from https://www.uffizi.it/en/artworks/birth-of-venus

[150] Helly Nahmad Gallery. (2005). Modigliani: the myth. Retrieved 2016, from http://www.hellynahmadgallery.com/exhibitions/modigliani-a-bohemian-myth?view=slider#2

[151] Cam, D. (2016, March 3). The Richest People in Europe. *Forbes*. Retrieved from http://www.forbes.com/sites/denizcam/2016/03/03/richest-people-in-europe/#2afbd5a71498

[152] Tully, J. (2018, June 12). 'It takes time to prove yourself': Joseph Nahmad on his New York gallery's fifth anniversary. *ArtNews*. Retrieved from http://www.artnews.com/2018/06/12/takes-time-prove-joseph-nahmad-new-york-gallerys-fifth-anniversary/

[153] ArtTactic podcast. (2009, May 27). *Michael Moses — Mei Moses Art Index* [Podcast]. Retrieved from http://www.arttactic.com/podcasts/latest-podcast/651-michael-moses-mei-moses-index.html

154 Mahler, L. (2015, January). Dutilleul, Roger | The Metropolitan Museum of Art. Retrieved from http://www.metmuseum.org/art/libraries-and-research-centers/leonard-lauder-research-center/programs-and-resources/index-of-cubist-art-collectors/dutilleul

155 Stamberg, S., Levitov, K., & Rothkop, K. (2011, June 25). A tale of two sisters and their serious eye for art. *NPR*. Retrieved from https://www.npr.org/2011/06/26/137368938/a-tale-of-two-sisters-and-their-serious-eye-for-art

156 Collecting Matisse and Modern Masters: The Cone Sisters of Baltimore / Stories. (n.d.). Retrieved from https://archives.nasher.duke.edu/matisse/stories.html

157 Powell III, E. A. (2010, April 6). *From Impressionism to Modernism: The Chester Dale Collection* [Video file]. Retrieved from https://www.nga.gov/audio-video/video/chester-dale.html

158 Modigliani's Nu couché (Reclining Nude) leads a night of records in New York | Christie's. (2015, November 10). Retrieved from http://www.christies.com/features/Modigliani-Nu-couche-Reclining-Nude-leads-a-night-of-records-in-New-York-6782-3.aspx

159 Freeman, N. (2015, October 22). Loic Gouzer promoted to Deputy Chairman, PostWar & Contemporary Art at Christie's. *Artnews*. Retrieved from http://www.artnews.com/2015/10/22/loic-gouzer-promoted-to-deputy-chairman-post-war-contemporary-art-at-christies/

160 Elaine Kwok biography, Christie's Education. (2016). Retrieved from https://www.christies.edu/hong-kong/hong-kong-faculty/ElaineKwok.aspx

161 Associated Press in New York. (2015, November 8). Modigliani's Reclining Nude fetches second-highest ever art auction price. *The Guardian*. Retrieved from http://www.theguardian.com/artanddesign/2015/nov/10/modiglianis-reclining-nude-fetches-second-highest-ever-art-auction-price

162 Impressionist & Modern Art. (2018, May 14). At $157.2 Million, Modigliani's greatest nude is also the most expensive painting ever sold at Sotheby's. Retrieved from https://www.sothebys.com/en/articles/at-157-2-million-modiglianis-greatest-nude-is-also-the-most-expensive-painting-ever-sold-at-sothebys

163 Net Worth. (n.d.). Liu Yiqian. *Forbes*. Retrieved from https://www.forbes.com/profile/liu-yiqian/

164 Fan, J. (2016, November 7). The emperor's new museum. *The New Yorker*. Retrieved from https://www.newyorker.com/magazine/2016/11/07/the-emperors-new-museum

165 The University of Chicago. (n.d.). Thorstein Veblen, Economics. Retrieved from https://www.lib.uchicago.edu/projects/centcat/fac/facch09_01.html

166 Auction results. (2008, September 15). Damien Hirst - Beautiful Inside My Head Forever (evening sale). Retrieved from http://www.sothebys.com/en/auctions/2008/damien-hirst-beautiful-inside-my-head-forever-evening-sale-l08027.html#&sort=lotSortNum-asc&viewMode=grid&size=m

167 Billionaire's son and Hollywood poker madam face court along with 32 others accused of running illegal gambling ring for wealthy celebrities and executives. (2013, April 19). *Daily Mail* [United Kingdom]. Retrieved from https://www.dailymail.co.uk/news/article-2311924/Billionaires-son-Hollywood-poker-madam-face-court-32-accused-running-illegal-gambling-ring-wealthy-celebrities-executives.html

168 Billionaire Gambler. (2016, October 4). Nahmad billionaire backgammon champion. Retrieved from https://www.billionairegambler.com/2016/10/nahmad-billionaire-backgammon-champion.html

[169] Fanelli, J. (2014, April 24). Math whiz busted in $100M gambling ring now teaching kids chess. Retrieved from https://www.dnainfo.com/new-york/20140424/east-village/math-whiz-busted-100m-gambling-ring-now-teaching-kids-chess/

[170] Holtfreter, K., & Meyers, T. (2015). *Challenges for Cybercrime Theory, Research, and Policy.* Retrieved from ResearchGate website: https://www.researchgate.net/profile/Travis_Meyers/publication/299594093_Challenges_for_Cybercrime_Theory_Research_and_Policy/links/5701439a08ae1408e15ea50b/Challenges-for-Cybercrime-Theory-Research-and-Policy.pdf

[171] Balmforth, T., & Kirilenko, A. (2013, May 31). For reputed crime boss known as Taiwanchik, Moscow is 'Paradise'. *RadioFreeEurope* [Russia]. Retrieved from https://www.rferl.org/a/russia-alimzhan-tokhtakhunov-taiwanchik-indictment/25003328.html

[172] Balmforth, T., & Kirilenko, A. (2013, May 31). For reputed crime boss known as Taiwanchik, Moscow is 'Paradise'. *RadioFreeEurope* [Russia]. Retrieved from https://www.rferl.org/a/russia-alimzhan-tokhtakhunov-taiwanchik-indictment/25003328.html

[173] *UNITED STATES OF AMERICA - v. - ALIMZHAN TOKHTAKHOUNOV, a/k/a "Taiwanchik," a/k/a "Alik," VADIM TRINCHER, a/k/a "Dima," ANATOLY GOLUBCHIK, a/k/a "Tony," MICHAEL SALL, STAN GREENBERG, a/k/a "Slava," ILLYA TRINCHER, HILLEL NAHMAD, a/k/a "Helly," JOHN HANSON, NOAH SIEGEL, a/k/a "The Oracle," JONATHAN HIRSCH, ARTHUR AZEN, DONALD MCCALMONT, DMITRY DRUZHINSKY, a/k/a "Dima," a/k/a "Blondie," ALEXANDER ZAVERUKHA, a/k/a "Sasha," ALEXANDER KATCHALOFF, a/k/a "Murushka," ANATOLY SHTEYNGROB, a/k/a "Tony," ILYA ROZENFELD, PETER SKYLLAS, RONALD UY, NICHOLAS HIRSCH, BRYAN ZURIFF, MOSHE ORATZ, KIRILL RAPOPORT, DAVID AARON, a/k/a "D.A.," JUSTIN SMITH, ABRAHAM MOSSERI, WILLIAM EDLER, PETER FELDMAN, EUGENE TRINCHER, EDWIN TING, a/k/a "Eddie," MOLLY BLOOM, WILLIAM BARBALAT, YUGESHWAR RAJKUMAR, a/k/a "Mateo Hermatte," and JOSEPH MANCUSO, a/k/a "Joe the Hammer,"* (13CRIM268). (n.d.). Retrieved from United States District Court, Southern District of New York website: https://www.justice.gov/sites/default/files/usao-sdny/legacy/2015/03/25/Tokhtakhounov%2C%20Alimzhan%20et%20al.%20Indictment_6.pdf

[174] Bernstein, J. (2016, April 8). Hiding money: the art of secrecy. *McClatchy* [Washington, DC]. Retrieved from https://www.mcclatchydc.com/news/nation-world/national/article70505092.html

[175] Khan, S., & Beament, E. (2018, March 7). Quarter of a million songbirds killed illegally at UK military base. *The Independent* [United Kingdom]. Retrieved from https://www.independent.co.uk/news/world/europe/songbird-killed-illegally-uk-military-base-cyprus-a8243006.html

[176] Munchies. (2015, January 12). *Cyprus's Songbird Massacre: The Politics of Food* [Video file]. Retrieved from https://www.youtube.com/watch?v=etlvWRMRPRQ

[177] https://www.spectator.co.uk/2017/03/the-cruel-criminal-industry-that-thrives-around-britains-cypriot-bases/

[178] Farolfi, S., & Kirchgaessner, S. (2017, December 24). FBI investigates Russian-linked Cyprus bank accused of money laundering. *The Guardian*. Retrieved from https://www.theguardian.com/us-news/2017/dec/24/fbi-investigates-russian-linked-cyprus-bank-accused-of-money-laundering

179 Kirchgaessner, S. (2017, March 20). Trump's commerce secretary oversaw Russia deal while at Bank of Cyprus. *The Guardian*. Retrieved from https://www.theguardian.com/us-news/2017/mar/23/wilbur-ross-russian-deal-bank-of-cyprus-donald-trump-commerce-secretary

180 Josef Ackermann. (2016, November 28). Retrieved from https://www.bankofcyprus.com/en-GB/who-we-are/directors-cvs/josef-ackermann/

181 Dayen, D. (2016, November 10). Trump presidency could be worth $14 billion to his troubled lender. Retrieved from https://theintercept.com/2016/11/10/trump-presidency-could-be-worth-14-billion-to-his-troubled-lender/

182 Arnold, L. (2018, October 18). Why you keep hearing the name Magnitsky in the news. *Bloomberg*. Retrieved from https://www.bloomberg.com/news/articles/2018-10-18/why-you-keep-hearing-the-name-magnitsky-in-the-news-quicktake

183 Greenberg, J. (2018, July 16). Putin wrong on $400 million to Clinton from Browder partners. *Politifact*. Retrieved from https://www.politifact.com/truth-o-meter/statements/2018/jul/16/vladimir-putin/putins-pants-fire-claim-about-400-million-donation/

184 Christou, J. (2014, February 26). Disputed €25m ring was a gift, Rybolovleva's lawyers say. *Cyprus Mail*. Retrieved from http://cyprus-mail.com/2014/02/26/disputed-e25m-ring-was-a-gift-rybolovlevas-lawyers-say/

185 Harris, C. (2016, December 27). The Murder of Rasputin, 100 Years Later. Retrieved from https://www.smithsonianmag.com/history/murder-rasputin-100-years-later-180961572/

186 Atchison, B. (n.d.). The Feodorovskaya Icon of the Mother of God - Blog & Alexander Palace Time Machine. Retrieved from http://www.alexanderpalace.org/palace/blog.html?pid=1214782701328517

187 Dolce & Gabbana Fall 2013 Ready-to-Wear. (2013, February 23). *Ginta Lapina, Daria Stroukous* [fashion show]. Retrieved from https://www.vogue.com/fashion-shows/fall-2013-ready-to-wear/dolce-gabbana/slideshow/collection#5

188 Rodriguez Marcos, J. (2013, December 25). Four centuries on from his death, time to meet the real El Greco. *El Pais* [Madrid, Spain]. Retrieved from https://elpais.com/elpais/2013/12/25/inenglish/1387992921_349206.html

189 El Greco. (1587). *Sts Peter and Paul* [Painting]. Retrieved from http://www.hermitagemuseum.org/wps/portal/hermitage/digital-collection/01.+Paintings/32730/?lng=

190 Kononov, A. A. (n.d.). Durnovo P.P. (1835-1919), statesman and public figure. In *Saint Petersburg encyclopaedia*. Retrieved from http://www.encspb.ru/object/2804020248?lc=en

191 The National Gallery, London. (n.d.). Albrecht Altdorfer | Christ taking Leave of his Mother | NG6463 | National Gallery, London. Retrieved from https://www.nationalgallery.org.uk/paintings/albrecht-altdorfer-christ-taking-leave-of-his-mother

192 El Greco (Domenikos Theotokopoulos). (1510). Saint Sebastian. Retrieved from https://www.museodelprado.es/en/the-collection/art-work/saint-sebastian/9b723f8f-0bae-4247-a52e-ed267ae70615

193 Art, Vision, & the Disordered Eye - El Greco. (n.d.). Retrieved from https://psyc.ucalgary.ca/PACE/VA-Lab/AVDE-Website/ElGreco.html

194 Christiansen, K. (2004, October). El Greco (1541-1614) | Heilbrunn Timeline of Art History. Retrieved from https://www.metmuseum.org/toah/hd/grec/hd_grec.htm

195 Smith, H. (2016, November 24). Four hundred years after his death, Greece reclaims the artist El Greco. *The Guardian*. Retrieved from

https://www.theguardian.com/artanddesign/2014/nov/26/domenikos-theotokopoulos-el-greco-spain-crete-exhibitions

[196] El Greco: Man of Two Worlds - and Beyond. (2016, December 16). Retrieved from http://www.asatours.com.au/el-greco-man-of-two-worlds-and-beyond/

[197] El Greco (Domenikos Theotokopoulos) - The Collection - Museo Nacional del Prado. (n.d.). Retrieved from https://www.museodelprado.es/en/the-collection/artist/el-greco/b031da57-6a7e-43f2-a855-293275efc340

[198] Luca, G. (1670). Expulsion of the money-changers from the temple. Retrieved from https://www.hermitagemuseum.org/wps/portal/hermitage/digital-collection/01.+Paintings/31947

[199] Disrobing of Christ, El Greco: Analysis. (n.d.). Retrieved from http://www.visual-arts-cork.com/famous-paintings/disrobing-of-christ.htm

[200] Caradec'h, J. M. (2017, September 23). Rybolovlev : l'oligarche qui fait de l'ombre au Rocher. *Paris Match* [France]. Retrieved from https://www.parismatch.com/Actu/Societe/Rybolovlev-l-oligarche-qui-fait-de-l-ombre-au-Rocher-1354064 Caradec'h, J. M. (2017, September 23). Rybolovlev : l'oligarche qui fait de l'ombre au Rocher. *Paris Match* [France]. Retrieved from https://www.parismatch.com/Actu/Societe/Rybolovlev-l-oligarche-qui-fait-de-l-ombre-au-Rocher-1354064

[201] Raya, A. (2017, October 13). "Monacogate" : la riposte de Tetiana Bersheda. *Paris Match* [France]. Retrieved from https://www.parismatch.com/Actu/Societe/Monacogate-la-riposte-de-Tetiana-Bersheda-1369328

[202] BestImage. (2013, May 31). *Tetiana Bersheda et Dmitri Rybolovlev lors de la soirée de célébration de la montée de l'AS Monaco en Ligue 1, le 31 mai 2013 au chapiteau de Fontvieille à Mona* [Photograph]. Retrieved from http://www.purepeople.com/media/tetiana-bersheda-et-dmitri-rybolovlev-lo_m3611392

[203] Moclard, E. S. (2018, August 27). 21 facts about Mark Rothko. Retrieved from https://www.sothebys.com/en/articles/21-facts-about-mark-rothko

[204] Mark Rothko - painter. (2014, April 2). Retrieved from https://www.biography.com/people/mark-rothko-9465194

[205] Guggenheim Museum. (n.d.). Mark Rothko. Retrieved from https://www.guggenheim.org/artwork/artist/mark-rothko

[206] Rothko, M. (1939). *Untitled (nude)* [Painting]. Retrieved from http://www.sothebys.com/en/auctions/ecatalogue/2018/contemporary-curated-n09909/lot.70.html

[207] *Rothko Chapel.* (n.d.). Retrieved from http://www.rothkochapel.org/learn/about/

[208] MacKay, A. S. (2017, September 5). Ten things you might not know about Mark Rothko. *AnOther Mag.* Retrieved from http://www.anothermag.com/art-photography/10126/ten-things-you-might-not-know-about-mark-rothko

[209] Chung, J., & Chazan, G. (2009, September 18). The Roman Empire. *Wall Street Journal.* Retrieved from https://www.wsj.com/articles/SB10001424052970204518504574418871692477730

[210] paradise | Origin and meaning of paradise by Online Etymology Dictionary. (n.d.). Retrieved from https://www.etymonline.com/word/paradise

[211] Impressionist & Modern Art. (2017, February 15). 'A new way of seeing the world?: Magritte's Le domaine d'Arnheim | Christie's. Retrieved from https://www.christies.com/features/Olivier-Camu-on-Rene-Magritte-Le-domaine-de-Arnheim-8096-3.aspx

212 The Domain of Arnheim by Edgar Allan Poe. (n.d.). Retrieved from http://www.online-literature.com/poe/28/
213 René Magritte (1898-1967), Le domaine d'Arnheim. (2017, February 28). Retrieved from https://www.christies.com/lotfinder/lot/rene-magritte-le-domaine-darnheim-6059215-details.aspx?from=searchresults&intObjectID=6059215&sid=0de2d03a-d811-443b-b858-247355a3712f
214 Goldberg, E. (2015, May 6). Meet 'Le Boeuf,' a painting of beef estimated to sell for over $20 million. *Bon Appetit*. Retrieved from https://www.bonappetit.com/entertaining-style/trends-news/article/soutine-le-boeuf
215 Reynolds, N. (2006, June 28). Hirst's pickled shark is rotting and needs to be replaced. Should it still be worth £6.5m?. *The Telegraph* [United Kingdom]. Retrieved from https://www.telegraph.co.uk/news/uknews/1522516/Hirsts-pickled-shark-is-rotting-and-needs-to-be-replaced.-Should-it-still-be-worth-6.5m.html
216 Muchinic, S. (1993, November 5). LACMA settles lawsuit With Senior Curator: Personnel: Maurice Tuchman will get his old job back and reportedly a cash award. *LA Times*. Retrieved from http://articles.latimes.com/1993-11-05/entertainment/ca-53662_1_senior-curator
217 Chaim Soutine (1893-1943), Le Boeuf. (2015, May 11). Retrieved from https://www.christies.com/lotfinder/Lot/chaim-soutine-1893-1943-le-buf-5895984-details.aspx

218 Dmitry Rybolovlev | ICIJ Offshore Leaks Database. (n.d.). Retrieved from https://offshoreleaks.icij.org/nodes/13011230
219 Kinsella, E. (2016, April 6). Billionaire collector Dmitry Rybolovlev denies 'Panama Papers' allegations. *Artnet*. Retrieved from https://news.artnet.com/exhibitions/billionaire-collector-dmitry-rybolovlev-denies-panama-papers-allegations-466880
220 Hammer, J. (2012, October 12). The Greatest Fake-Art Scam in History? *Vanity Fair*. Retrieved from https://www.vanityfair.com/culture/2012/10/wolfgang-beltracchi-helene-art-scam
221 Flader, J., & The Catholic Leader. (2014, January 13). The fall of the angels. Retrieved from http://catholicleader.com.au/people/guest-writers/the-fall-of-the-angels
222 Convicted forger claims he faked 'about 50' artists. (2012, March 7). *BBC*. Retrieved from https://www.bbc.com/news/entertainment-arts-17283458
223 Floradini, F. (2018, November 19). Notorious forger Wolfgang Beltracchi on ethics, the art market and how to make a great fake. *The Art Newspaper*. Retrieved from https://www.theartnewspaper.com/interview/beltracchi-his-own-work-in-his-own-words
224 Case of Rybolovlev's paintings: defence complaint for illegal records. (2015, July 15). Retrieved from https://monacowealthmanagement.com/2015/07/15/case-rybolovlevs-paintings-defence-complaint-illegal-records/
225 Ward, V. (2015, November 17). Did this billionaire get swindled out of millions in an elaborate art world scheme?. *Town & Country*. Retrieved from https://www.townandcountrymag.com/society/money-and-power/a4327/billionaire-defrauded-art-world-scheme/
226 Farago, J. (2017, August 9). Gaugin: it's not just genius vs. monster. *The New York Times*. Retrieved from https://www.nytimes.com/2017/08/09/arts/design/gauguin-its-not-just-genius-vs-monster.html

227 Glover, M. (2010, September 28). Gauguin uncovered. *The Independent* [United Kingdom]. Retrieved from https://www.independent.co.uk/arts-entertainment/art/features/gauguin-uncovered-2091234.html

228 Rodgers, P. (2011, January 23). Gauguin's British relative disputes artist's notoriety. *The Independent* [United Kingdom]. Retrieved from https://www.independent.co.uk/arts-entertainment/art/news/gauguins-british-relative-disputes-artists-notoriety 2191988.html

229 Searle, A. (2010, September 27). Paul Gauguin: guilty as charged. *The Guardian*. Retrieved from https://www.theguardian.com/artanddesign/2010/sep/27/paul-gauguin-tate-modern-exhibition

230 Richardson, J. (2004, February). Gauguin's last testament. *Vanity Fair*. Retrieved from https://www.vanityfair.com/news/2004/02/gauguin200402

231 Billionaire Leviev adds Zambia emeralds to diamond portfolio. (2017, June 5). *Lukasa Times*[Zambia]. Retrieved from https://www.lusakatimes.com/2017/06/05/billionaire-leviev-adds-zambia-emeralds-diamond-portfolio/

232 Heller, A. (2018, December 4). Diamond smuggling scandal spotlights shadowy Israeli tycoon Lev Leviev. *Times of Israel*. Retrieved from https://www.timesofisrael.com/diamond-smuggling-scandal-spotlights-shadowy-israeli-tycoon-lev-leviev/

233 Revolvy LLC. (n.d.). "Daria Strokous" on Revolvy.com. Retrieved from https://www.revolvy.com/page/Daria-Strokous

234 *Model Talks - Daria Strokous - Exclusive Interview - 2011 | FashionTV - FTV* [Video file]. (2011, August 11). Retrieved from https://www.youtube.com/watch?v=M0Uv0qiFV74&t=0s&index=3&list=LLlr3mHICzO oc9rBT_bLOmsA

235 Shaw, A. (2017, October 26). Swiss freeport king Yves Bouvier sells art storage company Natural Le Coultre. *The Art Newspaper*. Retrieved from https://www.theartnewspaper.com/news/swiss-freeport-king-yves-bouvier-sells-art-storage-company-natural-le-coultre

236 Abrams, A. R. (2016, September 14). Paris Art Complex R4 signs deal with new financial backer. *Artnet*. Retrieved from https://news.artnet.com/art-world/paris-r4-new-financial-backer-648308

237 Brun, R. (n.d.). Affaire Rybolovlev-Bouvier, encore des révélations. *Monaco Hebdo* [Monaco]. Retrieved from http://www.monacohebdo.mc/24507-affaire-rybolovlev-bouvierencore-revelations

238 Nemtsova, A. (2018, October 1). Mikhail Khodorkovsky, Putin's Most Powerful Critic-in-Exile, Says He's Living Under a Kill Order. *The Daily Beast*. Retrieved from https://www.thedailybeast.com/mikhail-khodorkovsky-putins-most-powerful-critic-in-exile-should-fear-for-his-lifebut-doesnt

239 Khashoggi: Saudi Arabia can never be a democracy 'on MBS watch'. (2018, October 3). *Al Jazeera*. Retrieved from https://www.aljazeera.com/news/2018/03/khashoggi-saudi-arabia-democracy-mbs-watch-180323103543171.html

240 MSNBC. (2018, October 13). *Mehdi Hasan* [Video file]. Retrieved from https://www.facebook.com/MrMehdiHasan/videos/2174091576182139/

241 Saudi anti-corruption drive generates $106bn in settlements. (2018, January 30). *BBC*. Retrieved from https://www.bbc.com/news/world-middle-east-42874245

242 History of the Louvre | Louvre Museum | Paris. (n.d.). Retrieved from https://www.louvre.fr/en/histoirelouvres/history-louvre/periode-4

243 Editors, H. (2018, August 21). Louvre Museum opens. Retrieved from https://www.history.com/this-day-in-history/louvre-museum-opens

244 Noce, V. (2017, September 6). Exclusive: the first interview with Louvre Abu Dhabi's French director. *The Art Newspaper*. Retrieved from https://www.theartnewspaper.com/interview/exclusive-the-first-interview-with-louvre-abu-dhabis-french-director

245 BeauxArts.com. (n.d.). *Louvre Abu Dhabi : Rencontre avec Manuel Rabaté* [Video file]. Retrieved from https://vimeo.com/244658094

246 M+ Matters | Keynote: Building Louvre Abu Dhabi - Announcements - e-flux. (2018, December). Retrieved from https://www.e-flux.com/announcements/223058/m-matters-keynote-building-louvre-abu-dhabi/

247 Lorch, H. (2017, November 12). Hissa Al Dhaheri frames the momentous opening of the Louvre Abu Dhabi. *Vogue Arabia*. Retrieved from https://en.vogue.me/culture/louvre-abu-dhabi-hissa-al-dhaheri/

248 Abu Dhabi Tourism Commission. (2018, August 9). *Emirati Voices: Noor Al Suwaidi on Louvre Abu Dhabi's Madonna and Child* [Video file]. Retrieved from https://www.theartnewspaper.com/video/emirati-voices-noor-al-suwaidi-on-louvre-abu-dhabis-madonna-and-child

249 Rowley, E. (2018, July 1). My lightbulb moment: Tetiana Bersheda, 34, realised that she wanted to help people divorce more easily. *Daily Mail* [United Kingdom]. Retrieved from https://www.dailymail.co.uk/femail/article-5907683/My-lightbulb-moment-Tetiana-Bersheda-34.html

250 Bersheda Law. (n.d.). Retrieved from https://www.bershedalaw.com/

251 LexSnap. (n.d.). Retrieved December 2018, from https://www.lexsnap.com/about-us